D0388262

Starting Your Career as a Wall Street Quant

A Practical, No-BS Guide to Getting a Job in Quantitative Finance and Launching a Lucrative Career

Brett Jiu, Ph.D.

Outskirts Press, Inc.
Denver, Colorado

Outskirts Press
http://www.outskirtspress.com

ISBN-13: 978-1-4327-0681-4

Library of Congress Control Number: 2007926790

Outskirts Press and the "OP" logo are trademarks belonging to
Outskirts Press, Inc.

Printed in the United States of America

Page Turners

Disclaimer

Please read the following disclaimer. If you disagree with the terms of the disclaimer, please do not read the rest of the book.

While every effort has been made in preparing this book and ensuring the accuracy of the information contained herein, neither the author nor the publisher makes any representations or warranties with respect to the accuracy, completeness, timeliness, reliability, or fitness of the contents of this book. The author and the publisher specifically disclaim any implied warranties of merchantability or fitness for a particular purpose. The advice, suggestions, tips, hints, and strategies contained herein may not be suitable for your situation. Neither the author nor the publisher shall be liable or responsible to any person or entity for loss or damages of any kind, including but not limited to special, incidental, consequential, or other losses or damages.

Some examples and samples in this book use fictitious names of individuals for illustration purposes only. Any resemblance or similarity of any kind these fictitious names may bear to identities of real persons or characters in other creative works is purely coincidental.

To Liangfen, Chongher, Ann, and Charlie

Acknowledgements

Foremost, I would like to thank you, my reader, for buying this book. (You did buy this book, didn't you?) This book was written for your benefit and I hope you do find something you like. Several people helped make this book possible. First, I would like to thank my dear wife Ann for her support and love. Without her encouragement and support, completing this time-consuming undertaking would have been painful. I would also like to thank my baby boy Charlie (who just turned 10 months as I was wrapping up the final draft of the manuscript), who proves himself the bright sunshine in my everyday existence. My parents, Chongher and Liangfen, did their best to raise me and made lots of sacrifices; now that I am a parent myself, I've come to truly appreciate everything they've done for me. Additional thanks go to my in-laws, Yi and Qing-luo, for generously providing me with a shelter as well as meticulously taking care of Charlie while Ann and I work full-time. A note of appreciation also goes to the fine folks at Outskirts Press, in particular my author representative Theresa. Finally, a heart-felt thanks to this great country, the United States of America, for providing immigrants like myself with boundless opportunities.

Table of Contents

INTRODUCTION: GET READY TO LAUNCH

Chapter 0: Why You Should Read This Book

Chances are, you already know you want to work as a Wall Street quant. By the way, when I talk about "Wall Street," I'm using it as a generic term referring to the financial investment industry in general, not just that specific downtown Manhattan area known as Wall Street. So whether you are in New York or Boston or London or Hong Kong, this book will be of equal value to you.

You probably already know you want to be a quant because of your education background – for example, you may have, or be in the process of getting, a Ph.D. or a master's in a quantitative field. Or you already know because you are sick and tired of your current non-Wall Street job and possess the quantitative skills to make more money. You know where you want to go. You just need some help in getting there. Well, you just found the right book. My goal is to help you find a quant job on Wall Street – hopefully a job you'll find much satisfaction in.

Even if you don't know whether you really want to work as a quant, this book can help you. For example, you may be thinking of becoming an investment banker, a *non*-quant type of job on Wall Street. (Sorry, being proficient in Excel alone does not you a quant make.) In that case, I'll talk about your options. In particular, Chapter 1 will give you reasons why or why not you'd want to become a quant.

As a working quant, I've been to both sides of the job search process: I've been to many job interviews where I found my palms sweating wet all day long, and I've also been on the other side of the desk interviewing candidates whose palms were probably sweating wet. In writing this book, my goal is to offer you practical information and advice that can prove valuable in your quest to get a quant job on Wall Street.

I call this book a "practical, no-BS guide" because that's what it is: lots of practical information you can use right away. I don't BS. I won't be selling you anything, and I don't have a hidden agenda like someone who is a professional headhunter might. I simply want to help you and others who are looking to start a quant career. It's that simple.

While this book contains loads of helpful tips, I have created a companion website dedicated to this book. The website, QuantCareer.com (http://www.quantcareer.com), features supplementary materials that will enhance your experience as the reader of this book. For example, on the website you can find out how to get the correct answers to the sample interview questions from chapter 4. You'll also find handy links to various resources.

This book is not only the *first* book (as far I know after searching on amazon.com and bn.com) that helps you find a quant job on Wall Street, but the *only* book of any kind that gives you complete, unbiased, comprehensive look at every facet of the job search process as well as what it's like to work on Wall Street. For example, this book covers the following topics:

- How much can you expect to make as a Wall Street quant (chapter 1)
- Why working on Wall Street can be bad for your health and mind (chapter 1)
- What not to do or say in your résumé (chapter 2)
- Where to turn to in order to find quant openings (chapter 3)
- When to ask about salary and bonus during interviews (chapter 4)
- What quant books to read for education and preparing for interviews (chapter 7)
- How to negotiate a job offer (chapter 10)
- What those funky titles (VP, MD, head this, head that) mean (chapter 10)
- And much, much more

After you finish with this book and follow at least some of the many tips I offer you, while I cannot guarantee you'll land the quant job of your dreams, I can say that you'll be a more informed and more shrewd job hunter, and you'll know how to handle interviews better than your peers who don't enjoy the benefit and competitive advantage of having read this book. (Of course, if this book becomes a best-seller as I hope it will, then everyone will be equally good, right? But by that time, you'll already be working on Wall Street, so you already got your money's worth!)

The book is divided into several parts, each reflecting the major section of a typical quant résumé. In Part 1, "Objective," I give you lots of general information and valuable tips on the why, where and how of launching a quant career. Part 2, "Education," details the kind of education you need to successfully get a quant job and the good books you *must* read (in addition to this one) in order to qualify as a quant. Part 3, "Experience," discusses the types of worldly experience that will help you get interviews and get offers. Part 4, "Bright Future" (admittedly not a standard section on a résumé), dispenses tips on how to evaluate and compare job offers, how to negotiate an offer, and where your quant career might take you in the future. In case reading this book alone doesn't quench your thirst for even more career tips, an appendix chapter on further resources closes out the book.

I welcome your comments as well as questions. You can contact me via the book's website, QuantCareer.com. I'll do my best in responding to every reader e-mail I receive. If you send me lots of valuable suggestions that can be used in future editions of this book, I may decide to send you a token of appreciation. So e-mail me, but please do not spam! (Spammers will be reported to the FBI and the FTC.)

"A thousand-mile journey begins with the first step." (Chinese proverb) Without further ado, let's get started on helping you launch a lucrative career as a Wall Street quant!

OBJECTIVE: GET A JOB AS A WALL STREET QUANT

Chapter 1: The Lure of a Quant Career

In this chapter:

You may or may not need a reason for why you want to launch a career as a quant. If you do, this chapter will help you make that decision by giving you a detailed rundown on what a quant career will be like and what its advantages and disadvantages are. If you don't need a reason – for example, if you are a Ph.D. in finance or economics, you already know that lucrative non-academic jobs are on Wall Street – you should still read this chapter to get a flavor of what it is like to work as a Wall Street quant in the "real world," so you know what to expect. (Hint: not all aspects of working on Wall Street are glamorous!)

Before I start, let me emphasize that all throughout this book, I use the term "Wall Street" as a generic reference to the financial investment industry. Your potential quant job need not be on Wall Street or in its vicinity in lower Manhattan. The financial investment industry is vibrant not only in New York, but in Boston, Chicago, Greenwich, Conn., San Francisco, London, Hong Kong, Shanghai, Tokyo, Sydney, among other financial centers. The industry encompasses various functions and services performed by financial firms ranging from global integrated banks (e.g., Citibank, HSBC, UBS, Deutsche Bank, Mitsubishi Trust) to investment banking giants (e.g., Morgan Stanley, Credit Suisse, Goldman Sachs) to investment management companies (mutual funds like Fidelity and Putnam, hedge funds like Citadel and Wellington, pension funds for government and private sector employees, etc.). I, for example, work for a 1,000-plus-person specialized equity brokerage firm that provides technology-driven equity trading services to institutional investors. I work in the firm's financial engineering department and conduct modeling research. I'm, therefore, a Wall Street quant.

A Rewarding Career

There is little doubt that working as a Wall Street quant can be a rewarding career. The reward may come in several forms:

- *Monetary:* Like other professionals working in financial investment, quants can make a lot of money – especially when compared to other white-collar professions. For a quant, a six-figure compensation (salary plus bonus, in U.S. dollars) is almost a given. Many quants make $200,000 or $300,000 a year, placing them in the highest Federal income tax brackets. A few lucky *and* bright quants can even make a million bucks or more each year.

- *Psychological:* Working on Wall Street can be like an aphrodisiac – just being in the center of all that money and power can make you feel good and excited and hot. (Take control of your emotions!) As a Wall Street quant, you are respected, by your non-quant colleagues, by people back in your graduate program, and by your friends (unless the latter group are mostly dotcom billionaires). Sometimes you may even feel you are invincible, especially around bonus time in a good year.

- *Spiritual:* Who knows, you may actually find the work as a quant gratifying, more so than good food or … you know what. Many quants love their work so much they go to work at 6 am every day, stay in their cubicles until 10 or 11 pm, and have to be dragged by the security guards to get out of the office. You may be one of those so enamored with the complicated mathematical equations and C++ code you see on whiteboards here and there that you feel compelled to write your own and show off to others. Indeed, if you love your job, that's the best reward you can get from a quant career – even better than the big, fat bonus you expect.

The above list is by now means exhaustive. The point is, working in quantitative finance can be very rewarding. Of course, it *is* also challenging; that's why Wall Street hire bright minds like you and pay you tons of money to build models. In finance, the most basic tenet is: "Where there is reward, there is risk." OK, I just made up this quote myself, but it does capture the omnipresence of the risk-reward relationship in finance. If you cannot see the risk to every potential reward, you should not be working as a quant – in fact, you shouldn't be considering a financial career to begin with. I'll talk about the risks later in this chapter.

What Is a Quant?

I've been talking about being a quant or having a quant career. But what exactly is a "quant"?

Adapted from the adjective quantitative, the word "quant" can be used as a noun or an adjective. As a noun, it usually means a quantitative analyst, researcher or trader; more on this in a bit. As an adjective, it's just a shorthand for quantitative, a word prone to typo.

A quant is a person who builds quantitative models. On Wall Street (remember, I use "Wall Street" as a generic term for the financial investment industry), a quant designs, constructs, implements, tests, and presents quant models in the specific financial area he or she works in. Some quants may do only parts of the modeling process, but most are involved in all the steps.

- *Model design:* The models Wall Street quants build are very diverse in kind. Whether it's a proprietary model adapted from some academic literature or an ad hoc model in response to a client's request, the quant is responsible for selecting the right modeling framework and technique. In other words, the quant is an architect of the model.

- *Model construction:* Once a model framework is decided on – for example, using multivariate GARCH to forecast a portfolio's risk structure – the quant needs to work out the details of the model. What variables should be used? What structure should the error term in an econometric model take? Should the mathematical relations be linear or nonlinear? Should Monte Carlo be utilized? The model construction step is crucial as it transforms the model from framework to implementable form.

- *Model implementation:* Depending on where he or she stands in the corporate hierarchy, a quant may or may not be directly involved in the actual coding of the model. This step just converts the model from its mathematical or statistical form to actual programming code. Most quants use C++ together with a mathematical or statistical package like Matlab, CPLEX, Mathematica, SAS, Stata, R, or S-Plus to implement their models. Most quants are also familiar with Microsoft Excel. Some may even use SQL for database-related tasks.

- *Model testing:* After the model is coded into a computer language, it's fed data and tested. The quant checks the results and works alone or with developers to improve the implementation. For example, if an optimization algorithm doesn't converge, the quant decides what to do next. The quant is also responsible for interpreting the results: for example, are the results meaningful or statistically significant?

- *Model presentation:* Presentation can mean two things in the quant world. It can mean being shown to upper management or clients. It can also mean being finalized into a product or service, to be used proprietarily by the quant's employer or sold to clients. The quant is often responsible for acting as the liaison between the model and the world outside of quantitative research (but quants rarely double as salespeople).

After the model is implemented, tested and released to its end user, the quant may or may not be involved in selling or supporting the model. Most quants aren't, although from time to time quants can be expected to be called upon to explain some of the intricate details in the model, especially when the model is cutting-edge or complicated, i.e., when it's something the sales guys can't put a good spin on in front of the client. For this reason, quants should possess reasonable communication skills in addition to all that knowledge in math, statistics, economics, finance, and programming.

The word quant is actually a quite generic term. Anyone who possesses strong quantitative skills and work with quantitative models is a quant. If you want, you can divide the quant workforce into several sub-classes:

- *Quantitative trader:* This is actually not a real title on Wall Street. Rather, such a quant will just be known as a trader, with the understanding that he or she employs cutting-edge (or not so cutting-edge) quantitative models to trade financial instruments. Quant traders are famous for their roles in making lots of money for their employers and themselves (and hopefully for their clients as well); but they are also infamous for the occasional blowups, such as was the case with the Nobel laureates-studded hedge fund Long Term Capital Management.

- *Financial engineer:* The financial engineer is the true research-oriented quant. Where a financial engineer works can be varied. For example, I work for a specialized equity brokerage, while other financial engineers work on trading desks or with investment bankers. Financial engineers are the closest form to Wall Street rocket scientists: they build models. These can be innovative models that no one else has done before, or models based on the latest academic research. Financial engineers are also heavily involved in the actual implementation of their models (hence the title "engineer").

- *Quantitative analyst:* The quants in this category tend to be more involved in model implementation than design. They are very concerned with the empirical robustness and viability of the model and with the ways in which the model can be applied to everyday situations. Quant analysts often possess superior *qualitative* knowledge as well. For example, a quant analyst specializing in swaps usually understands the mechanics of the swap market very well. (A financial engineer, in comparison, is more enamored with the math of valuing swaps, whereas a trader just cares about how he or she can make money in the swap market.)

- *Quantitative developer:* A developer on Wall Street is a professional who writes computer programs for a living, i.e., a programmer. A quant developer converts abstract modeling ideas into expertly written programming code for implementation and production. (Production means formalizing the code for regularly scheduled, possibly automated runs in the future to generate results that are delivered to the end user, such as a client.) While many non-developer quants also write code to test their models, large firms hire quant developers to focus on efficiently implementing the model – an important undertaking given the increasingly large datasets quants work with nowadays.

Of course, the classification here is not set in stone by any means. Many quants do work that cross into other categories. For example, many (if not most) quant traders build their own models, so they can be considered financial engineers as well.

A Typical Workday in a Quant's Life

Because Wall Street quants work in diverse fields, it's really not possible to talk about a "typical" workday. However, I have put together a schedule that I think reflects the workday of many quants. Most of the time, their diurnal rituals will probably be something similar to this hypothetical schedule.

7:30 am	Get into office, settle down in cubicle, get coffee or tea
7:45 am	Check e-mail and results of any overnight program runs
8:00 am	May need to participate in group Meeting, or meet with manager alone
9:00 am	Check e-mail again; open Internet Explorer to do some surfing
9:30 am	After bathroom break, continue working on modeling project
10:30 am	Annoyed (and annoying) client or manager calls regarding error messages in previous model; troubleshoot
12:30 pm	Lunch break for everyone except those

	working on the trading desk
1:30 pm	Feeling drowsy but still need to carry on working on model
4:00 pm	May need to meet with manager to go over status of project
7:30 pm	Leave office, run to train station to catch post-rush hour commuter train

Some people think that quant traders spend most of their time trading. They have this glamorized mental image that traders do nothing all day but bark into their telephones, sometimes two or three at a time, and move millions of dollars at the blink of an eye. Well, many non-quant traders do kill their days like that, although few actually move millions of dollars on a regular basis. But quant traders are ultimately modeling people – and, besides, quants are usually polite and genteel by trading desk standards – and their ultimate "weapons" in trading are the models they build, so they do spend most of their time toying with the models: refining them, improving them, calibrating them, testing them, having fun with them.

Financial engineers and quant analysts often lead a work life not unlike that of a graduate student (especially one in a Ph.D. program) or a newly minted, tenure-track assistant professor. There's tons of research to be done, but many projects don't have deadlines. (But again, many do, so all-nighters are not to be unexpected.) Many quants work closely together, so a lot of meetings take place where the quants can solve problems together or just talk about the latest episode of *The Simpsons*.

There's no doubt about it: quants work hard. If you are an employer and pays a guy several hundred grand a year, you expect him to work his ass off for you, period. Thirteen- to fourteen-hour workdays are typical for quants and others on Wall Street, although most non-trader quants do enjoy a one-hour lunch break and frequent bathroom breaks. A lot of people also surf the Internet at work, so even though you, as a quant, may have to put in 13 or 14 hours a day, you might end up doing real work just a few hours.

One interesting pattern about working on Wall Street is, as you climb up the corporate ladder, you'll be working harder and harder. A quant who becomes a manager will likely be less involved in building models, but he or she will now bear ultimate responsibility for the models his or her underlings build, which adds to the workload (esp. if he or she is a micromanager), pressure and stress. It's nice that, when you are a senior quant, you won't have to do all the "dirty work" of coding and testing models, but you'll be performing many other tasks equally boring. While some people like administrative type of work such as budgeting and horse-trading, most quants don't. Quants are smart people who want to spend their days productively building models, preferably making money, too!

Is a Quant Job Right for You?

Regardless of your conviction on whether a Wall Street-type quant job is right for you, you should be aware of the pros and cons of working as a quant in finance. You should also look into your inner self to decide if you really want to work as a Wall Street quant.

What are the advantages of working as a Wall Street quant? At the beginning of this chapter I mentioned the three major benefits. Let me reiterate them:

- Working as a Wall Street quant can make you a lot of money. Exactly what constitutes "a lot of money" is up to you. Starting compensation (salary plus bonus) for quants is almost always $100,000 or more (in U.S. dollars). If you want more and are willing to work hard to get more, you have plenty of opportunities to reach your monetary goals (assuming they are reasonable).

- Working on Wall Street is often perceived as prestigious, and working as a quant makes people respect you more because they think you are the brains, the intellect, the nerd who can help them reboot their PCs.

- Working with financial modeling in and by itself can be rewarding. Quant work is no cakewalk; it can be very challenging and tends to be tedious at times. (Just like graduate studies!) But if you are the kind who loves models and enjoys sifting through numbers to find order out of chaos, you'll love this kind of challenge. Besides, becoming an expert in one area makes you feel a tremendous sense of accomplishment – especially when the CEO calls you for your expert advice! (Nope, hasn't happened to me yet, but Bob, in case you are reading this book, I'm your man for modeling of trading tools – as well as how to optimize your Windows XP.)

Now, some of the disadvantages of working as a Wall Street quant:

- Quant work can be boring. You probably are already familiar with the research process. For a new research project, you'll need to do an exhaustive literature search. The usefulness of the Internet notwithstanding, lit search is still a royal pain most of the time. What keywords to you search for? Which articles should you take seriously? And which ones deserve your precious time and payment fee? Let's face it, most academic literature is crap, especially when it comes to economics and finance. If an article is published in a reputable journal, at least you know it went through peer review and deserves some quick read. But what about working papers? It's very difficult to judge the usefulness, and relevancy to your work, of these unpublished papers. But to be thorough in your research process, you still have to find them and read them. At least by reading a lot of papers, you become some sort of an expert, so it's not always time wasted. Opposite of lit search on the spectrum of research tasks is empirical implementation. This involves getting the data, cleaning the data, plotting the data to spot any problems or patterns, then estimating your model with the data. All these are chores for most people, even those of us who completed our Ph.D. by doing these things for years at reputable schools. I myself especially hate the data part, and every time I start a new project, I dread the weeks I'll have to spend writing Perl scripts to process the data into forms I can use for my model. If you need to write SQL statements, oh man, I can feel your pain. I truly can. But you just have to do it all, since you are the quant, and you are supposed to know the data well, really well.

- Quants often work in the middle or back office. Wall Street operations are usually divided into three parts: front office, middle office, and back office. The front office are the salespeople and the traders. These are the folks either selling products and/or services to clients (salespeople), handling clients' money and assets (asset managers, portfolio managers or traders), or betting with the firm's proprietary money in the asset markets (prop traders). They *generate* revenues for the firm. Middle office refers to groups that perform important support functions that have impact on the firm's revenue. Many research groups are considered middle office because their projects impact the company's bottom line, even if the projects aren't end products or services sold to clients. (To research departments, clientele can be internal or external.) Back office are all the non-essential, non-revenue-generating units. Accounting, trade checking, IT support, etc. are all part of the back office. Truth be told, the back office is not unimportant, but when you think about it for a minute, you realize that back office operations can almost always be *outsourced,* whereas the front office and most of the middle office can't. A trading desk often typifies this strictly observed hierarchy: you have the trader (front office person), a couple quant researchers under his or her command (middle office support), and IT and accounting to enable him or her to carry out the trading activity itself (back office support). In the Wall Street pecking order, front office people are the gods, period. They pull in the revenues and profits for the firm. They are the rainmakers. They are untouchable (unless they fail to produce, of course). Middle office are the quiet guys who do a lot of essential work but won't ever stand in the limelight to be recognized, and they make significantly less money than the front office folks in general. Back office employees are seen (and used) as cogs and treated with the least respect, and given the least pay. They perform functions that are important but can be outsourced. Quants, unless they are traders, often fall into the middle office group, occasionally even getting stuck somewhere in the back office camp. Hence, even though they are respected as brainy nerds, they aren't necessarily respected as powerful or important. And the pay reflects this reality, as does the career potential.

- Working in finance can be stressful and harm your body, soul, family relations, or all of them. Long hours can be detrimental to your health and/or sanity, especially long hours spent alone in front of a computer. Even if you are not alone and sit on a crowded trading desk instead, the open environment and foul languages around you can drive you nuts. So can the complete lack of privacy when you sit with ten other people around you, some nosier than others. (Luckily, if you feel the flow of foul language is impeding your work ability, you can complain to HR and they'll do something about it, or you can sue the firm and get rich. However, you can't complain about the open-environment nature of a trading desk.) Female quants in particular may find the overly macho atmosphere of Wall Street unbearable. Many of us also spend sleepless hours wondering exactly what social values we bring to the society. (The answer is: nil, except as well-off consumers.) You can also end up losing interest in a lot of other things in life. You might become too obsessed with money. You might become paranoid about everything and everyone. You might find yourself turning into a sycophant or eager beaver – types of people you despised in the past – in order to curry favors with your boss. In short, you may find the type of work and/or environment pernicious enough to destroy your well-being and self-respect. You know what the worst part is, though? It's that nobody else in the office cares how you are and/or what you think of the stress, the lifestyle or the working environment.

- Most Wall Street bosses are, yes, jerks. That's it. I said it. It doesn't matter what subfield of finance you get your job in. Chances are, you'll have to spend your working hours dealing with a demanding, pushy, difficult boss who often doesn't see you as a human being and treats you more like a human calculator. Worse, if the boss is not a quant himself, he'll have little sympathy for the challenging duties you perform as a quant. Of course, not all bosses on Wall Street are jerks, but I dare say that the nice, caring ones are truly a rare breed. When you think about it, this is not surprising. Money and power, the two driving forces that motivate those working on Wall Street, easily turn people into cold, greedy, ill-tempered half-demons. Of course, one can also argue that Wall Street attracts people of such dispositions to begin with. Either way, people in power on Wall Street are *not* nice in general. It's not unusual to hear employees describe their bosses as a "slave driver," a "fiend," a "usurper," an "egotistic arse," or worse. The situation is particularly exacerbating on trading desks, where trader-managers are notorious for speaking nothing all day but their particular "f*ckspeak." In Chapter 10, I'll discuss ways to deal with such lowlifes. By the way, if you ever become a manager (which you likely will someday), please treat your underlings with at least some degree of respect. All quants, regardless of their places on the corporate hierarchy, *are* human beings – smart human beings, too.

- Workplace competition is usually cutthroat. Money is the greatest motivator in the world, but it is also the root of all evils. Since the bonus pool is just so big each year, and only so many people can climb to the top (in earnings or in power), competition between you and your coworkers can be fierce. This necessarily leads to office politics, to internecine fighting, to coworkers just being nasty towards each other. Yes, this happens – a lot. You would be surprised how many quants have secretly read Sun Tsu's *The Art of War* and Machiavelli's *The Prince,* in hope of gaining an upper hand over their colleagues. Wall Street is largely a meritocracy, but like the rest of our society, just being the smartest or the most talented won't necessarily make you the star of your office. Instead, it's often that particular person who knows how to make himself or herself *look* smart and accomplished in the eyes of the boss and the boss' boss that eventually gets the big year-end bonus and the advancement. Part of this phenomenon has to do with the fact that quant projects usually involve teamwork, and when it comes to crediting time, it's often difficult to say who made the most contribution – and conversely, who made the least. (If you've ever co-authored a paper with others, you know how it is.) Suffice it to say that if you are used to the friendly competition of grad school studies, you'll be in for a big surprise.

- You have the potential to make a lot of money, but that's not guaranteed. A quant's compensation largely depends on three factors: the profitability of the entire firm, the profitability of the group to which you belong, and your perceived performance or contribution to the bottom line. (At small outfits such as most hedge funds, the first two are one and the same.) So, if the firm makes a lot of money *and* your group makes a lot of money, you stand to have a shot at making a lot of money, assuming your boss doesn't dislike you for some reason. A very few lucky quants – the ones you read about in the papers – may get such great packages as being paid a percentage of the money they rake in for their employers, but these are really the exceptions rather than the norm. If you work as a researcher in the middle or back office, it's very unlikely you'll see the kind of windfall you've heard about so much. Most Wall Street quants will be making a good living and probably be in the top 10% of all working Americans in terms of total compensation, but few will make into the top 5%.

You may have noticed that the above list of cons of working on Wall Street was considerably longer than the list of pros. Well, there's a reason for this. After all, just about the only "good" thing of working in finance is the money you *can* make. If you really enjoy quant research but do not care for the money, you can work in non-finance industries, or you can go into the academia if you have a Ph.D.

When it comes to the bottom of it, working on Wall Street is for people who can handle the stress – and often some degrees of abuse, from either the boss or competitive coworkers – and who have the discipline to take up the challenge and stay sane in a highly stressful, competitive environment. In addition, while it's not quite about "selling your soul to the Devil" as some cynics have opined, working on Wall Street does demand a healthy dose of skepticism about the social value of the work you do, and does require some degree of hard-ass aggressiveness if you want to truly succeed and make the big bucks.

Working as a quant researcher or analyst, as opposed to as a salesperson or trader, requires you to be comfortable with knowing that you're getting paid less than many non-quants while working harder than they. The level of stress and potential workplace abuse aside, the quant job is actually perfect for the researcher type – you know, people who just enjoy building models and reading up on the latest advances in the field. The quant has to be able to stomach the daily ennui as well as frustrations that always accompany model construction, implementation and testing. The quant must possess a positive attitude and be like a true scientist, remaining unfazed in the face of many failures. The quant must stay steadfast and hopeful in his or her endeavors. Last but not least, the quant *must* be honest and will never try to cheat his or her way out of a modeling project. If you did that, sooner or later you'll get caught, and the consequences can be severe.

Of course, the best thing about Wall Street is, you do have a shot at making it big. The potential is there. If you find the right job with the right group at the right firm at the right time, and if you work very hard, and if you are smart and creative, and *if you are lucky,* you might just win the Wall Street lottery, make seven figures a year and become the envy of the rest of us, yours truly included.

To sum up, the upsides of working as a quant are (1) money, (2) perceived prestige, and (3) doing work you may actually enjoy. The downsides are (1) boring work, (2) limited respect and recognition if working in middle or back office, (3) stress, (4) difficult managers, (5) intense competition, and (6) lack of certainty with respect to income or job satisfaction.

Non-Quant Finance Jobs

If you skipped over the previous section, this may come as a surprise to you, but many non-quant Wall Street jobs are lucrative, too. In fact, I think most of the highly paid people on Wall Street are *not* quants. They are usually lawyers or MBAs by training. Quant people tend to be the straight shooters and lack the necessary political skills to climb to the top, both in power and in money. Still, quants who can tie their compensation to performance have the potential of being handsomely rewarded, in money if not in power.

If you aren't sure whether a quant job is right for you, The following sections describe some of the other professional jobs you find on Wall Street.

Corporate Finance (Investment Banking)

You can get an MBA and work in corporate finance. Corporate finance is often known as investment banking, although the latter term can have a broader meaning encompassing both corporate finance and capital markets (trading). Those work in corporate finance are called investment bankers. Their jobs are to finance companies as well as other types of institutions such as schools and even governments. When a company wants to go IPO, it hires investment bankers to arrange the sale and to come up with a "fair" price. When a company looks to buy another company, or is being targeted for acquisition by another company, it hires investment bankers to assess the deal and strategize. When a government agency needs to issue bonds to finance the construction of a highway or homeless shelters, it turns to investment bankers.

The typical investment banker's career follows this path: After college, he or she joins the corporate finance department of an investment bank or integrated bank. He or she may rotate through various areas in corporate finance, such as M&A (mergers and acquisitions), equity financing, bond financing, municipal financing, etc. As a junior i-banker, most of your time will be spent doing background research and putting together Excel spreadsheets and PowerPoint slides.

After two or three years in the junior role, the junior analyst goes to business school to get an MBA. This is almost required of the junior analyst. After MBA, he or she returns to corporate finance, either with the same firm as before or a different one, and assumes more senior roles. As an MBA graduate, he or she will get to do more complicated Excel and PowerPoint in the beginning, but soon gains exposure to clients. Gradually, he or she is expected to become a "people person" and learn the art of schmoozing clients and convincing them to get in bed with their employing firm, so to speak.

Investment bankers are not quants. They do work with Excel, especially early in their careers, but they just use some pre-built valuation models the way a housewife follows a cookbook. The housewife (or househusband) can get creative from time to time, and so can the investment banker. But he or she does not deal with quant modeling. He or she likely doesn't even know what GARCH stands for, let alone the intricate details of such models.

Investment bankers work very hard. They put in a lot of hours and are on the road a lot, visiting perspective clients and existing clients all the time. As senior investment bankers, they are really just salespeople. They are part of the "front office," and therefore they get paid a lot, usually much more than non-trader quants.

Equity/Fixed Income Analysis

Equity analysts are the ones often quoted in the *Wall Street Journal* and other business publications making comments and predictions on various stocks. Their fixed income counterparts do so with regard to corporate bonds. Since equity analysts have a higher-profile presence on Wall Street, I'll focus on them in the discussion.

Equity analysts cover the performance of companies and their stocks. Each analyst focuses on a specific industry, such as consumer banking or Internet retailing or waste management. (There are over 100 industries according to various classification schemes.) The stocks an equity analyst follows are called his or her portfolio. Equity analysts spend their time staying abreast of what the companies in their portfolios do and trying to forecast what the "fair value" of each portfolio stock should be. For instance, an analyst covering Microsoft will follows all the news that comes out of Microsoft as well as meet with company officials and industry insiders in an attempt to figure out how Microsoft makes money and where the profit growth (or stagnation) may be. Every quarter before public companies release their quarterly earnings, equity analysts estimate what the earnings announcement might be.

Equity analysts can work for sell-side firms like investment banks, brokerages or dedicated equity research firms, or they can work as in-house equity experts for buy-side firms such as mutual funds and hedge funds. It's the former group – the sell-side analysts – that get all the press time. Why? Because they are really salespeople in a different form. Their "research" (in quotes because equity analysis is more or less a black art rather than disciplined science) enables their employing firms to sell products and services. Sell-side equity analysts don't become rich by simply becoming accurate in forecasting, which is extremely difficult to do on a consistent basis, but by doing a good job at publicizing their employers and attracting clients who are willing to pay hefty fees for investment banking products and services. That's why it's important for equity analysts to get press exposure: it gets their names out. And business journalists love to quote sell-side equity analysts because the analysts are exceptionally good at handing out pithy, colorful quotes that can help sell the paper or TV show or whatever.

Equity analysts, regardless whether they work for the buy side or sell side, can make good money, usually more than non-trader quants. They usually have an MBA, with some having advanced degrees such as Ph.D. or MD (medical doctorate) in the fields they cover, e.g., semiconductor fabrication or biotech. The tools they employ in their analytical work are rarely quantitative in nature. Like investment bankers, they use Excel a lot, but mostly to make financial earnings forecasting rather than doing complicated mathematical or statistical analysis.

Venture Capital and Private Equity

Venture capital and private equity firms deal with non-public companies, i.e., companies whose stocks are not traded on a public exchange. Venture capital (VC) firms invest in start-ups, while private equity firms invest in mature companies, including ones that may have been public at one point but was taken private by investors who thought keeping the company private rather than public was in their own best interest.

Both VC and private equity firms tend to hire MBA types, as well as accounting majors, who are good at poring over a company's financial books. They rarely hire quants.

Non-Quant Trading

On Wall Street, a trader is someone who buys and sells financial assets such as stocks, bonds, currencies, options, and futures. Beneath the surface of this simple definition, there are two functionally very different groups of traders – and their compensations reflect this deep distinction.

The first group are the bigwigs of Wall Street: the traders who bet money – their employing firms' money (prop traders) or their clients' money (money managers). The defining trait of these traders is they place financial bets and actively take on risks in order to earn high returns. These traders make decisions on which assets to buy and sell and how long to hold each position. They may employ whatever tool they see fit – including quantitative models – to achieve their money-making goals. Most traders in this camp do not use a quantitative approach; instead, they rely on any one or more of myriad qualitative techniques, from studying corporate financial books to looking for price patterns on stock charts, in their quest for returns.

Risk-taking, return-seeking traders can be found in every corner of the financial world, from investment banks to retail banks, from mutual funds (there they are known as portfolio managers) to hedge funds. They can even be found lurking in the offices of large companies; the infamous Enron, for instance, had a significant energy-trading division, and many large corporations maintain a full-time staff for trading commodities and/or currencies as part of their hedging programs. (Hedging means entering a secondary financial position in order to protect against a loss in the primary financial position; e.g., an export-oriented Japanese carmaker may trade currencies in order to avoid losses associated with the appreciation and depreciation of the yen which may negatively impact the value of the cars it exports.) Traders' compensations derive largely from the profits they make for their employers or clients. Conversely, if a trader fails to turn in an acceptable return in a given year, he or she may end up making little beyond the base salary.

The second group of traders are the clerical type who simply enter trade orders into computer systems or relay them to brokers. They are found mostly on the buy side: mutual funds, hedge funds, asset management operations of investment banks, and so on. They do not make decisions on what positions to take or what assets to deal with. They simply follow orders on what to do once the trading decision is made.

Where Quants Work

Wall Street quants work in all facets of a very diverse industry. Since the introduction of the Black-Scholes formula, which marked the dawning of finance as a quantitative discipline, quants have found work in every corner of Wall Street.

Most quants work for one of the following types of employers:

- *Global integrated banks:* Examples are Citigroup, Deutsche Bank, Société Générale, and UBS. These firms are like those Hindu gods with multiple arms and have their presence in all corners of high finance. Quants can be found in almost every part of these colossal organizations.

- *Investment banks:* Examples are Morgan Stanley, Goldman Sachs, Nomura Securities, and Credit Suisse. These firms focus on serving institutional clients as well as putting up their own capital in trading positions.

- *Specialized financial service companies:* Examples are State Street, MFS, and the company I work for which provides technology-driven equity trading services (including analytics) to institutional investors. These firms hire a lot of financial engineers to conduct modeling research and implement models that can be sold to the clients.

- *Mutual funds:* Most famous among the thousands of mutual funds are Fidelity, Putnam, T. Rowe Price, and Vanguard. These fund companies manage assets for both individual investors and institutional clients. They hire quants only in limited capacity, usually on teams that manage complex financial instruments or in portfolio optimization areas.

- *Hedge funds:* Many quants work for hedge funds, although many hedge funds do not employ quants.

- *Venture capital and private equity funds:* VCs and private equity funds like Blackstone and Bain Capital have limited opportunities for quants. These firms prefer MBAs, but occasionally they also hire people with strong quantitative skills to assist in portfolio optimization, risk management and other tasks.

Designing an Overall Strategy for Getting a Quant Job

The rest of the book is concerned with the nitty-gritty details of your job search process, from writing an award-winning résumé to negotiating a job offer. But first, before you embark on the journey, it's important that you have an overall strategy, a roadmap from where you are now (wanting to get a foot in the door) to where you want to go (having a foot in the door). This strategy is all about *you*. It will help you plan out exactly what you need to do. And it takes just a little time to do.

Before I began writing this book, I first created an outline. Before you begin writing a technical paper, you usually think about the overall structure of the document. (At least you should.) Same here. Take out a pen and a piece of paper now. We are going to make a few lists that will come in tremendously handy later on in the job hunting process – starting with the tasks in the next chapter.

Here are the things that you should write down:

1. What kind of positions are you interested in? For example, do you want to be a quant trader? Do you want to be a financial

engineer? Are you interested in a heavily programming position? Don't limit your list to just one or two positions; write down whatever quant work that may interest you. If you don't have a clear idea, that's fine, too. Just write down "any quant job!". (That's what I put down for myself years ago.)

2. List things you desire out of your job. High pay is one of them. What about good hours, no working weekends, limited amount of travel (or frequent business trips, if that's what you prefer), a clearly defined career path, a top firm (so you can impress people you meet in a bar), or little (or lots of) hands-on programming? List these characteristics from most important to least important. Alternatively, list them as they come up and later assign a significance score to each of them. This list will help you tailor your résumé.

3. Now list your qualifications. Include your education and past quant-oriented jobs. In the latter group, anything that involved number-based analysis or programming, or anything that demonstrates your ability to think independently, must be included. Write down your quantitative and analytical skills: for example, familiar with stochastic mathematics, proficient in Fortran and C#, member of the national mathematics Olympiad, etc. This list will serve to guide your résumé, too.

4. List anyone you know personally or have met in the past who works in Wall Street-type finance. If you have a personal stock broker, put him or her down. If your father plays poker regularly with an investment banker, write down the name. If you once met a Wall Streeter at a quant seminar somewhere, include him or her. Your goal here is to build an extensive contact list. Depending on your willingness to "cold-call," you may or may not include people you don't know personally.

5. Jot down places where you can find more contacts. If you are in school, the school's career office is obviously one such place. Your professors, the alumni office, and any investment-oriented student societies can help, too. As long as you can write to a person and say you came to him or her by way of a special relationship, you should be able to contact him or her to inquire about job opportunities. Of course, if you just write

someone whom you are not linked to any degree and ask for a job, you'll likely get a cold shoulder.

6. Finally, make a list of alternative options you'd take if you can't find the quant job you desire within a reasonable amount of time. I assume you need to make a living (otherwise you wouldn't have bought this book, right?). It's important to have a backup plan in case the grand plan itself falls through. This can happen through absolutely no fault of your own; for example, the stock market could crash and force Wall Street to lay off tens of thousands – exactly what happened post-dotcom bubble. Whether the alternative is another career (permanent or temporary) or starting your own business, think carefully about what your second choices are. What's more, how attractive you find these alternatives also serves to motivate you in your quant job search effort.

Chapter Summary

In this chapter, you learned the advantages and disadvantages of working in quantitative finance. I served up a little warning because it's my true belief that a Wall Street career is not for everybody, and the Wall Street environment is not for everybody. You also learned where quants work and what they do in general. Finally, you took the first steps in formulating a strategy for getting a quant job.

In the next chapter, you'll find out how to write an impressive résumé that can help you get a quant job.

Chapter 2: Brushing Up Your Résumé

In this chapter:

Finding a job, any job, is really about selling something – this something being yourself, or rather, your labor and your skills. If you want to hold a yard sale, you post some nice-looking posters around the neighborhood. The posters have to be nice-looking in order to entice your neighbors to come to your yard sale. If you don't post any announcement or don't make the posters look enticing, few people will show up to buy your ware.

Same thing with your résumé. The résumé is more than your life's summary. Actually, it shouldn't be your life's summary. What you did last summer in the backwoods of Vermont, unless it has a direct bearing on your quant qualification, should not be listed, even if what you did was helping homeless kids learn to tie shoelaces and start a fire with rocks. The résumé is the first thing an employer sees about you. I know it sounds sad, that your fate, at least in the initial stages of looking for a job, all comes down to a piece of paper. But employers are busy people, especially if they are quants themselves. They can't possibly meet with every potential candidate in person, so they have to rely on résumés for the first screening of these potential candidates.

So to be successful, your résumé must stand out. By this I don't mean you should dress up your résumé in fancy fonts or put a picture of you and Britney Spears on the first page. Quants are down-to-earth people. Most have a science-based training background. This is not to say they are not vain people like you and me. Rather, it means they won't be easily swayed by eye candy. They demand and look for substance.

Therefore, your résumé can stand out by succinctly highlighting your quant qualifications. To achieve this, your résumé should possess the following characteristics:

- *Use a clean layout.* Think of your résumé as a painting, or a photograph. When someone looks at it, he or she should feel good. Layout is all about visual elements. Your résumé should look clean to the reader and present a clear structure. Obviously, you wouldn't put everything into just one giant paragraph or one colossal bullet-pointed list. On the other hand, don't get fancy with the layout, either. If your bold headings get down to the 5th level, you have way too many headings. Two heading levels usually suffice: level 1 headings define the sections – Skills, Education, Experience, etc. – and level 2 headings typically list the places where you gained your education or worked in the past.

- *Stick to classic fonts.* In the descriptive text, it's perfect okay to use **boldface** text to highlight important details that you want your reader to see right away. Do not pepper your résumé with too much boldface text, though; overuse distracts the reader and can be annoying. Furthermore, be consistent in the use of fonts, and use no more than two typefaces – e.g., Arial for headings and Times New Roman for text – in the document. Above all, never commit the cardinal sin of résumé writing by using 10-point fonts and stuffing the page with small letters from edge to edge. Use large fonts; for instance, 12-point Arial for Level 1 headings and 12-point Times New Roman for Level 2 headings and text. Why? Because many résumé readers are 40 or older, and they'll have a hard time reading small fonts. Even if the reader is under 40, as a quant he or she might have had a long day staring at the computer screen, so the last thing he or she wants is a résumé packed with tiny text.

- *List only the important items.* This means leaving out that Vermont backwoods activity from last summer. Also omit any part-time jobs or entrepreneurial endeavors that don't emphasize your quant background. I often find it puzzling why many candidates list every single course they took in school. If you are getting a Ph.D. in economics or finance or statistics, I know what courses you *should have* taken. If you have a master's in physics and tell me what subfield you specialized in, I would have an inkling of what courses you *might have* taken; given I'm not a physicist by training, I really have no interest in knowing exactly what physics courses you took. However, for non-economics and non-finance majors out there, it does make sense to list quant-oriented courses (financial modeling, Monte Carlo methods, etc.) that you did take and that have a direct impact on your qualification as a future Wall Street quant. When you list your past job experiences, only list jobs that gave you a leg-up in quant qualification.

- *Be concise but be concrete.* This is probably the hardest part about writing a successful résumé. You have to be concise, because your reader, a quant guy who's looking to hire you, is a busy person. In addition to his regular work, he probably has dozens of other résumés to read. Say what you have to say, in as few words as possible. Don't cram your résumé with tiny fonts running to the edges of the paper. On the other hand, you want to be concrete in detailing your education, experience and skills. If you completed a dissertation or thesis, put down some details. If you just list the title of your dissertation as "Three Essays on Financial Derivatives," that kind of tantalizes the employer's interest but he or she may be too busy to call you and ask you exactly what you wrote. Flesh it out. Similarly, when you describe your last summer job as an intern at a mutual fund, provide details on your projects and describe what concrete results your work achieved. Even if you didn't achieve anything concrete, try to say something concrete without lying or making up stories. If you have specific skills you'd like your reader to know, offer details. For example, "bilingual" – okay, tell me what two languages you are fluent in.

- *Use action verbs.* I bet you've heard this one before, but it's so very true. Résumés that employ action verbs do read better and grab the reader's attention and interest. "Designed and implemented VAR model to forecast exchange rates" sounds so much better, and more concrete, than "Worked on time series model for exchanges rates." The action verbs actually reflect your can-do attitude. Use as many as you can. Consult a thesaurus or expert if needed.

- *One page or two pages?* Some headhunters are religious about this and insist you keep your résumé to one page or they'll not send your résumé to employers. I don't think you should let the number of pages screw up your résumé layout and content. Tell the adamant headhunter that you have advanced skills and/or extensive experience and/or lots of publications, and these are very important for proving your strong qualification as a quant candidate. If the headhunter has any sense, she'll relent and let you have your way. If she doesn't, prepare a one-pager just for her to handle.

- *Proofread, proofread, proofread!* Make sure you proofread your résumé. Proofreading means checking your document for errors in spelling, grammar and punctuation. Common typos like spelling the as teh, receive as recieve, and principle where you mean principal (and vice versa) must be avoided. Another thing to do is try to get feedback from the headhunters you work with. Some of them can be helpful in giving you editorial feedback to help you improve your résumé. I highly recommend you get a good dictionary. I personally use an electronic English dictionary made by Sharp, model PW-E550, that features an American English dictionary, a thesaurus as well as an English grammar guide. When I'm online, I also consult the Encarta dictionary at `dictionary.msn.com`. Its one salient feature is employing sophisticated, natural-sounding text-to-speech technology to speak out aloud the words you look up, so if English is not your native language, you'll hear how a word is pronounced, in addition to seeing its pronunciation key.

The above list can, and should, be used as general guidelines as you begin writing a quant-oriented résumé. The rest of the chapter will delve into the details of composing and formatting a good résumé that fits your needs. The appendix at the end of this chapter has a sample résumé I've put together. It looks clean and makes it easy for the reader to see what the candidate has done and what skills he possesses.

Now, let's take a look at how you can create your own job-winning résumé.

Traditional vs. Creative: My Hard-Learned Lesson

A résumé, especially one used to find a job on Wall Street, is more or less a standardized document. It should have a certain look and structure to it, so the reader can immediately pick out the important items literally right off the paper.

I know, you are not a machine; you are a breathing human being, and you may even be a creative soul. But take your creative energy elsewhere. Trust me, the résumé is not the place where you try to be creative. If you did, it *might* work with some employers, but chances are, it won't work with most employers. Why? The reason is simple: Wall Street people are stodgy types. They generally tend to look at creative types with a high sense of suspicion. Besides, what you think is creative and tasteful may look childish or obscene or just plain weird to someone else.

I myself learned this the hard way. When I was graduating from Harvard College quite some years ago, I decided I wanted to find a job as a trader. I went to Harvard's Office of Career Services and looked through a book of sample résumés. "Boring!" was my reaction. What did I do? I went back to my dorm room and quickly typed up a résumé in Word. Then I did something no one else had ever done: I put a mug shot of myself – with my thick-rimmed glasses and geeky good looks – at the top of my résumé, under my name. As I looked over my résumé, I felt very proud, not of its substance, but of the black and white photo at the top of the page.

Well, I didn't get many interviews. My "wall of shame" in the room quickly filled up with rejection letters from all the big and small firms on Wall Street. I was pissed. I had good grades. I had taken challenging classes in math, statistics, economics, finance, computer science, and German. I had co-founded a student organization, led two others, and helped edit the campus daily newspaper. Anyway, I thought I had a strong background for a top-paying job on Wall Street. So why didn't anybody want to just interview me?

Then it hit me. Maybe it's that picture? In those days, quantitative finance was not in fashion. Most of the firms recruiting at Harvard were "white-shoe" investment banks. Quant geeks and Asians alike were seldom welcomed into the rank and file of these firms, let alone a crazy Asian kid who put his photo on the résumé!

Things sure have changed since then, but things haven't changed a bit since then. Doing non-conventional things like putting your picture on the résumé is still not acceptable. People expect you to stick to the true-and-tried. Now that I have read others' résumés from the point of view of an employer, I can kind of see the point. (God, maybe I'm just becoming old and stodgy.) A classic-looking résumé does please the eye more than a strange-looking one, especially at the end of a busy working day. Plus, a classic-looking résumé almost conveys a sense of awe, as if the writer tried hard to demonstrate his or her interest in working in a stodgy environment.

(Some hedge funds allow their employees to show up in the office in jeans and flip-flops every day. Don't let that fool you, though. When it comes to screening candidates, they still expect you to fit into certain mold. Play conservative, even when you apply to a hedge fund located in Hawaii.)

So, as you put together a new résumé or edit an existing one, make sure you give it a standardized, widely accepted look. For example, the résumé templates you find in Microsoft Word are usually okay.

Components of a Résumé

A quant-oriented résumé usually consists of the following sections:

- *Personal info.* At the top of the page (or the first page if you have more than one) you need to spell out your name and provide your contact info. I see no reason to give out your home address, although you can list your current city and state (or country if you are outside of the U.S.). In fact, if you plan to post your résumé online at various job sites, it's highly advisable that you omit your home address and even your phone number, so your information won't be easily lost to spammers and identity thieves. A phone number and e-mail address are necessary and sufficient; for the former, a cell phone number is perfectly acceptable. To prevent potential identity theft, you should definitely *not* give out your Social Security number or your date of birth; neither of these is needed for the initial screenings for employment. Likewise, there's no reason to tell people whether you are married or have kids.

- *Objective.* You may be surprised to find this included here. Indeed, most career advice guides ridicule the inclusion of an objective section. After all, they claim, isn't the fact you are looking for a job (e.g., a quant job) itself the objective? I beg to disagree. I think the objective section can be helpful for two reasons. First, it can serve as a guiding light as you look for an interesting position. Second, it gives the headhunter and the potential employer an immediate idea of what kind of position you are interested in. Having a clearly defined career objective reflects both your thoughtfulness and maturity. Of course, the objective should probably be left in fairly general terms. So instead of saying something like "I want to find a quant trading job," a general statement like "I want to find a challenging and stimulating quant position that leverages my quantitative knowledge and skills" will expose you to more opportunities – unless the narrower objective is absolutely what you want.

- *Quantitative and technical skills.* This section can be placed at the beginning (my preferred place) or at the end of the résumé. List skills that you truly possess and can substantiate. Anything that's related to math, statistics, finance, economics, programming, etc. can be listed here.

- *Education.* If you are still in school or fresh out of school, the education section should come before the experience section, although this is by no means a rule set in stone. This section lists the post-secondary education you have received; in other words, don't list your high school or middle school or anything before that. Include any awards and honors you have been bestowed. If you have been in school all your life so far, you may want to include significant extracurricular activities that demonstrate your quantitative experience or leadership quality.

- *Experience.* Here you list the jobs you have held in the past. If you have spent your entire life in school, you can list research projects you have actively participated in as well as internships and part-time jobs. List only jobs that showcase your quantitative and technical experience and/or skills. If you have absolutely no such experience either full-time or in school,

- *Publications, working papers or academic activities.* This section is optional and pertains mostly to people who have pursued an active academic research career, including newly minted Ph.D.s.

- *Other relevant info.* If you are a U.S. citizen or permanent resident, you may wish to mention that fact. (Otherwise, there's no need to list your country of citizenship.) If you speak multiple languages, list those languages. If you have been awarded any highly visible public honors such as the Presidential Medal, be sure to list them. (Note: school honors should be listed in the Education section.) Anything that tells others that you are smart and accomplished should be listed. On the other hand, leave out awards or honors from high school or before – nobody is really interested in those, and even if you won the gold medal in some international math competition back in high school, you'll probably find yourself more burdened than helped by mentioning this fact (i.e., you may be asked to solve some difficult math problems on the spot!). The key here is to include *relevant* information only.

- *References.* This section is optional but can lend a sense of credibility to your résumé. If you do choose to list references, list two or three. No more, no fewer. If you don't – I never do, for instance – leave out the rather useless "References available upon request" line. Keep in mind that almost all firms ask for references at some point of the job application process (in part to satisfy post-9/11 financial industry regulations).

By the way, although most people omit it, it's perfectly okay to list your top hobbies – if you have healthy hobbies that you actively participate in. You can list them in the relevant information section, or in a separate hobbies section. For example, playing sports, playing chess, playing an musical instrument, singing or dancing, collecting stamps or coins, solving crossword or sudoku, and shooting your own digital short films are all good-to-list hobbies. On the other hand, passive hobbies like surfing the Internet or watching sports on TV, questionable pastimes like gambling or cock- or cricket-fighting, and downright offensive activities like amassing a huge adult video collection or growing pot in the backyard garden, have absolutely no place on a résumé. What's more, whatever hobby or hobbies you list, make sure you are familiar with their ins-and-outs. It would be really nice if you meet an interviewer who shares the same hobby – but if he or she finds out that you barely know anything about the activity, he or she will suspect you listed it simply to pad your résumé, and this will definitely do your candidacy more harm than good.

The following sections will walk you through creating and improving each of these sections in detail.

Writing Your Résumé

Follow these steps to create a quant-oriented résumé (estimated time needed in parentheses); be sure to save your file often – and back it up to another storage device regularly.

1. If you have a current résumé or CV, highlight the important items that you think should make it to the final résumé. Anything – an advanced quantitative class, a summer job, a research project, a published paper, etc. – that demonstrates your ability to work with quantitative models. Don't worry about having too many items for now. Just circle the ones you think are important – and add any that you might have left out earlier. (~10 minutes)

2. If you do not yet have a résumé, don't panic. Take a blank piece of paper and start jotting down a list of qualification items that you think will make you a great future quant. See #1 above for some hints. BTW, this step is most effective when you do it with pen and paper instead of on a PC. (~20 minutes)

3. After you compiled your skill/qualification list, fire up Microsoft Word and create a blank document. (By the way, if you don't already have Microsoft Office, you can get Office 2003 Student and Teach Edition, with three licenses, for around $130. Here's the direct link to the product page on Amazon: www.amazon.com/exec/obidos/ASIN/ B0000C0XT1/pd_bk-20) Choose a résumé template (you may need to be connected to the Internet to do this). It's going

to save you a lot of time if you use a template instead of creating your own design. (Remember the story I told earlier?)

Type your name and contact info. If you have a preferred name that you want your future coworkers to know you by, you should put it down here instead of your full legal name. For instance, say your legal name is Charles William Morrish but you'd like to be known as Chuck Morrish, use Chuck Morrish. If you want to go by C.B. Morrish, put that down. As another example, say you are from China and your real name is Zhengxing Lu. As you know, the *Zh* and *X* sounds in Mandarin Chinese (Putonghua) are impossible for others to pronounce. So you adopt the Western name Aidan and would like to be called that on a daily basis. On your résumé, simply put down Aidan Lu as your name. There is really no need to do something like Zhengxing (Aidan) Lu or, worse, Aidan LU Zhengxing a la Hong Kong-style. When you fill out background check and other official forms later you'll have ample opportunities to let the employer know your legal name – so, for instance, you'll be able to deposit future paychecks! For the résumé, feel free to use the name you want to be known by.

Speaking of adopting a Western name, make sure you pick a sensible, "normal" first name. Once I saw someone calling himself "Welldone Zhou." I couldn't help but laugh my head off – and I still laugh every time I recall this name. Do you suppose I took the guy seriously? (It didn't help his background wasn't a good fit.) Similarly, a name like "Playstation Wang" would make potential employers think twice about your maturity (and sanity). Ask some American friends for help if you need it. One more thing, don't forget that, in most Western countries, one's given name (Zhengxing) comes before the family name (Lu); the form "Lu, Zhengxing," while acceptable in some countries, does not look natural to an American reader. Plus, if you want to attach a suffix such as PhD to your name, you'll definitely want to use the first name first form, e.g., "Zhengxing Lu, PhD," not "Lu, Zhengxing, PhD" or "LU Zhengxing, PhD." Bottom line: when in Rome, do as the Romans do. Follow the local custom, and you'll find your résumé going a longer way than if you didn't.

Next, you may leave out your home address if you want

to keep some privacy – in fact, I recommend you omit the home address – but be sure to write down your telephone number (cell is fine) as well as e-mail address. Do not worry about any formatting right now. Just type out the content first. *Hint:* If you are in school, be sure to use your official school e-mail address, one that ends with the domain name ".edu." Use a free web-based e-mail account like Hotmail *only if* you are already working and don't want your current employer to know about your job search, or you don't otherwise have an official-looking address. Employers do tend to take official-looking e-mail addresses more seriously. It's just human nature. (~5 minutes)

4. Put down the section headings: Objective (optional), Skills, Education, Experience, Publications (or Academic Activities; both optional), Certifications (optional), and Personal Info. I think these are sufficient, but feel free to leave out any that doesn't apply to you or add a section or two that reflect your truly unique qualification. For instance, if you are a grad student and have never had a "real" job – TA-ships and RA-ships don't count as real jobs! – you may substitute the Experience section with a Research Projects section.

   Earlier – back on page 32 – I already gave you the rundown on what each section contains. Here are more specific details. Remember, at this point we are not filling in the all the section contents yet; we're focusing on putting up the framework of the résumé.

   Some people like to have an Objective section. I used to think it was superfluous – after all, I thought, if I submitted my résumé to a hedge fund, wouldn't my objective already be to find a job there? But I've had a change of heart since. Nowadays it's not uncommon for us to work with headhunters, and these people often submit a résumé to multiple places. By putting down your objective, you actually clarify what you are looking for. My advice is to make the objective broad enough so you don't pigeon-hole yourself into a niche field, but also make it narrow enough so you don't come across as somebody who doesn't know what he or she wants. See the sample résumé in the appendix to this chapter for an example.

   I highly recommend putting the Skills section up front,

so anyone reading your résumé can easily see what essential skills you have. This is especially true if your résumé spans more than one page. Should Education come before Experience? There's no right or wrong answer on this one. If you are currently in school, or fresh out of school, or a graduate of a top-ranked school – think Top 20 in your field or in general reputation – it makes perfect sense to put down Education first. If you have already had some significant experience in quant, you may choose to list your experiences first. Either way is fine, as long as your most important qualifications are highlighted and easy for the reader to spot.

In terms of the phrasing of the section headings, I think it's advisable you stick with the words I have here. It's unnecessary to use such words like "Skill Set," "Educational Background," or "Professional Experience" (the recruiter will only be interested in your professional experience anyway!). By the way, the Personal Info section at the end is where you might want to put down things like "U.S. Citizen" or "U.S. Permanent Resident" to distinguish yourself from other candidates. The truth is, if two identically qualified candidates go for the same job, it's likely the employer will pick the one already eligible to work in the U.S. (or whatever country you seek the position in), since hiring that person is so much cheaper and more convenient. Of course, if you need an OPT or H-1 in order to start working, you shouldn't mention this on the résumé. Most large employers will not discriminate against candidates who don't have a green card – after all, most quants these days are foreign-born and went through the H-1 and green card processes themselves.

5. Now transcribe qualifications you wrote down earlier (in step 1 or step 2) to the computer. Don't worry about formatting or the details; those will come next. Just enter the list into Word. When done, read back the list to make sure you didn't leave out anything important. (~20 minutes)

6. With the list done, it's time to fill in the details. For now, provide as many details as you can. Do not worry about the verbiage; we'll fix that later. Don't worry about the length of the résumé, either. It's okay if it ends up on two or three pages. The key here is to *not* miss any important aspects of your life

and background that may help you get a quant job. So type away. (~30-60 minutes)

    a. For every institution on the list (education and experience), give its geographic location as city, state or country. If a city is well known – e.g., Boston, New York City, Shanghai – you may omit the state or country name.

    b. For each activity (education, experience, publication, research project, etc.), give its time frame. For example, "City College of Wasteland, Wasteland, Abscondin Republic, 2000-05." Again, we do the formatting in a later step.

    c. For each activity (education, experience, working paper, publication, etc.), give a detailed description of what it was about and what you achieved. If it was a degree, say so and list any honors or awards you received. Then list any significant learning you achieved. If it was a major research paper, give its title and briefly describe what it was about. Remember, use action verbs wherever you can.

    d. For each skill set (quantitative, financial, etc.), list the specific skills that you *already* have. Do not list a skill if you can't demonstrate it in front of an interviewer. This point is so important that I will devote an entire section later (starting on page 56) to the issue.

7. You don't need a line that says "References available upon request" (because their availability is always implicit!), and you don't really need to list any references, but if you do choose to list references, list two or three. For each reference, provide his or her name, title/position, affiliation, and phone number and/or e-mail address. Be sure to talk to the references first! You want to get their permission to be listed on your résumé. You also want to make sure they'll have positive things to say about you when they are contacted.

8. Finally, format your résumé. If you picked a template as I suggested in step 3, this should be straightforward. Or you may use the sample résumé in this chapter's appendix if you wish. If you have decided to do your own formatting, follow the general guidelines provided earlier on page 28. Still, I highly

recommend you use a Word template or follow the style of my sample résumé. Why reinvent the wheel when others have already done the work for you? (~30 minutes)

9. Look over your résumé on the computer screen. Did Word flag any spelling or grammar issues? You can also press the F7 key to start a spelling and grammar check manually. In fact, I would ignore or turn off Word's grammar check; it's just not good. But pay attention to the red wavy underlines. These alert you to potential typos. Fix all typos. If you aren't sure what a correct spelling should be, right-click the word and Microsoft Word will show a list of suggestions. (~5 minutes)

Congratulations. You just completed a solid draft for your résumé. And you did save and back up your precious résumé file, didn't you?

Now, it's critically important that you close Word and put your résumé out of your mind for a while. You may want to surf the Internet; you may want to go play a game or two on your PS3 (or Wii or Xbox 360); you may want to go out for a walk and listen to your favorite CD; you may want to call up your significant other and complain about your current finances (but don't talk about the résumé!); etc. The idea is, you want to avoid thinking about your résumé for some time – this "some time" can be a few hours to a few days. That way, when you move to the next step as detailed below, you'll be able to start from a semi-clean slate, so to speak. This makes it easy for you to edit your résumé into a stellar one.

Improving Your Résumé

After the break (which can last as long as you want – in fact, the longer the better), you are ready to take a hard look at your résumé and make some edits and improvements. It's not yet time to ask somebody else to read your résumé. You want to make sure your résumé is already in a good shape before you send it to a friend or professional editor for additional fine-tuning. Remember, "garbage in, garbage out": if you send someone else garbage, they can dress it up in pretty formatting, but it'll still look and smell garbage! Always make your own edits first. After all, you know yourself better than anyone else does, right?

Important: print out your résumé! We wouldn't want to edit such an important document on the computer screen, because it's easy to miss errors on the screen. You want to print it out on paper. Make sure you print in standard mode, not economy. Now is not the time to save on ink or toner.

Even if you think your first draft was already a winner, trust me – it ain't yet. *Every* first draft can be improved. After the hiatus, you'll benefit from having a pair of critical eyes, and this will allow you to read your first draft from an outsider's point of view and spot problems easily.

We divide this action item into two parts. In the first part, we improve on the content of your résumé. In the second, we improve its layout (formatting). Actually, you can do these two things in either order; it doesn't really matter.

Our approach will be top-down. Take out a red pen and follow these steps to improve the content of your résumé:

1. Read through your résumé quickly. Are there any obvious spelling, word usage or grammar errors? Are there sentences that don't read well or don't make sense? Highlight these and any other problems you spot. In this step, you rely on your critical eyes to identify obvious problems – problems that literally pop out of the paper.

2. Take a look at the *logical flow* of the sections. If you are still in school, haven't worked full-time for more than two years, or have never worked in finance, you should put the education section before the experience section. If you already have some full-time finance-related or quantitatively analytical experience, you should list experience first. Either way, I recommend the skills section be the first section of your résumé. That way, a recruiter or employer can *immediately* see what quantitative skills you possess, without having to read through your other section and make the inference himself or herself. Remember, the easier you make it for the reader to see your qualifications, the better your chance of getting an interview.

3. For each section, go down the list of items you've written. Are the items essential? Did you cover all the bases in each section? At this point we won't edit the actual contents of the

list items yet; that'll come next.

For the skills section, did you list more than six skills? If you did, you may want to break them down into categories: quantitative skills, business skills, programming skills, etc. If there are fewer than six, do *not* break them down into categories, or the list would look kind of ridiculous. If you had put down fewer than three skills, you should think hard and bring the list up in count. After all, you are smart, you are a future quant, and you doubtless have a lot of skills to offer to your future employer.

The education section is usually straightforward. One frequently asked question is "Should I list out my educational trainings by school/institution or by degree?" I say it doesn't really matter. If you went to top-ranked schools – think Top 20 – it might be advantageous to use them as boldfaced item headings. If you went to so-so schools but would like to emphasize your degrees and/or certificates, feel free to do so. If you have advanced degrees – read, post-bachelor – it's best to list your most advanced degree first, all the way back to that B.A. or B.S. (Bachelor of Science).

For the list in the experience section, you need to ask yourself, "Is this one relevant to my qualification as a quant?" Try to think from the POV of an employer. If you see someone who worked at this or that job, or did research in this or that area, would you hire the person? It's not an easy task, trying to think like somebody else. But do your best. Pretend you are reading a stranger's résumé. Better yet, pretend you already dislike this person and want to find every reason not to offer an interview. Use the red pen to jot down or highlight any changes to the list you want to make. Again, we are not editing the actual content for each item yet; we are just doing an exercise to make sure you have the most relevant and powerful items listed in this section. When done with this step, take a good break before moving on to the next.

4. We are now ready to work like a surgeon and perform precise edits on the body text. Here's one great tip for ya, my dear reader: instead of re-reading what you already wrote and trying to use that "critical eye," I highly recommend you just cover up the text under each list item and re-write the whole thing! No

cheating here. Just look at an item (e.g., your master's education or your most recent full-time job) and pretend you hadn't written up the details yet. Then create the details as if you were writing them for the first time.

Let me offer an example. Say you spent your last summer interning at a high-tech start-up doing mostly C# programming to analyze traffic data. (Surprisingly, quite a few candidates I have come across seem to have had this kind of experience!) Your listed item probably reads "Farcix Data Corp., Newport, RI, summer 2006." Now without trying to recall what you typed on the PC before, use that red pen and quickly jot down what you right at this moment think were the highlights from this job. What did you do exactly? What tasks did you tackle? What praises did you manager shower on you at the farewell party? So on and so forth. See my point?

Your mind works differently when you write with a pen and when you type on a PC. Working this way, you attain two benefits: one, you ensure you are not missing out on any important details; two, you can later compare the two descriptions you've written and decide what to include, both content-wise and wording-wise. You can simply compare the "old" version with the "new" version and choose the best elements from each version.

Using the same example as before, let's say previously you put down "Summer intern [title] – wrote C# programs to analyze traffic patterns," whereas later, with a clearer mind, you penned "Summer analyst [wow, already so much better!] – completed C#-based project to analyze real-time traffic patterns and create efficiency matrix." It's obvious which version you would use, isn't it?

If you are the lazy type who just doesn't want to re-do everything, fear not. No résumé is going to be perfect. All you want is a good résumé, one good enough to get you the job you want. In this case, use your red pen freely and mark any additions or deletions or changes of wording you want. This is the time to check whether you are doing everything you can to "empower" your résumé. Pay attention to job titles (e.g., "software engineer" [good] vs. "entry-level programmer" [not good]) In the Education section, under the degree and honors line, you can list or describe your achievements in school. The most recent educational experience should get the most space. As you go back in time, reduce the amount of description. For example, if you got your Ph.D. three years ago and your B.A. 12 years ago, there's really no need to mention all the undergraduate societies or fraternities you belonged to (unless you know that many of your frat brothers work on Wall Street – then be sure to mention it!).

The precise editing step will take a lot of time – and deservedly so. The body content is the "meat" of your résumé. The previous two steps improved the "skeleton," and this step has enhanced the real thing. Feel free to spend as much time as you need on each item, especially items that you consider very important.

5. Now, read through your entire résumé and assess its content as your read – once again, pretending you are a potential employer who's reading this for the first time. Use that red pen to highlight anything you think can be improved.

6. Go back to Microsoft Word and make the changes to your electronic résumé. If Word flags any spelling mistakes, be sure to correct them right away.

Congratulations! Chances are, the current draft of your résumé is significantly improved over the first draft. Feel free to repeat the above steps one more time: print out the draft, mark changes with a red pen, implement the changes in Word, and so on. Just be aware of the law of diminishing marginal returns: after two thorough edits, further efforts likely won't add much value without getting some outside help.

We are not done with enhancing your résumé yet. We just improved the substance of your résumé. Now we need to make the résumé look good. It's time we formatted the résumé for a professional look.

When it comes to résumé formatting, a couple of ground rules should be kept in mind:

1. *Keep it simple*. Stick to the basic fonts (Arial and Times New Roman) and avoid any fancy typefaces – the reader of your résumé will be a quant or professional recruiter, not an artist. (And if the reader *is* artistic, he or she likely won't be impressed with your choice of fancy fonts.) Bold only the

section headings (Education, Experience, …) and list headings (school name, company name, published article title, …). If you *had to* bold certain phrases in your résumé for emphasis, keep them to a minimal.

2. *Keep it consistent.* Use the same typeface and style for job titles and education degrees. For instance, you can use italicized Times New Roman for these things: *Research Scientist, Senior QA Engineer, Ph.D., JD/MD,* etc. Of course, all headings should be consistent on the same level. Once I saw a résumé with one section heading in caps and left-justified and another (on the second page) underlined and centered. It just didn't leave me a good impression of the work quality the candidate would bring to my group. If somebody is so sloppy about his résumé, would he be thorough and detail-oriented (two qualities quants should possess) when he does real work? I think not. In addition, I think this lack of editing shows a perfunctory attitude, something that a reader may interpret as lacking respect for other people. The reader may decide that "If you don't care enough about getting this job, why should I consider you for this job?"

To format your résumé, we'll follow the same top-down approach we employed when editing the content. Ready? Here we go:

1. First, let's plan out the overall appearance of your résumé, from layout structure to choice of fonts.

    a. Even though résumés all follow the same logical structure, there are many ways to lay out a particular résumé. For example, do you want all the headings to flush left? Or do you want them centered? For list items, would you like to use bullet points, or just bold them but use no bullet points? At this point, you can take a look at the built-in résumé templates that came with Microsoft Word to get some ideas.

        To do this, first you need to be connected to the Internet, as Word will be getting the templates from a Microsoft website. Open the File menu, then select "New…". Under the Templates heading, either search for *résumé* from the "Search online for:" search box, or click the "Templates on Office Online" link. Browse through the résumé templates and see if there's a particular style you like. If so, download it for a closer look or emulation.

You can also look at the sample résumé in the appendix to this chapter for a layout and format with a clean, modern look. Or you can buy low-cost software programs like *Resume Maker* to get additional ideas. Still not satisfied? If you have access to a career office, go there and browse through their sample résumés. Personally, I don't think you should spend too much time on this step. Remember, it's really the *content* of your résumé that matters. When it comes to the look, as long as your résumé appears clean and easy on the eye, it's good enough.

b. One feature which I have seen on only a few résumés – and a feature that I have just started emulating myself – is utilizing a page header on a multiple-page résumé. The header is the one-line text that's placed above the main text of a document. This book uses headers to let you know which chapter you are reading, as well as to show you the page number. If your résumé spans more than one page, it's a good idea to put your name, and a page number, in the header on all pages except the first page. (A header on the first page would look awkward.) So if you have two pages, put a header on page 2. If you have three pages, both page 2 and page 3 should have a header.

For the header, put your name on the left, in a bold font. Then on the right edge of the header, put down the page number. Here's how you generate such a header in Word 2003 or earlier: Open the View menu. Select "Header and Footer" (5th item from the bottom when you have the full menu open). A header box with dashed borders appear at the top of the page. When the blinking text cursor is aligned to the left edge, choose a bold font (e.g., Times New Roman bold) that's one size larger than your body text, and type your full name. Do *not* make your name all caps or in small caps; that would just look pretentious. Do append any titles (Ph.D., MD, CFA, etc.) you may have. Now press the Tab key twice or thrice so that the blinking text cursor is positioned at the right edge. On the "Header and Footer" toolbar, the first small icon to the right of "Insert AutoText" looks like a dog-eared document with a pound (#) symbol on it. If you hover your mouse pointer over this icon, an "Insert Page Number" tooltip will appear. That's the button you use to insert an automatic page number (so in the future if your résumé takes on more pages, Word will automatically number each page correctly.) Click it, and a page number will appear. Click "Close" on the "Header and Footer" toolbar. Right now, page 1 also gets the header, which makes the page look ugly. It's also redundant since page 1 already has your name at the top. To make the header not show on page 1, open the File menu, select "Page Setup…", and click "Layout" at the top of the dialog box. On this Layout tab, the second section is titled "Headers and Footers," and there are two checkbox items here. Check the second item, "Different first page" to turn it on. Then click OK to save the change. Voila! Now your beautiful and informative header will only appear on pages subsequent to the first page, and your résumé all of a sudden looks so much more professional – even though you haven't done anything else!

c. When it comes to the choice of fonts, the ground rules laid out previously should be adhered to strictly. It's totally okay if you stick to one font – but make that font a serif font like Times New Roman or Georgia. *Serif fonts* are fonts that have little ornamental projections ("serifs") at the start and end of each stroke. *San serif* ("without serif") fonts like Arial and Tahoma look like they are made up of bare sticks, with no projections ornamenting the each stroke. It's common for writers to use a serif font like Times New Roman for the main text and a san serif font like Arial for headings.

My recommendation? Use Times New Roman

for your contact info (see the next step for formatting details) and the main text, and use Arial only for the section headings (Education, Experience, etc.). Above all, avoid non-conventional fonts like Comic Sans MS; they'll just make your résumé either difficult to read or facetious-looking.

2. We now format the personal contact section of your résumé. Obviously, you want people to see your name. It should be boldfaced, and it should be in a larger font than the rest of the document – but don't make it too large! If you do, people may think of you as an egomaniac – which is a "good" thing on a trading desk after you've proved your worthiness, but not now when you are still a "lowly" job seeker. If your body text is going to be in 12-point Times New Roman (which, incidentally, is what the text you are reading now uses), then you can put your name in 14- or 16-point Times New Roman. Whether you want to left-flush, center, or right-flush your name is totally up to you. Try them all and see which one you like the most.

    If you have a doctorate (Ph.D., D.S., M.D.), a JD, an MBA, or a professional chartered title like CFA or CPA, put the title or titles down, and separate your name and the title with a comma, e.g., "Morris Quant, MD, PhD, JD, CPA, CFP" – note that when used in headings, the dots in the abbreviations are best left out, so PhD looks better than Ph.D. here. (Whether you prefer to use the dots or not in the body text is up to you.) If you have a master's other than MBA, whether to include the degree title is up to you; people usually omit it.

    Now, here comes a great tip for those who don't have an advanced degree or professional certification title yet but are working on getting one: under your name, in a smaller font than your name (e.g., 11- or 12-point Times New Roman), write down "XXX Candidate," where XXX is the certification you are pursuing. Examples: "Ph.D. Candidate in Finance"; "CFA Candidate – Level 2"; "MBA Candidate." The key thing here is to include the word "candidate," which tells the reader that you will achieve the title in the future. When I first saw someone do this, I was very impressed and wondered why I hadn't thought of it when I was still in grad school and hadn't got my Ph.D. yet. I think it can make your resume stand out from the other "candidates."

A special note to Ph.D. students: you are considered a Ph.D. candidate *after* you've passed all your qualifying exams. Before that, you are a Ph.D. student, not yet a Ph.D. candidate. If you are still a Ph.D. student, it's perfectly okay to – in fact you should – put down something like "Ph.D. student in applied mathematics" under your name. More information is better than less in this case.

Now, what if you are an undergrad or are not in the process of getting a title of any sort? Worry not. Very few people working on titles use this technique, so your résumé won't be at a disadvantage vis-à-vis most of your competitors, even those working on a CFA or Ph.D. Remember: never invent a title you don't have. People will surely find out if you tried to mislead them.

For your home address (if you put one down; see page 32 for discussion on why you might want to leave out your address – I, for instance, never give out my home address) and your phone number(s), use the same font as your name but use a size that's either the same as your main text or slightly smaller. You can italicize these but do not bold them. For the e-mail address and web address (if you have one), you can use the main-text font, or you can use `Courier New` to add a geeky flavor to this information. If you do use Courier New, keep in mind that this font is bigger than the other fonts size-for-size, so you will want to choose a smaller size, e.g. 10-point.

3. A nice layout touch at this point is to put a *divider rule,* which is just a horizontal straight line, between the personal information section and the main body of the document. This lends a simple-yet-elegant stylistic element to your résumé, and also shows off your sophistication and good taste. You can format the line however you want. I prefer a double-line style, with a thin line above a thicker one.

Microsoft Word makes this task easy to accomplish. Here's what you do in Word 2003: Open the View menu. Select "Toolbars" then "Drawing." (Omit this step if the Drawing toolbar was already turned on. It's located at the bottom of the window by default.) Now, at the bottom of the Word window, the Drawing toolbar appears. (You can reposition this toolbar anywhere you want by dragging its handle.) The icon to the right of "AutoShapes" looks like a line; yep, that's the line-drawing tool. Click it to select it. Now you can just draw a straight line by holding down the Shift key and dragging your mouse (with the left button held down) horizontally across the page. You can fine-tune the line's length and position on page. You may need to hold down the Alt key to make small, subtle adjustments to length and position. (Without holding down the Alt key, you'll find the adjustments take place in predefined steps instead of in pixels.) To change the line's style, click the icon on the Drawing toolbar that looks like three lines; it should be located to the right of the A icon. I use the "4 ½ pt" style. Finally, resize the "object box" that encloses the line so it won't push the rest of your résumé all the way to somewhere near the bottom of the page. By the way, you can do this for your header as well; when your text cursor is inside the header, any "objects" (such as the divider line) drawn will be positioned in the header and show up on every page. (Remember: Word 2007 uses an entirely different interface, based on "ribbons," from all previous versions. Fortunately, Office 2007 includes a vastly improved help system.)

4. You've probably already done the formatting of the section headings in Step 1a on page 45, when you planned the overall look of the résumé, e.g., via Word templates. These headings should stand out clearly from the body text, so as long as you **boldface**, *italicize*, ALL-CAPS, or <u>underline</u> them, it should be sufficient. Believe it or not, I have seen résumés where the headings were meshed together with the rest of the text, which made those résumés look cramped and disorganized. Don't make that mistake. Ensure that the reader can easily identify the major sections of your résumé. (Tip: Try to give your résumé draft a read-over at the end of a tiring day, when your eyes and mind are fatigued. Can you make out the major parts of your own résumé? Can you easily pick out the important things? If you can't, you can bet that the typical employer won't be able to, either.)

5. For the Skills section, let's say you have listed three groups of three skills each (for a total of nine skills). Format the group heading (e.g., "Quantitative") first, in the same font as the body text but probably italicized. The skill items themselves can be done either as bullet points (my preferred format) or included in a descriptive sentence.

    The bullet points can each occupy a single line, in which case you can elaborate on that particular skill. For example, under the Quantitative group heading, the first bullet point might read "Time series methods: stationary and non-stationary models, GARCH, ACD, high-frequency returns modeling."

    Alternatively – especially if you want to keep your résumé fit on one page – you may want to bundle the bullet points in one line together. To do that, you'll need Microsoft Word's Format → Columns function to divide a line into *n* columns (where *n* is the number of bullet points you have; it should be no more than 3) and put one bullet point in each column. Regardless of your choice, as long as the skills are listed or described clearly and jump right off the page in the eyes of the reader, you've accomplished the desired effect. Use the "fatigued eyes" test mentioned in step 5 if necessary to judge whether your skill listing and descriptions are effective.

6. We've now come to the Education section. (I assume your Education section comes before the Experience section.) Let's say you followed the traditional structure and first listed out the schools you went to and under each school the degree(s) you received or are expecting to receive. The school names should be in bold. Sometimes people use italics for the school names, but personally I don't think that looks effective on paper. Your degree and major (e.g., "Ph.D. in nuclear weapon design" or "B.A. in feminine studies") can be in italics, or you can just leave them in a plain font. If your bachelor's was honored with *summa cum laude* or *magna cum laude,* be sure to mention that. If it was just *cum laude,* you may or may not choose to mention it; you should be aware that, at many schools, everyone who graduates with a bachelor's automatically gets *cum laude,* so this "honor" doesn't carry much weight at all.

    A few words for foreign university graduates: graduates

of U.S. colleges (post-secondary schools that bestow the four-year bachelor degree) are given the title of either B.A. (bachelor of arts) or B.S. (bachelor of science). If the bachelor title in your home country goes by another designation (e.g., SSB), you should tell your reader what it means by spelling out its entire name. You might also want to put down, in parentheses, what the U.S. equivalent may be. (All this is, of course, assuming you are applying to a U.S. firm.) In the past I've seen non-U.S. degrees that made no sense to me or my colleagues, and it was a bit frustrating for us to have to guess whether it was a four-year degree or something of greater or lesser value. If you paid an accredited American educational evaluation service to certify your foreign degree(s), that's even better, and be sure to mention it in your résumé.

For the elaborative description of your educational experience, use either bullet points or simple sentences to highlight your achievements. (I've already covered what's considered essential here in the content-editing section a few pages back.)

7. Formatting the Experience section is similar to doing the Education section. Company names should be in bold. Job titles can be in italics or plain; your choice. Use bullet points effectively to highlight your accomplishments on each job. If there's a word here or there that you feel compelled to boldface because you believe they should really be noticed by the reader, go ahead and do so, but do it sparingly or you risk ending up with a "crying-wolf" résumé.

8. For the remaining sections such as Publications, Working Papers, Research Activities, and Honors, use bullet points. Publications should be cited in this format: "Title," *Journal,* volume number (publication date): page numbers (coauthors) [award, if any]. For example:

Crystal-Balling the Stock Market: Evidence from a 120-Year Study of the Dow Jones Industrial Average," *Journal of Financial Wizardry,* volume I no. 2 (summer 2007): 3-321 (with A. Shih) [awarded best paper of the century by *JFW*'s board of editors]

It's also fine to use the accepted standard bibliography format for your field of study. The only point of departure I recommend is to omit the authors listing at the beginning of the entry; instead, put your coauthor's names in parenthesis a la the example here. If you had more than two coauthors, say "with John Doe, et al."

After all the sweat and work, you are done! Now give your résumé to someone who can honestly critique it: your significant other, a professor, a trusted friend (who's not looking for the same kind of job as you!), a professional editor, a recruiter you've been talking to, etc. It would be best if one or more of your readers are familiar with the financial industry. But even if none does, you will still benefit tremendously from other people's comments. When feedback comes in, be selective! While other people can often spot obvious mistakes and provide a fresh set of eyes, you have to be aware that sometimes their suggestions may not make much sense or may not be relevant for a quant résumé.

If you need to print out your résumé for submission, I recommend two things: (1) Use a laser printer. Even though inkjet printers have improved dramatically in the last few years, they are still behind laser printers in print quality when it comes to black text. Entry-level name-brand laser printers like Okidata, Konica Minolta and Brother often cost under $50 at Staples or Office Max, so get yourself one if you don't have ready access to a laser printer. (Always buy a name-brand.) (2) Print on good-quality paper, preferably the kind specifically formulated for résumés. When I see a résumé printed on a piece of see-through paper, I usually just throw it into the recycle bin. Remember: you have to show respect for your reader, and the paper quality reflects your attitude, a lot.

Tailoring Your Résumé to a Position

One popular route many job hunters follow is to have multiple versions of their résumés, each version tailored for a particular type of job. For example, say you are highly skilled and experienced in both programming and high-level modeling. For each skill you have enough experiences to fill two pages, so you don't want to put everything down into a four-page résumé that would end up reading like a laundry list. In this case, it makes perfect sense to have two résumés, one promoting your programming talent and the other advertising your modeling expertise. You would mention the other skill, too, but only in passing.

This approach essentially places a practice focus on your résumé. Each version tries to sell you into a particular field in quant finance, be it mathematical modeling (e.g., asset pricing), econometric analysis (e.g., microstructure), or data mining (e.g., volatility pattern identification). It makes it easy for the reader to identify quickly your qualifications in the hiring area, without getting bombarded with extra information that he or she does not need to know and in any case is not interested in knowing. This ultimately benefits you because your skills relevant to the job are highlighted.

You should create multiple versions only after you're done with the master résumé, which includes all your qualifications as a potential quant. In other words, the master résumé contains everything you can think of that's relevant to potential quant jobs. Then create tailored versions that present you as a master of a particular trade (the one the employer is interested in!). When you have a single master document to work from, it's easy to produce and manage the "slave" documents. If, instead, you tried to write multiple versions at the same time, making changes can become a headache as you struggle to maintain consistency across the different versions. So, create an all-inclusive master résumé first, then just cut-and-paste into focused versions.

The caveat of this approach is, when you have multiple versions of your résumé, you might end up sending the wrong version to the wrong employer. You must be the meticulous kind to avoid this potential catastrophe. Of course, if your versions differ little from one another, the damage won't be fatal, and most likely the résumé reader won't have a clue. However, if you send a version that heavily advertises your C++ skills to a job that requires no programming but does demand time series knowledge, you can be sure your résumé will go into the recycle bin in no time. So, before you click the Send button in your e-mail client, always double-check to see that you attached the right version of your résumé.

Another customization technique – one that can also help mitigate the version confusion problem discussed in the previous paragraph – is to tailor your résumé to each position you apply to. This is very simple to do. First, highlight the skill requirements in the job posting. Next, modify your master résumé so that those specific skill areas are emphasized while you other skills that are periphery to this particular position are either deemphasized or left out completely. The advantage of this approach is the résumé you submit will make you look like a perfect fit and will allow you to stand out from the rest of the pack. The potential disadvantage, a rather minor one IMHO, is the reader may actually want to hire someone with a broader background. Of course, this can be easily addressed by including (but not emphasizing) your other skills. The most critical issue about this fit-the-position approach, though, is making sure you tell the truth about your skills and being able to demonstrate you do have those skills. See page 56 for a thorough discussion on this.

From CV to Résumé

If you are an academic – a Ph.D. candidate, a post-doc, a professor, or a researcher – it's likely you already have a CV (curriculum vitae). Should you submit your CV in lieu of a résumé to a potential employer?

The answer is no. You should – actually, you must – take the time to convert your CV to a résumé. There are a few reasons for this:

1. The résumé format is easier to read for potential employers. Remember, the first person reading your résumé may not be a quant himself or herself. This could be an HR (human resource) representative who does the first-level screening of résumés. Or this person could be a non-quant assistant to the hiring manager. Or it could even be a programmer on the team who's not familiar with the CV format. The point is, many people in the industry just aren't familiar with the content and layout of a CV. If you submit a CV and it lands in front of a non-quant, it'll likely look strange to the person and may be escorted to the recycle bin promptly. Don't risk it. Follow the industry standard and write up a résumé – a good-looking résumé.

2. The résumé tells a better story of your qualifications for an industry job. A typical CV is laid out in a plain format and lists your educational background, your teaching and/or research experience, your current projects, and your publications and working papers. You rarely use action verbs in a CV. A CV is judged good if it has a long list of published papers in

respected journals. However, employers on Wall Street rarely care about a laundry list of all the research projects you've ever participated in or the academic conferences you've presented at. Instead, they want to know what important things you have been doing and what practical skills you can bring to the table, *their* table. A properly laid-out and worded résumé draws the employer's attention to your achievements and thus makes a strong case for your candidacy.

3. Many headhunters (professional recruiters) simply do not accept CVs. Again, these folks never had the kind of advanced academic training you had or are gaining, so they do not understand the purpose of the CV. And, you know what? They are right. Different industries have different standards, and on Wall Street, a résumé is what counts.

I hope you are now convinced you should convert your CV to a proper résumé. Even if you aren't, just follow my advice and do it. It's better to spend a couple hours creating a résumé than sending out your CV to dozens of firms only to never receive a reply.

How do you convert your CV into a proper résumé? It's not difficult at all. First, review the earlier section on the parts of an effective résumé. Then, use a pen to mark your CV into the relevant sections: education, experience, publications, research activities, etc. Looking over your research experience and papers, summarize the quantitative skills you acquired from these activities. Did you write a paper on differential equations? Did you implement a Monte Carlo over a large dataset? Did you conduct data mining? Did you write a 10,000-line Matlab program for linear programming? Spend a few minutes thinking hard about what you did on each project and what you learned, and you'll reap plenty of benefits from this effort. Finally, follow the steps given in the previous sections to create and edit your résumé.

The Single *Most* Critical Aspect of Your Résumé

Now, here's a very practical tip that I think is worth this book's weight in gold: when you put down a skill on your résumé, **make sure you can back it up with concrete evidence.** This applies not only to academic achievements such as a Ph.D. or professional certifications like CFA, but skills and proficiencies as well. Let me give you a real-world example.

Not too long ago, I interviewed a candidate who claimed he was an expert in C++ and SAS, two commonly used tools among quants. I happen to be proficient in one and know something about the other – enough to ask some advanced-level questions and know the answer to those questions! So I asked him one question each on the two languages, questions that were actually very basic, nothing tricky at all. For example, on SAS, I asked him "what are the two major types of programming blocks in SAS" (answer: DATA steps and PROC steps). No matter how I rephrased this question or what hints I gave him, he couldn't answer it. When I finally gave up and asked him what a DATA step and a PROC step were, he didn't know! For an SAS "expert" to not know this most basic concept, that's simply beyond belief. Needless to say, he didn't get the job. (After he failed to answer any of my simple questions, I spent the rest of the interview just chitchatting with him. (But see Chapter 4 to find out what you should do in case you can't support a skill claim on your résumé.)

Way too many candidates make the fatal mistake of listing skills they don't really have. They do so because, one, they've heard these skills (such as C++ proficiency) are "sexy" in the eyes of employers; two, they took a course years ago and think they are still an expert; and three, they believe that interviewers won't actually ask these questions. The last belief is simply misguided and wrong. Quant interviewers such as yours truly spent their careers dealing with various quant topics, from panel data to numerical methods to non-stationary time series. We want to hire people who have the concrete knowledge to contribute to our projects. We don't need people who *think* they know something. And we definitely don't want people who pad their resumes with fluff or lie about their backgrounds.

So, listen up! If you say on your résumé you can speak Chinese fluently, make sure you do as you may come face-to-face with a Chinese speaker. (Pretending to a Mandarin speaker that you speak the Cantonese dialect won't work, either.) If you claim you are an expert in time series, make sure you can answer any question related to the subject, from GARCH to VAR to co-integration to stationarity tests. If your résumé presents you as a SQL (usually pronounced "sequel" for historical reasons) master, make sure you can show off some advanced SQL queries. In short, your résumé must be truthful and every fine point must be supportable with evidence. Never assume your quant interviewer is stupid.

(Yes, there *are* stupid and incompetent quants, but they are few and far between. Besides, you will likely meet with more than one quant during the interview process. If every one of the quants on a team seems dumb to you, you'd better cross that place off of your desired job list.)

Missed all that? Let me repeat: Be truthful on your résumé. Make sure you can back up every single claim you put down on paper with proof.

Creating a Cover Letter

Strictly speaking, the cover letter is not a part of the résumé. Not all employers even bother to read cover letters. But, when properly written, it can significantly enhance your candidacy. Why? A good cover letter can serve to convince the reader why you are different from the other candidates. Let's face it: most people with quantitative skills really have more-or-less similar backgrounds. Oftentimes, one résumé just reads the same as another. Sure, you can dress up your résumé or boldface a lot of keywords in an effort to try to attract your reader's attention, but if he or she is tired (or in a bad mood), there's no telling if that attention will indeed be grabbed.

A good, properly written cover letter, on the other hand, can be that icing on the cake. It can serve to highlight your quant qualifications. More important, it can convey to the reader why you want the job and why you deserve the job. It's your first chance at convincing potential employers to take a good look at you.

When it comes to writing an effective cover letter, there are three rules to follow: keep it short, keep it clear, and keep it simple.

Keeping it short: first of all, never go over one page, with plenty of rooms for margins as well as using fonts no smaller than 12-point Times New Roman. Quants are busy people. They don't have time to plod through a four-page cover letter detailing everything the writer has done in life (unless the writer is already famous, but in that case you wouldn't need to write a cover letter to begin with!). If you forget everything else from this book, do *not* forget this rule: keep your cover letter short!

Keeping it clear: this means both having a clean layout and making your points come across. Don't use fancy fonts or fancy languages. Stick to the basics. You are writing a business letter, not a love letter or suicide note. Be cordial and forthcoming.

Keeping it simple: only talk about why you want the job and why you are qualified, and nothing else. No need to mention your SAT or GRE scores – trust me, most quants aren't impressed by those numbers. If you are an undergrad at a good school who's taken a lot of graduate-level courses and managed to get a GPA very close to 4.0 (out of 4.0, which is the university convention in the United States), you can mention both facts; otherwise, leave out your GPA. If you won the International Mathematics Olympiads or something equally significant, you may mention it if doing so does not make your letter too long. Otherwise, no need to laundry-list all those college honors you received. Chances are, most other applicants to the job also had the same feel-good honors. (Besides, you list them on your résumé, not here.)

Now, let's talk about exactly how you can write an effective and succinct cover letter. I'll cover both content and formatting as I go along.

If you print your cover letter, it should have a classic business layout like this:

88 Unknown St, Apt 8W
Brooklyn, NY 11288
(718)555-8888
wfgwfgixix@hotmail.com
September 24, 2007

Dr. Charles J. Jewel
Chief Quantitative Strategist
Doolittle, Doomore, Donothin Securities
188 Wide Lane Ave, 188th floor
New York, NY 10008

Dear Dr. Jewel:

[Body text]

Sincerely,

William F. Gates IX, Ph.D., CFA, CPA

There are three blank lines between your contact section and the addressee's section, and also for the signature area between "Sincerely" and your name. (You can also use "Sincerely yours," "Cordially," "Cordially yours," or the effusive "Respectfully at your service.") Whether you tab over the lines in your contact and signature sections (as in this example) or left-align them is up to you. In Europe, the former is more acceptable. In the United States, either one is totally fine.

One thing to notice here is how I included the home address in the cover letter. Unlike the résumé, the cover letter is individualized for the specific addressee, and if you omitted your return address, the letter would look incomplete – and the recipient might get suspicious of your intention! Since cover letter is likely to be read only by the addressee (or his or her assistant), the chance of your address and phone number falling into the hands of spammers is negligible. By the way, be sure to include your return address on the envelope as well: security measures at many Wall Street firms mandate automatic destruction of incoming mail that does not carry a proper return address.

Also notice how I saluted the recipient as "Dr. Jewel." Find out if the person has a Ph.D. or another doctorate. (Note: JD, or Juris Doctor, is *not* a doctorate. It's the lowest-level degree lawyers in the United States receive. But if someone is JSD – Juris Science Doctor – or DJS – Doctor of Juris Science – he or she can be called by "Doctor.") If so, address the reader as "Dr. <Surname>." It probably sounds a little pretentious to non-Ph.D.s, but won't hurt your chance at all. If anything, it shows that you respect the reader, which is a very good thing. After all, who doesn't like a little bit of flattery? Be sure to include the recipient's official job title as well – and make sure you have it right! Finally, after you print out the letter, don't forget to sign it with a pen.

For e-mail cover letters, you should use the same header (your contact info and the addressee's title and address), although obviously you won't be signing the letter.

For the body text, four brief paragraphs would be sufficient. A typical cover letter goes like this (although you can always be flexible): In the first paragraph, tell the reader why you are interested in a position with his or her group. The second paragraph briefly lists the reasons why you are qualified. The third paragraph can be devoted to either expanding a little bit on your qualifications (such as listing your published papers), or explaining how you've come to know about the position or the reader, e.g., through a personal referral. The closing paragraph simply thanks the reader for his or her time and reiterates your *strong* interest in working for him or her. That's it, short, clear and simple.

Here's a sample cover letter body text:

Dear Dr. Jewel:

Currently a Ph.D. candidate in finance (degree expected this summer) at the Wharton School of Business of University of Pennsylvania, I'm writing to express my strong interest in the full-time position of quantitative research analyst in your group. It is my belief that my solid quantitative background is a good fit for this challenging position.

During the four-and-a-half years of my finance Ph.D. studies, I have gained both valuable finance knowledge, from asset pricing to continuous-time modeling, and practical research skills that I believe prepare me well for a Wall Street quant career. For example, my dissertation explores non-conventional ways of pricing equity and fixed income, and I have come up with innovative methods to pinpoint the equilibrium pricing of such assets. Two of my papers have been accepted by the *Journal of Finance,* which, as you know, is the top journal in academic finance.

In addition to this solid foundation in financial concepts and models, I have extensive training in employing various econometric and time series techniques in real-world research contexts. My advisor, Prof. Anne Saxon, mentioned that she knows you well and thinks your group could use a highly qualified researcher like myself. She strongly encourages me to seek a position under your tutorship.

Enclosed please find my résumé for your inspection. If you would like to see my CV, which has a more extensive listing of my publications, working papers and conference presentations, I would be more than happy to furnish it. At your convenience, I look forward to discussing with you how my skills can contribute to the growth of your group. Thank you very much.

Sincerely,

Two things of note regarding the sample cover letter. First, I adopted the old-fashioned business letter writing rule that a sentence should never start with "I" or "my." The rationale behind this rule is starting a sentence with "I" sounds pretentious and egotistic. This rule is no longer followed strictly in business today, so it's your call whether to follow it or ignore it. Second, I left-flush the paragraphs and separate them with a blank line. This is a common practice in the United States. Alternatively, you can indent the first line of each paragraph (like in this book). The choice is also yours.

If you have met the addressee in the past – by "having met" I mean you actually talked to him or her and have reasons to believe he or she would at least recall the event where you met, if not who you are – it's best to mention this upfront in the cover letter. This grabs the reader's attention pretty well. Here's a sample opener for this case:

Dear Dr. Pavlov:

At last month's Society of Insane Quants meeting in Manhattan, I had the honor of attending your seminar and speaking to you afterwards about the importance of kicking government regulators out of the finance industry. Your depth of knowledge and sense of humor impressed me greatly. At the end of our discussion you encouraged me to seek a quant-oriented career in finance, and I'm writing to express my gratitude for your guidance and also to express my strong interest in the quantitative analyst position in your group.

[Rest of letter]

If the person who referred you to the addressee knows the addressee very well, you may want to play to this fact instead of bringing it up in the third paragraph as in the earlier "Dear Dr. Jewel" example. Here's how you might want to open your cover letter in this case:

Dear Dr. Agwal:

Dr. Jay Pattison, a golf partner of my father's and a long-time mentor of mine, recently brought to my attention the fact that his close friend Dr. Agwal is a prominent working quant. Dr. Pattison encouraged me to contact you for advice on how to start a quant career on Wall Street.

[Rest of letter]

Whichever approach you take, remember to keep your cover letter short, clear and simple. Be sure to sign your printed letter before mailing or faxing it.

In the next section, we'll go over the art of fine cover letter writing in some more detail.

Refining the Cover Letter

In this section I will give you some more specific tips on how to make your cover letter an effective tool.

The ideal cover letter should be both business-like and personal. By "personal" I don't mean your saying "how are you?" in a dozen different fashions or inquiring after the addressee's family (which, by the way, is none of your business, at least not at this point). Personal means your letter is addressed specifically to the recipient, *not* a canned or template-based letter that contains only general content. If the recipient of your cover letter suspects that you simply changed the name and address of a canned letter, you can bet that he or she won't take your candidacy seriously (unless he or she bothers to read your resume anyway and then finds your background to be stellar).

Let's compare two cover letter openings. The first letter reads as if it was based on a template (because it was), and the second is tailored to the addressee, the head quant at a large hedge fund.

Opening 1 (generic content):

To Whom It May Concern:

I'm writing to express my strong interest in the position of quantitative trader at your company. I believe I offer the necessary skills this position requires and I'm confident I will be able to do a good job if given the opportunity.

[Rest of letter]

Opening 2 (tailored content):

Dear Dr. Akaike:

Three months ago I had the opportunity to hear you speak on the topic of advanced convertible arbitrage techniques at the NYU Trade 2007 Forum. Your speech not only piqued my strong interest in quantitative modeling, but opened my eyes to a possible career in convertible arbitrage analysis and trading after I obtain my Ph.D. in physics this coming July. After doing more homework, I decided to write you to inquire about potential opportunities at your fine company, possibly under your direct tutorship.

[Rest of letter]

Isn't it obvious which letter Dr. Akaike, the recipient, will want to keep reading? Even though the opening paragraph of the second example is much longer, it is much more effective because it focuses on the recipient (Dr. Akaike), rather than on the writer (the job candidate). As the Dale Carnegie principle puts it, people want to hear you talk about themselves, not about you. By flattering Dr. Akaike subtly, the second letter makes Dr. Akaike feel good about himself or herself, and makes him or her inclined to talk to the candidate in person.

In contrast, a person like Dr. Akaike who's in an important position will likely be turned off, or even disgusted, by the first example opening, which shows no respect for the addressee. First of all, it's a cardinal sin to start your cover letter with the anemic salutation "To whom it may concern." Avoid this, and its variants "Dear Madam/Sir" or "Dear Manager" or "Dear Quant," at all cost. Frankly, such a salutation has its place in a complaint letter to your local cable company, but absolutely *not* in a cover letter when you want the other person to give you a job. Always address the person by his or her name, prefixed with "Dr.", "Mr." or "Ms." (By the way, these days "Ms." Is more acceptable than either "Mrs." [used for a married woman] or "Miss" [used for a single woman], since it does not presume the marital status of the female addressee.) Once again, it's advised that the reader keeps the Dale Carnegie principle in mind; specifically, that the sweetest-sounding word in the world to any person is his or her own name.

The opening paragraph of the first sample letter also makes it clear that the letter was based on a template, possibly lifted off the Internet. [Legal disclaimer: this particular example was constructed entirely by myself, the author, adopting a template-like style.] While such a generic opening is not as offensive as the "To whom it may concern" salutation, it will not help the candidate at all. At best, the reader might quickly go over the rest of the letter and, if interested enough, take a look at the writer's résumé. At worst, the writer's letter and résumé get trashed. Don't take this risk! Whatever you do, take the time to craft a personalized cover letter for each recipient.

How exactly do you set about writing a personalized cover letter? It's not difficult at all. First, you should do some quick research on the person and the position. With regard to the recipient, what position does he or she hold? What's his or her title (e.g., SVP or chief quantitative analyst)? What kind of background does he or she have (e.g., quant vs. general management)? Does he or she have a doctorate or CFA or CPA? With regard to the position, what skills are required and what do *you* have to offer to the hiring group? In other words, how and what can you contribute if you are given the job? Thinking through these simple questions will allow you to write an effective cover letter, one that will complement your resume well or even do more than your resume to land you an interview.

I'm often asked how one should close the cover letter. I believe the closing paragraph should be neither generic nor pretentious. Let's look at three examples:

Example 1 (generic closing)

I look forward to speaking with you about the position. Thank you.

Example 2 (pretentious closing)

I trust that you will find my résumé, which is enclosed, interesting and look forward to being interviewed by you and your colleagues at your convenience. Thank you.

Example 3 (effective closing)

Enclosed please find my résumé. As I believe that I will be a good fit for the position, I look forward to the opportunity to speak with you further regarding my candidacy. Thank you very much for your time.

Example 1 suffers the template syndrome, but overall it's a rather innocuous closing. Personally I would avoid starting a sentence – and definitely avoid starting a paragraph – with "I," as discussed previously on page 62.

Example 2, however, is quite a turn-off. The letter writer easily comes off as over-confident, bordering on being pretentious and even arrogant. The phrase "I trust" is usually reserved for addressing subordinates or making threats (e.g., when a lawyer pens a notice of potential legal action), not when you write someone who's your superior in the job-search hierarchy. More problematically, saying you look forward to being interviewed implies that you think the reader should interview you. Well, you know what? He or she may disagree with your assessment of what he or she should do. Never tell an interviewer what he or she should do. Your job is to offer and request, to nudge him or her into a favorable action with subtle persuasion, not to demand.

Example 3 offers a balance between politeness and expression of confidence. I think it's an effective closing that will be well-taken by any reader in any mood.

Two more quick notes regarding the closing: First, always say "thank you very much" at the end. This is a business letter, and you are asking for a favor, so be sure to express your gratitude. Second, for those readers of this book whose native language is not English, notice that the word or phrase that comes after "to look forward to" is a noun, not a verb. So it's incorrect to say "I look forward to speak with you" or "I look forward to meet you." It's "I look forward to speaking with you" or "I look forward to the opportunity to meet you."

Finally, as with your résumé, after you write a cover letter, you may want to sleep on it for a while before you go back and review it with a fresh perspective. For example, if you want to send out the cover letter today, give yourself a half-hour or longer break after you first draft it so you can review it from a more critical angle. If you don't have to send it out today, literally sleep over it for a night or two or more. By doing this, you can often catch unintentional errors or institute some effective improvements. Remember, even the best writers can find plenty of room to improve in their first drafts of anything.

Chapter Summary

This chapter has walked you through creating and improving your quant-oriented résumé. I also discussed the most critical aspect of your résumé that can make or break your candidacy for a quant job. You learned how to convert a CV to the résumé format, as well as why you should always write an effective cover letter and how to do so.

Appendix to Chapter 2: Sample Résumé

The sample résumé on the next page shows you some of the important elements of a good résumé I talked about in this chapter. Clean layout, easy-on-the-eye formatting, judicious use of emphasis and action verbs, and concrete examples make this résumé worth reading a second time for the busy employer. This sample is a completely fictitious résumé and any similarity it may bear to any real person, living or dead, is purely coincidental.

I created the sample résumé in Microsoft Word 2003. I only used Times New Roman as my font. To make the résumé fit on one page in this paperback book, I chose a small font size. (You should definitely use a size no smaller than 12-point for serif fonts such as Times New Roman.) Feel free to use this example as a template for your own résumé. In other words, I grant you a free license to use the *structure and format* of this sample résumé. You must supply your own bio details for your résumé!

To do the shading for the section headings, I put each heading in a table. I then went into the Format → Borders and Shading… function. First I chose None for borders and applied this setting to the entire table. Next I picked "Gray -10%" as the background shading color and applied it to the cell with the heading text. Alternatively, you can do the shading without using tables by applying the fill shade to the paragraph, since each heading is also a paragraph on its own. Using the table method, albeit more involved, does give you more control over the exact formatting (such as how wide across the page you want the shading to span). Either way, using the background shading really lends an elegant stylistic touch to the overall look of the résumé.

You can e-mail me for the Word .doc file; see the book website for contact information.

Charles X. Jewel, PhD

Cell phone: (212)555-5555   *E-mail: cxj_2006@quantcareer.com*

Objective
To find a quantitative position where I can leverage my **superb** quantitative and analytical skills

Education
Stamford University (Stamford, CT)
*Ph.D. in astrophysics, July 2006. **Ph.D.** in English literature, June 2003.*
- Astrophysics dissertation on plasma properties
- English lit dissertation on obscure English poetry
- NSF Grant #2005333-AB348, for plasma studies
- Awarded best dissertation by university in 2003
- Coursework in financial time series, MCMC modeling, investment theory
- Ranked #1 among 181 astrophysics Ph.D. students in class

Hardvard College (Hardvard, MI)
B.A. in women's studies and mathematics, summa cum laude, *December 2001.*
- Completed honors senior thesis on careers of female mathematicians
- Coursework in numerical methods, econometrics, C# programming
- President of Financial Fraud Investigation Club

Experience
J.P. Moregam Capital Markets, Inc. (New Yard City, NY)
Project leader for advanced equity research, summer 2005.
- Efficiently **managed a team of six** to apply CAPM to alpha research
- Successfully created binary-tree pricing system with proprietary models
- Collaborated with JPM traders to **make more than $350 million**
- Played key role in launch of $130 billion option-trading hedge fund

Publications
- "Properties of Plasma in Space," *J. Not Advanced Astrophysics,* Aug. 2006
- "Why So Many British Poets Were Unknown," *J. Obscure Poetry Studies,* Sept. 2004

Special Information
- **U.S. citizen** with British, Canadian, Iraqi, and Thai permanent residency

Chapter 3: Hunting for Openings

In this chapter:

Looking for a new job is inevitably an anxious and stressful exercise. This is especially true of the first job out of school. Only a very lucky few have jobs looking for them instead of them looking for jobs – these are usually the people who have had publications in top finance journals (*Journal of Finance* and *Journal of Financial Studies*), or who stand to benefit from nepotism. The rest of us mere mortals? We need to work hard to get a job.

For many potential quants, the most difficult part of the job hunt process is probably finding where the job are. This task actually has two aspects to it: one, you need to know where the openings are; two, you need to know what the companies do. For example, one day, out of nowhere, you saw a small ad on the bus that reads in part "Ambitious quants needed for fixed income research – Smithe Weston Capital." What do you do now? You need to get more information about the position, of course, but you also need to find out exactly what kind of firm Smithe Weston Capital is. (I made up the name, in case you were wondering.) Is it a big trading firm? A hedge fund? An investment advisory provider?

Much of the time you can just log onto the World Wide Web and do a search on the name. Many hedge funds and private equity firms, however, do not have a presence on the Web, or their websites are private access only. In the latter case, you'll often see a website with little information on the home page except a "Client Login" form.

So in addition to the Internet, you need to be creative in tracking down lesser-known firms.

I know, many a reader of this book would like to work for a large firm like J.P. Morgan or Bank of America or Morgan Stanley. But many small companies offer equally attractive opportunities for quants. If you have your heart set on hedge funds, then you'll likely be looking at small operations, often with just two or three people. Unless you are absolutely sure you won't like one type of firm, it simply makes sense to cast your net wide.

When to Start Looking

The answer is simple: start looking as early as possible. Be an early bird. Don't worry about market downturns. In fact, it's probably better to get hired when general market conditions are bad but picking up than to start a new job at the top of a bull market. In the former case, there's an upside waiting for you, whereas in the latter case, things can only get bad. Of course, you can't time the market (otherwise you would not need to look for a job and work for somebody else), so the best course of action to take is simply start early on the job hunt.

Most large firms hire new people all year round. Of course, the particular kind of job you want may not be available at a given point in time, but if you are flexible enough to consider a range of positions, chances are you'll be able to find openings somewhere. At some firms, even if they are not actively hiring into particular areas, if they consider you good enough, they'll hire you anyway – assuming the times are good or at least picking up so they foresee enough work for you to do.

Smaller firms, as well as many research departments within big firms, look for new hires only when they need them. With these employers, it does matter when you submit your résumé. If you submit at a time when they don't need anyone, they simply won't take your candidacy seriously. One thing to be aware of is even though some employers claim they'll keep your résumé on file for consideration for future openings, I have yet to come across anyone who does that. Of the many financial firms that I have submitted my résumé to in the past and been told by that I was good enough to be considered for a future opening, to this day I have yet to hear back from a single one of them. Of course, in this modern age of e-mail and World Wide Web, it costs virtually nothing to send your résumé to a potential employers, and no employer I know of holds any grudge against people who send them résumés, so there is little harm in submitting your résumé to a firm even though you know they are not hiring. You just never know whether the principal might take a strong liking of your background and actually break the rule and consider creating a position just for you! So, feel free to send in your résumé; just don't fret when no response ever comes your way.

If you are in school, you are probably aware that most big firms, as well as a few small ones, observe the annual ritual of running a recruiting season that starts in the early fall and lasts into late winter or early spring. These programs were originally created for MBAs, as firms were eager to line up the country's best future business leaders before these future leaders went somewhere else. As more and more quants migrated onto Wall Street, now many firms recruit freshly minted Ph.D.s and masters the same way. This really works to the great advantage of the firms: by running a single recruiting season, they get the largest pool of qualified candidates at the same time each year and can thus compare these candidates all at once. Without a unified recruiting season, firms would have had to look at each candidate individually, without the benefiting of comparing him or her with his or her academic peers.

The recruiting season also works to the great advantage of the students, as they gain access to a large pool of potential employers all at once and save time, effort and money in getting an audience with these employers. If an offer comes in, the students can also enjoy the rest of their last year in school with a job in hand. In addition – especially for Ph.D. candidates – firms can be flexible in setting the start date of the new hire, so if you need an extra month or two to finish your dissertation defense, they'll probably accommodate that and let you start working in the fall. This is so because firms participating in a campus recruiting program are hiring way in advance and understand that sometimes a student may have special needs in terms of scheduling the first day at work six or seven months from now.

Most Ph.D. candidates in economics and finance, as well as in a few other social science fields, are well aware of the annual ASSA (Alliance of Social Science Associations) meeting, held each early January in a major American city. This huge gathering comprises the annual member meetings of various academic social science organizations, the most prominent of which (at least in the present context) are the American Economic Association (AEA) and the American Finance Association (AFA). When you hear people talk about "the AEA meeting" or "the AFA meeting," you know they are really referring to this annual ASSA event.

The ASSA annual meeting has become *the* place for Ph.D. students to look for a job, academic or otherwise. Besides the many universities and other academic institutions that look to hire assistant professors and post-docs, many Wall Street firms, consulting firms and other private employers (as well as government agencies from all over the world) also use this opportunity to meet and interview candidates for their openings. Over the years, the private sector interviewers have come to overwhelm the academic ones, and the ASSA job fair has become, at least in the eyes of students on the job market, nothing more than a chance and place to land job interviews. (In other words, nobody seems to care for the presentations any more!)

I personally think the ASSA meeting is really good for both Ph.D. candidates and holders on the job market (and by "job market" I don't mean just academic positions, but all kinds of employment positions) and the employers. For the job candidates, the ASSA event provides a good opportunity to contact a large pool of potential employers and to meet as many in one place as possible. It can really save the Ph.D. student looking for a job a lot of time and money, as he or she can put everything together and send the materials out at once, instead of doing them piecemeal, spending tons of time looking for employers to send the application materials to, and traveling to each individual employer's location for interview. Later on, it's also a good thing for the student to get multiple offers at roughly the same time, so he or she can compare them and potentially negotiate them. For the employers, there's the abovementioned benefit of having access to a large pool of candidates and not missing out on the good ones. It also enables smaller firms to come across as legitimate and respectable by having a presence at this meeting. In short, if you are in graduate school, especially if you are getting a Ph.D. (but even if you are not), definitely consider attending the January meeting in the year you expect to graduate.

Ph.D. students usually do not know exactly when they can officially graduate, as they need to first schedule their dissertation defense and then find out how much work there is left to do in terms of improving the dissertation to the point of winning the advisor's seal of approval. (Without this seal of approval – in the form of his or her signature on the defense form – you cannot graduate.) But most final-year Ph.D. candidates have a decent idea of when they can finish. In fact, you do not need to know whether you can finish in, say, June or July, before you can look for a full-time job. All you need is a fairly good idea that you'll be done with your dissertation writing and major revisions by some point, and try to start a full-time job around that time. Of course, you should be aware that (1) many Ph.D. advisors highly disapprove of their students getting an industry job, thus your advisor might try to use whatever leverage he or she has to steer you away from an industry job, and (2) you'll still need to finish your Ph.D. education, go through the defense and get that degree. If you don't, some employers may have second thoughts about you. (In fact, many large firms condition their offers on Ph.D. candidates' getting their doctorates.)

You might say to yourself, "But that's easy. After I finish writing my dissertation, I'm as good as done, right?" Not quite. Rewriting parts of your dissertation to satisfy your demanding advisor may consume a lot of time, time you won't necessarily have when you start working full-time on Wall Street, where hours tend to be long. (But one good thing about working as a quant is you probably won't have to work weekends or travel much on business trips.) As a final-year Ph.D. student, you must work hard *now* to try to get that degree before your start working. At the minimum, try to schedule your defense for a date before the start of your full-time job.

If you missed the recruiting season, or if you are already working full-time, you may find this following tip valuable: the best time of the year to look for a quant job is in January, February or March. These three months are when the year-end bonuses are paid and a lot of people either switch jobs or quit the industry altogether, resulting in a lot of available openings – many of which need to be filled urgently (after all, somebody's got to do the work). Whether you are a greenhorn with respect to finance or if you already have a finance job but want to go for a better one, winter is the hot season when it comes to job hunting on Wall Street.

Where to Find Job Openings

This is probably *the* question every job seeker asks.

First of all, forget about mass-appeal job websites like Monster or Hot Jobs. I have seen very few high-quality jobs advertised on these websites. If you search for keywords like "quantitative," too many suspicious listings come up. Besides, you'll be sharing your information with companies and people you have no idea about, and the chances of you getting a real quant job are pretty slim.

Here are where you should be looking:

- The annual ASSA ("AEA" or "AFA") meeting. I covered this in detail in the previous section. To sum up: if you are a final-year Ph.D. candidate or recently received your Ph.D., you cannot afford to miss this big job fair.

- Your graduate-study department. Jobs are often posted on the announcement boards. Even if you already got your degree and left school, you should consider checking them out if you can get back to the department office physically (i.e., you are not in a different city or there's no hostile security guard who would only let in people with a valid school ID). Be sure to find out whether your department has a job posting service via e-mail or on its website.

- Your school's career office. This is true if you are still in school or just recently graduated, but even if you have been out of school for a while, it may still be worthwhile paying an alum's fee and gaining access to their job listings. The career offices at the top-ranked schools usually have a surprisingly large number of quant job postings.

- Career or job fairs. These can be on-campus or open to the general public. Obviously you want to go to one where quant openings are available. If a fair is hosted by a quant-related professional society or targets a specific field (e.g., a job fair for econ Ph.D.s), obviously the chances of finding something you want are much higher than at a general-purpose fair.

- Niche websites that cater to quants. I'd say you'll have a better chance with these sites than the mass-appeal sites. Part of the reason is some of these sites are run by headhunting firms, so they have people who actually read your résumé as opposed to using a Pentium 4 PC scanning for keywords among many résumés. The sites I have used are `JobsintheMoney.com`, `Wilmott.com` (with lots of general career advice),

`AnalyticRecruiting.com` (run by a leading headhunter firm), `QuantFinanceJobs.com`, and `QUANTster.com`.

What about websites that you find via a search engine that seem to have quant job listings? Personally I'm wary of such sites because, in this day and age of rampant identity theft, you just never know if these sites are for real, or if they are run by some kids in Russia intent on stealing your social security number and other personal info. (No, the search engines won't check websites they compile into their databases for legitimacy.) So I advise caution when you take this route. Visit this book's website (`www.quantcareer.com`) for updates on websites that I have personally used. (Yep, consider me your guinea pig.) In any event, when you do post a résumé, leave out your social security number, your date of birth and even your home address; no employer requires these pieces of information on a résumé, period.

The AEA (American Economic Association) runs a web-based service called JOE (Job Openings for Economists, at `www.aeaweb.org/joe`). It has monthly job listings for both academic and non-academic positions, and more and more Wall Street firms (including the company I work for) advertise openings there. For full-time non-academic jobs (the types discussed in this book), look at section 5 for each month's listing.

Similarly, the AFA (American Finance Association) has a job listing webpage (`www.afajof.org/association/jobs.asp`). Jobs are posted on a rolling basis. Regardless of whether you have an advanced degree (master's or Ph.D.) in finance or not, I highly recommend checking out the AFA recruiting page regularly for potential opportunities.

- Professional societies for finance workers. If such a society or association has a local office, visit them to see if they have job listings. Or check the societies' websites; many, indeed, have a jobs section. Or attend one of their events and talk to other attendees about job opportunities.

One of the best known is the group of financial analyst societies worldwide that are affiliated with the CFA Institute (`www.cfainstitute.org`). In fact, if you ever want to get the CFA title, you'll need to join one of the affiliated societies first. (I'll talk about the CFA – and whether it's worth your time and effort getting the certificate – in chapter 7.) For example, in New York, the CFA-affiliated society is called the New York Society of Security Analysts (NYSSA, at `www.nyssa.org`). In Boston, it's the Boston Security Analysts Society (BSAS, at `www.bsas.org`) Chicagoans have the CFA Society of Chicago (`www.cfachicago.org`) In San Francisco, it's the CFA Society of San Francisco (`www.cfasanfrancisco.org`). In the UK, you have the United Kingdom Society of Investment Professionals (UKSIP, at `www.uksip.org`) For the complete directory and contact information, navigate your Internet Explorer to `www.cfainstitute.org/society/societies.html`.

Besides the CFA-affiliated societies, there are other prominent (and not-so-prominent) finance professional associations in the major financial centers. A prominent and popular U.S.-based organization is the Society of Quantitative Analysts (SQA, at `www.sqa-us.org`), with membership open to financial academics and practitioners alike. The SQA sponsors regular finance seminars and other events, and its website features an active Job Postings section (`www.sqa-us.org/jobbankdisplaylistings.cfm`). In Boston, Chicago, Johannesburg, London, NY and a few other cities across the globe, there are active chapters of a non-CFA-affiliated society called QWAFAFEW (Quantitative Work Alliance for Applied Finance, Education and Wisdom, at `www.qwafafew.org`).

There are also professional societies formed by people sharing the same ethnic or national background. For example, a New York-based association called TCFA (The Chinese Finance Association, at `www.aimhi.com/VC/tcfa`) is well known among Chinese-speaking finance professionals but welcomes members of all nationalities; you do not even need to speak Chinese to join and enjoy their fabulous annual meetings (each with at least one panel discussion on finding quant jobs, featuring some of the best known people – many non-Chinese and non-Asian – from Wall Street).

One thing to be aware of is that all of these professional

associations and societies charge membership fees for services such as access to their job boards. In most cases (but not all cases), the membership due is quite reasonable, often discounted for full-time students.

- Bloomberg terminals, if you have access to one (many business school have it; check the library). A lot of firms and financial headhunters post on Bloomberg. Just type the keyword "jobs" to go to the job listing board. The problem with Bloomberg is the jobs are listed in chronological order, and you'll often find the same job listed each and every day. Some headhunters really jam the board with the same positions, making the board look more resourceful than it actually is. Another disadvantage is you can't do a keyword search but instead must browse through the listings one by one.

- The *Wall Street Journal* and major daily newspapers as well as their websites. Before the age of the Internet, the *Wall Street Journal* and the Sunday *New York Times* were the places where you'd be looking for a Wall Street job. These days there are fewer job listings in the papers (because advertising in them is more expensive than on the Internet), but you can still find gems there. I highly recommend you do not skip over these valuable resources.

- Headhunters, but of course. Wall Street is heavily dependent on professional recruiting firms (headhunters) to fill openings, especially outside the regular school/ASSA recruiting season or when experienced candidates are desired. Most of the people in my financial engineering group, for example, came by way of headhunters, including myself. I'll talk about how to work with headhunters in detail in the next section, including where to find them. They are important enough to deserve a completely individual section of their own.

- Listservs and websites run by student organizations at your school or other schools. Many ethnic student organizations, for instance, have their own member mailing lists (called listservs for list servers) or websites. These Internet-based services feature lively discussions (politics, online bargains, surviving in America, sex, etc.) as well as classifieds ranging from apartments for rent to job openings. I myself belong to an

English-language listserv catering to Chinese students (but open to all ethnic groups) run by the Columbia University Chinese Students and Scholars Association (CUCSSA, at www.cucssa.org, the Columbia chapter of the worldwide CSSA organization). You do not need to be affiliated with Columbia University in any way to register on their website or sign up for their regular listserv mailings. This is but one example, and I'm sure there are similar listservs and websites catering to Indians, Russians, Turks, Colombians, Brazilians, and other national groups. Ask around your campus or search on the Internet.

- Any contacts you can think of. People in your graduate program who are already working on Wall Street, your alumni relations office, your current and past professors, your friends, your full-service broker. It never hurts to ask them if they might know of any available positions or if they might know someone who would know of such positions. You just never know where you might hear about openings that you would not have found out any other way. As they say in job hunting: the best jobs always go to people who know people.

- Cold calling. If you are the aggressive type, you may want to look up the head quant in a practice area – e.g., fixed income research, equity agency desk, prop options trading, risk management, hedge fund research – at each firm you are interested in seeking a job with. Of course, the one hundred grand question is, "where do I find these people's names?" You need to be creative.

    The first obvious place to look is the company's website, but that's usually not fruitful as I have yet to come across a company that actually lists all its personnel. However, it's still worth trying as many firms feature certain employees from time to time, and sometimes quants get a chance to be quoted (to say how great their firms are, of course). Also, you should poke around the research webpage of a company site to see if they list any research papers written by staff. My company, for example, has a publications page buried a couple levels deep down from the corporate home page, but once you find it, you'll see papers written by me and my colleagues in analytical research and financial engineering.

A second place to find prominent quants is a finance professional society such as a CFA Institute-affiliated local finance society or the TCFA mentioned earlier. Attend one of their seminars or annual meetings – many societies allow non-members to attend for a higher fee than paid by members – and get the business cards of the speakers.

The third place to look are finance-oriented journals and trade magazines. Academic finance journals such as *Journal of Finance* and *Journal of Financial Studies* mostly carry articles written by true academics, but occasionally have papers contributed by industry practitioners. A company called Institutional Investor (`www.institutionalinvestor.com` or `www.dailyii.com`) specializes in publishing an amazingly large number of trade journals such as *Journal of Portfolio Management* and *Journal of Wealth Management* as well as special issues on various topics of interest to Wall Street professionals. Their journals and the flag-ship *Institutional Investor* magazine are widely read on Wall Street, from trading desks to research centers. By "trade magazines" I mean publications like *Euromoney* and *Bloomberg Markets* that cater to the Wall Street audience (thus excluding popular magazines like *Money* and *Forbes*). Of course, you can also scrounge the *Wall Street Journal* and other popular finance publications, as well as watch CNBC, for names of quants featured or quoted. If you have the time and energy, it doesn't hurt to cast your net wide, especially if you are looking for a job outside of the regular recruiting season of large firms.

As you can see, the number of places where you can look for job openings is very large and varied. In fact, if you try to cover all these bases, you'll find yourself quite stressed out as you struggle to compile a large list of applicable positions and associated contacts and try to keep track of where and when you sent your cover letter and résumé. Instead, in order to maximize your chances of landing a good job and saving your sanity, I recommend that you focus in your job seeking effort.

Here are some specific tips:

- *If you are in school:* Undergraduates and master's students usually know exactly when they graduate, and it's most likely in May or June of your last year in school. In this case, it's relatively easy to schedule your job search process. Your top priority would be to rely on the annual fall-season recruiting program as much as possible. As I said before, this gives you access to a large pool of potential employers and saves you time, effort and money in reaching out to many of them. At the earliest possible time, start preparing your résumé – and take courses you think can enhance your standing! As the recruiting season approaches – in the summer time, for instance – re-read this book and begin writing down the kinds of jobs you'd like to get. Be sure to subscribe to your career office's announcements regarding the upcoming recruiting season. Visit the career office often to stay abreast of the latest happenings. In short, your goal is to try to get as much out of the recruiting season as you can. If, and only if, after you've mailed (or e-mailed) your résumé and cover letter out to all the employers that participate in your school's recruiting program, should you consider looking outside on your own. You can read the next bullet point, for non-student types, for some tips.

As mentioned earlier, Ph.D. students usually have only a rough expectation of when they can finish. As long as you expect to be done or very close to being done by the end of the summer, you can participate in the recruiting season for that summer, including attending the annual SSRN meeting.

(If you won't graduate anytime soon but would like to find an internship, check out Chapter 8 for details specific to internships and part-time jobs in quantitative finance.)

- *If you already have a job, missed the campus recruiting, or just want to search on your own:* Hopefully you've written a polished résumé as explained in chapter 2. You are on your own, so how extensively you search is up to you. When you feel ready, sit down at your desk, pick your own brains and quickly write down a list of people whom you might be able to contact about opportunities. Review the previous section and decide which venues you'd like to take. I recommend you start your search by contacting a few headhunters; see the next section on headhunters for more details and tips.

Working With Headhunters

A headhunter, according to the *New Oxford American Dictionary* used in my Sharp PW-E550 electronic dictionary, is "a person who identifies and approaches suitable candidates employed elsewhere to fill business positions." The definition aptly captures several features of a headhunter:

- The headhunter screens candidates for suitability for a position or a number of positions. He or she will read your résumé and decide if you are the right person for the positions in his or her dossier. In my experience, some, but not many, headhunters will actually honestly tell you whether you are qualified and, if you are not, what you can do to your résumé or training to make yourself qualified. In the real world, headhunters vary tremendously in how carefully they consider your background and potential openings. The sad truth is, most of them simply speed-read through your résumé and then blindly submit it to as many hiring firms as he or she can find, hoping at least one of these firms will have an interest in your candidacy.

- The headhunter may also approach candidates deemed suitable. He or she may attend professional seminars or presentations, or may peruse trade journals such as the *Journal of Portfolio Management* to compile a list of author names. After I published an article in an Institution Investor special issue on algorithmic trading, for example, the number of headhunter calls I received more than tripled (and they all called me at work, because my work phone number was listed in the article).

- The headhunter is independent of the firms they recruit for. A person who is employed by a Wall Street firm to hire for that firm is known as an in-house recruiter and is usually affiliated with the firm's HR (human resources) department. A headhunter, in contrast, works for himself or herself, or for a company that specializes in headhunting. This independence from the hiring firms carries two implications: one, headhunters have access to positions from many different firms; two, headhunters do not necessarily know the firms or the positions well. This means while you can potentially reach a large number of firms all at once through a headhunter, he or she may (and usually does) blindly submit your résumé (assuming you possess the minimum required background for a quant position) to a lot of places, which is a worse practice than helping you focus on a narrow range of firms or positions.

What the dictionary definition does tell you is how headhunters are paid. This is important to know because once you understand what motivates a headhunter, you'll know how to deal with one.

Headhunters are usually paid a finder's fee by the employer depending on the *success* of finding a candidate for a position. Success is defined by the candidate's receiving the offer letter *and* accepting the offer. So if a candidate fails to get the job, or declines the offer, the headhunter won't get paid. This compensation arrangement, however, usually doesn't apply to high-level positions; in those cases, a headhunter will get a retainer's fee and get paid simply for looking for a suitable candidate. Regardless of whether the high-level candidate succeeds, the headhunter goes home happy with a nice, fat paycheck. Of course, chances are you won't be looking for a high-level position (think management director) at this point in your career, so the headhunters you work with won't receive a dime from working "for" you unless you succeed in landing a job.

Please note that legitimate headhunters are *always* paid by the hiring firms for their services, never by you, the job hunter. If someone approaches you and offers you access to job openings in exchange for your paying him or her a fee, tell them to scram. Let me reiterate: you, the job candidate, should *never* pay a headhunter, period.

Headhunters from different recruiting agencies sometimes work together, especially during Wall Street downturns when new jobs are scarce. In that case, the headhunters will split the commission they receive for a successful hire. Again, you, as the candidate, will never need to pay a dime for working with them. Of course, whether you decide to send your headhunter(s) a nice gift for getting you a job successfully is entirely up to you.

How headhunters get paid has one serious implication: it determines how personal they'll make their services to *you.* And to be honest, since you'll likely be working with headhunters who are on finder's fees, you'll have trouble getting their full attention unless they deem you a "sure bet" for certain positions. Because they receive stacks of résumés every day and only get paid when they succeed in getting a candidate an offer (assuming the candidate will take that offer), they can only devote a very limited amount of time to each candidate. And they spend this limited amount of time: quickly reading your résumé, calling you up to see if you are interested in a certain position they happen to have, and trying to set up an interview with the employer for you. If your résumé doesn't pass the employer's screening or if you come back from your interview empty-handed, you may or may not hear from the headhunter again. Well, if you fail to get an offer after two or three tries, you likely won't hear from the same headhunter again.

I used to think of this practice (limited attention to a candidate) as impersonal and "cruel," but now I can understand perfectly why headhunters *have to* do it this way: they have to bring the bread home, and they can only earn the bread if they succeed in placing candidates. If a candidate can't get a job, they just have to move on to another who might have a better chance of succeeding. The headhunting business is a highly competitive business, and the turnover rate is high, with many people giving it a try and then leaving after finding out they can't make a good enough living as a professional recruiter. This means not only that the headhunter you work with today may have left the field by next week, but also that he or she may have jumped ship and joined another headhunting agency.

How much do headhunters get paid for successful recruits? The amount varies by hiring firm and geographic location. In New York, for example, what I hear is that headhunters usually get between 50% and 100% of the base salary of the successfully filled position. Given that as of winter 2006-07 many junior quant positions pay a base of $90,000 or more, that's actually a lot of money. Now you know why headhunter can't afford to spend more time with candidates that fail to attract potential employers early on.

I cannot emphasize enough the importance of headhunters on Wall Street. Unless you participate in an on-campus recruiting program (e.g., if you are still in school and your school offers such a program), you'll most likely come into contact with headhunters during your job hunt. In fact, many openings posted on the web or in print are from headhunters. The Bloomberg jobs section, for instance, is notorious for teeming with headhunter-placed ads, to the point that few openings are posted directly by hiring firms. Wall Street firms, always flush with money (even in bad times, contrary to what you might have read in the press in early part of this decade after the dotcom bubble burst), are very fond of working with headhunters. Chalk it up as part of the national trend toward outsourcing. (In fact, I've received headhunter calls from outside of the U.S., from countries as near as Great Britain and as far as India! No surprise there, I suppose.) Headhunters, for better or worse, will always be an integral part of the job scene on Wall Street.

Knowing whether a quant-wanted ad is placed by the hiring firm directly or by a headhunter is important in at least one aspect: if the former, you'll need to tailor your cover letter specifically for the position; if the latter, you can be general in your cover letter (because it'll be sent to the headhunter, not the hiring firm) – it's entirely likely that the headhunter will not pass on your cover letter to the hiring firm, even if you wrote a Nobel-worthy one. The difference also has implications on whether you should aggressively follow up on a response to your application (or the lack thereof), and on how you pursue the follow-up.

Before I discuss how you can work effectively with headhunters, let me tell you where you can find them. A little earlier I alluded to the fact that many job openings are posted by headhunters. So one place to find them is by answering these ads: on quant jobs websites, on Bloomberg, in newspapers or trade journals, etc. Sometimes it's easy to tell if the job poster is a headhunter; he or she will list the name of the firm he or she works for, either directly or as a web address or e-mail address, that you can look up on the Internet. If it's something you can't find, chances are it's a small headhunting firm without a web presence. Other times, the ad won't tell you anything about who posted it; it would just say something like "a prestigious Wall Street investment firm" or "a leading global asset management firm." Actually this is the telltale sign that this is most likely a headhunter-posted ad, because ads placed directly by Wall Street firms usually do state, with pride, which firm it is. Conversely, though, even if an ad does mention "J.P. Morgan" or "Credit Suisse" or "Nomura Securities" or "Bank of China," it doesn't necessarily mean it's placed by that firm. The best way to find out? Just answer the ad with a nice cover letter. If it turns out to be a headhunter at the other end of the line, you'll know eventually.

You can also find headhunters at career fairs, meetings organized by professional societies, and after-work happy hours hosted by some fun-loving Wall Street-types. It's usually easy to identify who the headhunters are: they are the garrulous ones who seem to try to talk to everyone in the room, sometimes accidentally spending 15 precious minutes with another person only to find out the latter is also headhunter, a competitor! Seriously, though, headhunters are usually pleasant to talk to. After all, they are a kind of salespeople (there's nothing wrong with that, mind you), and an important aspect of their job is to schmooze potential candidates and identify the ones that'll likely be positively received by employers.

Many headhunter firms maintain websites where they tell you about themselves and post some (but not all) of the jobs they are recruiting for at the moment. Some of the more popular headhunter firms include Analytic Recruiting (www.analyticrecruiting.com) and Pathway Resourcing (www.pathwayresourcing.com) .

As you receive e-mails or calls from headhunters, save them in your address book. Next to each entry, make a note of what areas they recruit for, if you know the answer. (In Microsoft Outlook, for example, you can simply use the notes area for each contract entry to jot down anything you want.) Some headhunters focus on trading desk recruiting, while others specialize in a particular area of quant research, yet still others (probably most of them) are generalists. Your strategy is simply to avoid sending your résumé to a headhunter recruiting exclusively for mutual funds if you want to work on the sell side. (The exception to this rule is if you are truly desperate; then it doesn't hurt to contact as many headhunters as you physically can. Remember: headhunters are aggressive; so should you.)

Let's say you just found the name of a headhunter, probably from a quant help-wanted ad or at a happy hour. What should you say to the headhunter? And what should you ask? If there's a phone number listed, you should probably call him or her up and have a quick chat, to introduce yourself and build up some rapport. Headhunters are human beings who desire social acceptance. If you call them in person, as opposed to just firing them an e-mail, they may feel more "connected" with you and give you some extra time or assistance, both of which can be valuable and helpful. Indeed, as most quants are either shy or unwilling to talk on the phone – e.g., English may not be their first language – those who do make that call will have a slight edge over those who rely on e-mail alone.

I speak of this from first-hand experience. I've found that when all that I do with a headhunter is exchanging some e-mails, we inevitably lose interest in each other quickly. But if I talk to them on the phone, I usually receive more tips from them, or at least a quick hello once in a while telling me that they still remember me and they still work as headhunters. I personally think this connection matters if your goal is to cast your net as wide as possible. Of course, social rapport with headhunters only goes so far. In the end, they have to eat, and only those candidates who they deem having a high chance of getting an offer will get the most attention from them.

When you approach the headhunter for the first time – either on the phone (preferred) or via e-mail – introduce yourself by telling them what you are looking for (your objective) and what your background is (your skills, education and/or experience). That first contact is basically a verbal or e-mail summary of your résumé. Be sure to only mention the most salient parts of your qualifications. You have to remember that the attention span of a headhunter is very short. If you give him or her a laundry list to chew through, he or she won't remember much, if anything at all. Instead, the buzzword is once again *focus*. Focus on your best skills. Focus on your most advanced degree. Focus on that one experience that really makes you an outstanding quant candidate. You want to pique the headhunter's interest, not to drown him or her in a thousand words.

For example, this is what I may say when I call up a headhunter for the first time.

"Hi, Dorothy? My name is Brett Jiu and I'm currently a senior financial engineer with XXX [my company's name]. The reason I'm calling is I saw an ad you placed on the SQA website, for a senior quant position at YYY [hiring firm's name]. I'm *very* [stress 'very'] interested in the position. I have a strong background in quantitative analysis, with a Ph.D. in economics and over 10 years of industry quant experience. ..."

You get the picture. Depending on how suitable Dorothy thinks of me for that particular position and for the other positions she recruits for, she may spend the next ten minutes getting more details out of my work life and qualifications. If she is not interested, she'll ask me to send her my résumé by e-mail. When I do send that e-mail, I'll keep the cover letter short and emphasize my quant qualifications, using HTML formatting if needed so I can utilize *italics* and **bold** for emphasis. (Many popular e-mail programs, such as Outlook, Outlook Express, and the web-based free Live Mail [mail.live.com] which gives you 1GB of mail storage, can send HTML-formatted messages.)

After that first contact, give the headhunter a few days to match you with an employer. He or she may or may not ask for your permission before sending your résumé to an employer. If you don't hear back within a week of the first contact, call or e-mail him or her to follow up. Make sure you log the dates on which you contacted a headhunter so you can keep track of the details; otherwise you may forget when you did what. Worst, you may easily forget which headhunter covers which job opportunity or whom you have talked to in the past week. The last thing you want during a stressful job hunt is to turn the process into a mess which would only add to your stress!

Another important thing to remember is, when you get the headhunter's e-mail address, be sure to add it to the "safe list" of your e-mail account. That way, messages from him or her will not be sent to the junk mail (spam) folder or, worse, deleted without your ever seeing them. To be extra-safe, add his or her company's domain (e.g., "quant-hunters.com") to the safe list, so anyone from his or her company can e-mail you. You may also want to add his or her phone number to your cell phone's phone book, so you'll be able to tell which headhunter is calling you with one glance.

Here's how I would follow up with Dorothy, my imaginary kind-hearted-but-forgetful headhunter:

"Hi, Dorothy. This is Dr. Brett Jiu [I call myself "doctor" just to pique her interest and emphasize my educational superiority!] from XXX. We spoke last Wednesday about that senior quant position at YYY you were recruiting for. I was just wondering if you got my résumé and had a chance to look it over. Oh, you did. So what do you think? Oh, you mean I'm not a good fit? Can I ask why? [I'm pissed as hell but I try to stay cool and cordial.] You know, I must respectfully disagree with what you just said. I have over 10 years of solid industry experience, much of which was with top firms on Wall Street. …"

I concocted this example to give you a flavor of what to say if the headhunter turns out to be less than thrilled about your candidacy. If this happens to you, the important thing to remember is: be firm, but don't lose hope and don't lose your cool. Emphasize your positives. Insist that she take another look at your background. Ask her to keep you considered for other positions – and give her the reasons why ("Because I'm really qualified!"). Do whatever you need to do to leave an impression with the headhunter – even if it means keeping her on the phone for longer than she wanted! Obviously, you don't want to veer into harassment. If a headhunter shows little interest in you after you made a good presentation of yourself, move on. There are many other headhunters and some are bound to be interested in what you have to offer.

If a headhunter has reservations about your candidacy, be sure to ask him or her why. "Do you think there's something missing from or unclear about my résumé?" If he or she doesn't volunteer to help you improve your résumé, ask. "Would you mind giving me some tips on how I can enhance my résumé? You know, I really want to work with *you.*" Again, if the headhunter is less than responsive, move on.

Here's a question that a headhunter will ask of a candidate who's currently working full-time, a question that the candidate likely feels uneasy about: "How much are you currently making?" This question worries many candidates because they don't know what the "right" answer should be. They usually worry that if the number they give is too low, the headhunter may not think highly of them and be unwilling to work with them. Nothing can be further from the truth. If you are asked this question, give the headhunter an honest answer. Tell him or her that "my base is XXX and my annual bonus is (or is expected to be) YYY." Don't worry about what the headhunters *might* think of your current pay. They usually ask for this information to make sure they won't match you into a lower-paying job. They also use this information to gauge your experience (beyond what your résumé says about your experience). They might also use this information to prod the hiring employer into offering more money to you (whereby giving themselves a higher commission, too!). The bottom line is, you don't care, and shouldn't care. Tell them the truth. No matter what you tell them, never lie. Don't tell them you are making $200,000 a year if it's really $170,000. You just never know if the headhunter or the potential employer might ask to see your last paycheck stub. (It has happened to people!) The last thing you want is getting caught with your pants down when it comes to telling the truth about how much you are currently making.

It's your right to ask the headhunter how much the new position will pay. In fact, only the headhunter can tell you how much you can expect the job to pay before you actually go in for an interview. This information is part of the service headhunters provide. As you are probably already aware, most job postings do not tell you how much the jobs pay. Oftentimes you see something like "commensurate with experience" or "$100,000 plus." Knowing how much a position pays is especially important for people who are already working – in particular, those who are looking to move up on the pay scale (e.g., someone who's been working in non-quant finance but aspiring to move into a quant position). The headhunter can offer this information, or at least give you a range, so you can decide whether it'll be worthy of your time and effort to pursue that opportunity. So if you work with a headhunter, be sure to ask about expected pay for each opening he or she refers you to.

However, there is a tricky side to this coin: the headhunter may *not* tell you the truth about how much the position will pay! My experience has been that, headhunters tend to exaggerate the potential pay early on in the application process. I think they always want to make a position sound attractive, and part of doing this is to make you think there is a lot of money to be made so to arouse your strongest desire and interest. To avoid getting called liars, they usually give you a range: "It pays $100,000 to $500,000, depending on experience." That's the typical answer you'll get. Obviously, you have no idea what level of experience deserves the lower bound and what level commands something closer to $300,000 or $400,000. You hope you won't get the lower figure. In this case, you should make sure the lower figure is something you can accept. (A couple times, the actual offer I received was even less than the lower figure the headhunter had quoted me!) If it's too low for your taste, tell the headhunter so and see if he or she is willing to come back with a higher figure. Any time you don't like something about a job opening, be it expected salary or location or working hours, move on to something else. (Obviously, you don't want to be too picky or you'll scare away a lot of potentially helpful headhunters.)

Before we leave this section, I would like to re-emphasize the importance of recognizing the revolving-door nature of working with headhunters. To headhunters, candidates come and go, and the headhunters simply hope to catch the few "big fish" who can score quick offers and get them the commission fees. To candidates, headhunters are often necessary to work with, but there's no point in feeling attached (or loyal) to a particular recruiter (unless he or she goes out of the way to help you). What this all means is that if you never hear back from a headhunter after one or two rounds of contact, don't feel you are neglected. Well, yes, you are probably neglected by that particular headhunter. But after all, he or she is only acting out of her self-interest, which is to maximize his or her chance of scoring a big commission. So forgive him or her if you are not deemed the "optimal" candidate. On the other hand, if you don't want to talk to a headhunter, no need to feel bad at ignoring him or her or just telling them "no." That said, I wouldn't burn my bridges but instead would at least keep up the appearances and stay in e-mail contact with the headhunters that I have spoken with.

Leveraging Contacts for Job Search

If you are or have been on the dating scene, you know how it is: the good ones are *always* already taken. The same can almost be said about the job market. The most attractive jobs are often taken before the public (that's you and me) knows about them, and the jobs that are publicly posted are usually just okay. The fact of life is, the best jobs often go to the insiders – job hunters who know someone inside the hiring firm with knowledge, and probably influence, of the hiring process.

Incidentally, this appears to be true in many professions, where nepotism can always have an ample presence. But hiring an "insider" doesn't necessarily mean nepotism, and nepotism is not always a bad thing. (It's bad when an unqualified person is given a job solely because of his connection.) Firms do prefer to hire someone referred by an existing employee because:

- It saves money, in a big way. As I mentioned before, headhunters are very expensive, and when a candidate is hired, the hiring firm shoulders all the costs (which also include incidental expenses the headhunters and all the candidates incur). Even if a firm doesn't use a headhunter but relies on advertising instead, it can still get expensive, as well as time-consuming. Many firms pay employees a referral bonus, usually between $2,000 and $5,000, which is peanuts compared to employing a headhunter or advertising.

- The candidate has already been "pre-screened" by the referring employee. This not only makes it easier to trust the candidate than someone who just walks into the door to interview (e.g., making sure the guy is not a terrorist), but gives the employer more confidence that the referred candidate is qualified for the position. If the referring employee works in the same group as the potential hire, the fact a candidate is referred also increases the odds he or she will get along well with the referring employee and the other coworkers.

Of course, because of the referral bonus policy, current employees often have a strong incentive to refer their friends or acquaintances – or even a friend's friend's friend – to open positions. Sometimes, in the hope of getting the bonus, employees blindly refer friends, betting at least one of them will get the job. But for the most part, employee referral programs work well and help firms get qualified candidates without expending a lot of money and effort.

What does all this mean to you? Two things.

First, it pays to have contacts on Wall Street – including headhunters. Even if you don't know a Wall Street person well, as long as you make your presence known and ask them to keep you in mind for future openings, you may be able to get a head start on the competition and find out about job openings before the rest of the world does. The key here is to make these contacts remember you. You can often accomplish this by staying in regular contact with them. How frequently you should contact them depends on your relationship with each of them. If a Wall Street quant is a close buddy of yours, naturally you'll be talking to him or her a lot. If the person went to the same school as you and you knew him or her, say hello once every month or two. If you didn't know the person while in school, you might keep your contact to no more than two or three times a year, but each time subtly mention your qualification for potential quant positions at his or her firm. For example, in your e-mail or phone call you can mention the progress you have been making in education or other quant-oriented endeavors: "By the way, I just finished a paper on stochastic innovations in emerging-market stocks and had a great presentation this morning. One of the guys who attended my presentation was Prof. Nobel Winner, the guy who won the economics Nobel last year. He seemed pretty happy with my findings." No, you don't need to have met a Nobel prize winner to highlight your achievements. As long as you can leave the contact the impression that you are gaining skills and qualifications as a future quant, you've achieved the objective.

Second, when you have contacts, be sure to utilize them. I know, a lot of quants are socially shy and loath to being aggressive. In fact, we quants usually dislike aggressive people. We are intellectuals, we are scientists, we are highly educated people. We believe in meritocracy, not aggressive selling or sycophantic servitude. But Wall Street is not ivory tower, where one's career advancement largely depends on the number of peer-reviewed publications (at least before tenure is attained). Wall Street, like the rest of the "real world" out there, is heavily dependent on connections for its daily workings. From getting a sale to receiving investment tips to finding a job, whom you know is very important – often much more important than what you know. The fact is, if you want a good job, you just have to work hard to get it, including contacting people whom you don't know or don't know well but who may be able to help you.

Connecting With Contacts at Seminars or Happy Hours

We now find out how you can approach a potential contact at a seminar, presentation or happy hour. I want to emphasize that you really do not need to be a smooth operator to "work the room," so to speak. In fact, if your goal is to meet other quants, it's better you not try to be smooth. If you are the nerdy quant type, great – just be yourself. If you are a sociable type, be yourself but be careful not to sound too ingratiating – most quants are uncomfortable with any kind of close encounter with a stranger, even those quants who've made it to the managing director level. Whatever you say, never get into an argument. You don't have to always defer to the other person's opinions if you don't agree with them, but you should always be polite and respectful. You have to remember that you are talking to an intelligent person who's in a position you'd like to be in.

If you are going to a conference, seminar or presentation, look over the speaker list beforehand to see if there's anyone you are interested in approaching. Try to think of something in common between you and these people. For example, maybe you and they went to the same school, or maybe you share a common ethnic background. Maybe his or her research topic falls into one of your own research areas; indeed, talking about research is usually the most enjoyable and comfortable thing for quants to talk about and share ideas on. Don't worry if there's nothing in common between you and any of the speakers, though. The fact you and they are quants already qualifies you to speak with them. (Plus you are attending the meeting also for its substance, right?)

If you are going to a social gathering, or any event where you don't know who's going to be there, then you'll just need to improvise. The same applies when you step into the reception room at a conference or seminar. I always become nervous when I enter such a room full of strangers – strangers whose IQs are likely much higher than mine, strangers each of whom thinks of himself or herself as an intellectual deity. What I usually do is just shrug – a simple act that is surprisingly effective at calming myself down. I tell myself that I'm not an intellectual laggard. I tell myself that I have nothing to lose by approaching one or more of these people to strike up a conversation. I tell myself that the worst that can happen is I don't like someone (or they don't like me) and I just walk away. I tell myself that no matter what happens, 100 years from now *everyone* in the room will be dead. See if any of this positive thinking helps you, and come up with your own. You should feel good about yourself, period. You've survived countless exams and presentations and what-not in your life. You've got various knowledge, skills and experience (academic or industry) under your belt. You are a future quant, which makes you a smarty. Talking to strangers shouldn't scare you – even if you are nervous about presenting yourself to potential employers.

Once you make up your mind to approach a person, just do it. You know the drill. Introduce yourself. Make some small talk if you can: about the weather, about the meeting, about the other people in the room (but don't gossip!), about recent happenings in your field, etc. One topic to stay away from is politics. No matter what your view on the Iraq invasion or Taiwan independence is, keep it to yourself. Even if the other person seems to agree with you on a controversial topic, you have to steer clear of that topic because, one, you may soon realize that you two don't actually agree on all the details, and two, someone else (a potential employer, for example) may be listening in on your conversation and may become offended by your remarks. You can always engage the person on these hot talks *after* you get the job! For now, you are looking for a job. You want to be yourself but avoid offending others unnecessarily.

When talking to a person who could potentially offer you valuable help in finding a job, you may want to consider the Dale Carnegie method. You can read about this in detail in his classic social networking book *How to Win Friends and Influence People* (Amazon link for the most recent print: www.amazon.com/exec/obidos/ASIN/0671027034/pd_bk-

20), first published in 1936 and later updated by him and his associates. Basically, his idea of making someone like you is to refrain from talking about yourself; instead, get the person to talk about himself and herself, and you just listen and provide some positive feedback by nodding or saying "yes, that's really interesting" or "wow, that's great." I know, this sounds empty and bordering on being sycophantic; but it's not. If the other person is willing to share with you his or her thoughts or life experiences, it's because they are interesting to *him/her.* You simply reinforce what he or she says from *his or her point of view.* Carnegie's idea is simply that people like to talk about themselves and their achievements, not yours or mine. (If you think about it, this applies to yourself, too. Like Carnegie says, it's human nature.) By encouraging them to talk about themselves and thus making them feel good, you make them like you. Carnegie thinks this works all the time. Does it? I'd say no, but it works often enough – even (and probably especially) among hardcore quants – that I think it's a socializing technique that I highly recommend you follow as you look for contacts who can come in handy during your job search.

But what if you really find someone and/or his stories boring? What if you just can't stand someone who gossips about other people? What if the other person is a shameless braggadocio? What if you find the person's mordacious comments offensive? Simple. Just walk away when you get a chance. Pretend you need another drink. Pretend you want to use the restroom. Or pretend you saw a friend in another corner of the room. You don't need to put up with a stranger you don't like. Move away and move on to somebody who's more interesting, and who's possibly interested in hearing *your* story rather than telling his or her own non-stop. By the way, if someone truly offends your senses, you wouldn't want to work for, or work with, him or her anyway, right?

As you talk to the person, you may or may not want to bring up the fact that you are looking for a quant job. It's up to you. If you are making good rapport with the other person, I think it's a good idea to let him or her know that you are on the job market. If the person feels he or she is connecting with you, he or she might offer help or tips. If the person seems rather remote, then don't bring up your job search. You may still want to ask for his or her business card, but quickly try to find someone else who seems a warmer person. The truth is, the odds of meeting a solid contact at any one event are pretty slim. That's why if you are the shy or cynical type, you should only go to events where you can both enjoy the presentation topics and/or the atmosphere and find people whom you feel you can connect with. I personally don't think you should force yourself into doing anything you don't like or being someone you are not just in order to find a job. I'd like to encourage you to find your own comfort zone and stick with it. All roads lead to Rome. There are more than one way to skin a cat. It's always more cost-effective when you expend your energy on job search venues you find comfortable with.

After you've made the connection, be sure to keep it warm. Regularly contact the person to say hi. E-mail is the preferred way these days, as more and more people (except headhunters, of course) feel uncomfortable about getting a phone call from people they don't know well – and they'll think that you are trying to "use" them in some way, which no doubt will not help your chances of getting useful information from them! A brief e-mail that simply says "how are you?" serves to remind the person of who you are. If you can send it from an official e-mail address with a domain name from your institution (e.g., a .edu domain or that of your company) also helps them remember where you go to school or currently work.

Speaking of e-mail and domain names, be sure to add the e-mail address of an important contact to your e-mail safe list, so his or her messages will not be wrongly classified as spam (junk mail) by your e-mail program. The last thing you ever want is meeting a great contact who is genuinely interested in helping you, only to have your e-mail program blocking his or her messages and end up hurting the person's feelings. Likewise, you may want to add his or her phone number to your cell phone's contact book for convenience of calling him or her as well as utilizing the caller ID feature.

Occasionally, if it's a contact with whom you feel comfortable and at ease, you may want to ask them to have lunch or drinks with you, or you may invite them to a seminar or happy hour that you know of. Again, I think the key here is be sincere and be genuine in your attitude. If you truly want to be friends with the person, you shouldn't feel constrained by the fact that you met them in the first place because you were looking for a job search contact. As long as you are willing to treat the other person like a friend instead of looking at him or her as an "investment" of sort, you'll have nothing to lose.

Here I'd like to offer a word of caution if the other person is a member of the opposite sex (or the sex whose members you feel attracted to) – especially if he or she is in the same age group as you:

be careful how often and how you contact the person. If your approach is ever construed as a sexual pass or harassment, at best you end up offending the person and being told to lay off, and at worst you may face encroachment charges that you'd rather not deal with at this stage of your life (or ever). Conversely, if a contact appears to harbor ulterior motives or seek sexual favors in return for giving you help, you should immediately walk away from the relationship. The general rule is, if the person belongs to an older generation and seems genuinely interested in helping young people launch their careers, you can contact them more often for advice. Otherwise, keep the contact cordial until you feel confident the relationship is a healthy friendship. No matter what the case may be, always be cautious about how you approach the other person. Best friends and lovers can turn into worst enemies overnight.

Chapter Summary

This chapter explored when you should start looking for a job and where you can find job openings. For current Ph.D. candidates, the annual ASSA meeting (aka "AEA" or "AFA" meeting) is the most important venue and surely not to be missed. For anyone who's still a student, the fall-season campus recruiting program should be taken full advantage of. If you are on your own, be sure to explore the finance professional societies in the area you are interested in as well as try to link up with headhunters who recruit quants. Finally, identify people you know or have met who may have inside information on quant jobs, and don't be bashful about asking them for help.

Chapter 4: Acing the Quant Interview

In this chapter:

W hew! After searching hard and wide and making contacts left and right, you finally landed a job interview. (Hopefully, you'll have a bunch of them lined up.) After the initial rush of euphoria – which is well deserved given the amount of hard work you've put in – you are suddenly overwhelmed by a mixture of fear, anxiety and self-disbelief. "How am I going to deal with the interview? What am I going to say? Are they going to test me on my math and stats? Will they like me?"

I'm not going to sugarcoat the fact: of the entire recruiting process, the interview is the hardest part. This is, unfortunately, especially true of quant interviews, because quant jobs require highly qualified people who can meet high expectations – and only interviews can reveal a candidate's true qualification. Quant employers can overlook typos and grammatical mistakes on your résumé. They can tolerate the unusual formatting and 8-point fonts on your résumé. They can be skeptical of but choose to ignore the encomiastic introduction from the headhunter. But if they find fault with your depth of knowledge or skills during the interview, you won't get the job, period.

On the other hand, there *are* ways to ace a quant interview regardless of whether you are new to the interview scene or have been on the circuit for a while. There *are* things you can do to make yourself the best candidate in the eyes and minds of your interviewers. You can do it. You are smart, you are ambitious, you are savvy – that's why you want to be a Wall Street quant! In this long and tip-packed chapter, I'll show you how to ace quant interviews of all stripes and colors.

Types of Interviews

In terms of medium, there are two types of interviews: phone interviews and in-person interviews.

Employers often conduct phone interviews with candidates who come through headhunters or third-party contacts (e.g., an employee referral). The purpose of the phone interview is to get an initial sense of the qualifications of the candidate beyond what's written in the résumé. Phone interviews are easy to set up and save the employers time and money during the initial round of recruiting.

In-person (or face-to-face) interviews can be on-site or off-site. On-site means bringing the candidate to the office, which can be the headquarters of the company or the location where the opening is. Off-site refers to a place other than the company's premise; it can be a job fair, a school career office, the ASSA (AEA/AFA) annual meeting, or any other location not controlled by the company.

On-the-phone interviews usually last half an hour to one hour – although once in my life, a hedge fund gave me an extremely tiring three-hour interview over the phone (at the end of which I decided these guys were slave drivers and absolutely not the type of people I would ever want to work with). In-person interviews can take as little as 15 minutes (at a job fair, for example) and as much as an entire working day, which can mean up to 10 hours at some firms! Later on, I will discuss the strategies of dealing with these interviews.

In terms of content, interviews can be categorized as informational interviews, technical interviews (also known as analytical interviews), case interviews, or a combination of the three. Informational interviews are the easiest kind to deal with: you and the interviewer just exchange information about each other, with you giving him or her a rundown on your qualifications and him and her briefing you on the job and the company. Informational interviews are what every job candidate secretly wishes every interview to be. They are relatively stress-free, although we shall see later that some informational questions from the interviewer can be tricky, tough, or stressful (and you'll learn how to deal with such questions).

Technical (or analytical) interviews, on the other hand, place the candidate in the hot seat by bombarding him or her with questions that test his or her analytical and technical knowledge. These are, without a doubt, every candidate's nightmare. Depending on the position's requirements, the technical questions asked can range from esoteric C++ concepts to proving the Ito's Lemma to identifying econometric problems in a regression model. While some interviews hand out relatively easy questions ("How do you read in a text file in SAS?"), others can ask really hardcore questions ("What are the tests for stationarity and what are their limitations?").

Case interviews, popular with management consulting firms, involve giving the applicant either real-world problems to solve on the spot or brain-teasers (puzzles). Real-world problems can take the form of a specific modeling question, such as "We have a client who wants to build a domestic swaps portfolio and his risk tolerance is x%. What would you do to help him achieve his objective?", or they can involve a broad-context scenario, such as "My group wants to get into the options trading business. How should we start the process?" These questions differ from technical tests in that they try to examine both your technical knowledge and your problem-solving skills at the same time, with an emphasis on the latter. (A word that comes to mind which describes case questions is *holistic*, as in "taking a holistic approach.") A candidate who knows the ins and outs of every C# feature doesn't necessarily know how to put a small development project together. Depending on the position, the "big picture" ability may be of paramount importance. Brain-teasers are IQ-testing puzzles unrelated to work. For example, a Sudoku puzzle is a type of brain-teaser, as is something like "Why are manhole covers round?" (purportedly a question that originated at Microsoft). Some interviewers like to give case interviews because such questioning gives the interviewer some insight into how the candidate thinks about and solves problems, as opposed to being a number cruncher – and in the long run, a person who can think logically and solve problems effectively will contribute significantly more to the firm's bottom line than a pure "quant geek" who only knows how to follow specific commands.

Many interviewers, myself included, conduct a combination of the three interview styles in each interview, especially when face-to-face. I typically start an in-person interview with information exchange. I ask the candidate about his or her background. I often make small talk in an effort to make him or her feel at home. (By the way, from the standpoint of an experienced interviewer, helping an interviewee relax not only constitutes a nice gesture, but can get the interviewee to let down his or her guard and inadvertently reveal sides of his or her true personality that he or she wouldn't have otherwise shown at a job interview. Hmm, did I just give you a valuable tip or what?) I also try to gain a better understanding of the person's qualifications than can be gleaned from the résumé. I give the candidate some details about what my group does and how we work together. From this information exchange I get a chance to gauge the candidate's communication and interpersonal skills. I then move on to the technical tests by asking specific technical questions. For instance, my group uses Perl extensively in our daily work, so I often test a candidate on his or her Perl programming skills. I may also ask topical questions from mathematics, economics, econometrics, or finance. I often throw in a case question. Depending on the amount of time I have, the case question may be a general problem-solving one or a brain-teaser. (I usually prefer short brain-teasers.) Finally, I spend the last five to ten minutes reverting back to the informational style: asking the candidate questions, or letting him or her ask questions.

Interviewer Styles

By interviewer style I mean *how* an interviewer conducts an interview, not what he or she says or asks during the interview. Some interviewers can be very friendly and easy-going, and give a lot of positive feedback and encouragement even when the candidate stumbles on a question. Some are there in the interview room simply to do a job, and they usually follow the "typical" interview routine without much enthusiasm but also without much hostility. Some interviewers act bored and want to go through an interview quickly. Others – you'll no doubt bump into them at some point – can act hostile or brusque or impatient, casting a negative light on everything the candidate says. Indeed, there are true stories about candidates, male and female, being pushed into tears by nasty interviewers. Who said life was fair?

If you meet a friendly interviewer, consider yourself lucky. But you should still be on your guard 100% throughout the interview and not become cozy with the interviewer. Behind the façade of friendliness and warmth is often a cunning person who tries to lure you into a sense of complacency. If you do something stupid – many candidates do when they are misled into believing that the interviewer is their friend – the interviewer *will* note it down and report it back to the big boss. You have to keep reminding yourself that the interviewer is *not* your friend, or even your advocate. (Unless, of course, you two are already real friends.) The interviewer will treat you like he or she treats all other candidates. Yes, he or she may find your personality (or appearance) more agreeable than another candidate, but at the end of the day, he or she will judge you based on your performance and qualification, not whether you two had a pleasant chat.

For instance, I'm usually a friendly interviewer. I'm so because I'm generally a cordial person, and I enjoy helping a candidate wade through the interview process. But my job as an interviewer is to gauge whether the person will be a good fit for the team and for the type of quant work we do. My job as an interviewer is not to play nice simply for the sake of playing nice. Personally, I want the candidate to feel as little stress as possible in front of me, but that doesn't mean that I'm not judging him or her constantly, or that I won't throw in a tough question or two when I see fit. On more than one occasion, a candidate would feel so at home in front of me that they would get carried away when telling a story and use the absolutely forbidden F--- word. (Yes, you'll hear the F--- word on trading desks all the time, but in an interview, it's not accepted, especially if it comes from the interviewee!) When that happens, the word "foobar" pops into my mind, and I'm pretty sure I don't want this person on my team no matter how smart he or she is. (In case you didn't know what foobar meant, it's a spelling play on the word "fubar," which in turn is a management science acronym standing for "f*cked up beyond all recognition.") Why wouldn't I want this person? Because someone who gets carried away so easily lacks maturity, and there's no telling that, someday, when a project bombs and the big boss comes to town looking for a scapegoat, this immature person won't try to sell me or other team members out.

The moral of all this is, don't ever let your guard down during a job interview. Always be on your toes. Treat every interviewer with respect but keep a healthy dose of skepticism at all times. If the interviewer is super-friendly or constantly flatters you, tell yourself that the interviewer is probably up to no good (even if that's not true – but you'll never know what's truly going on in his or her mind!).

If an interviewer behaves as if he or she is just doing a chore by interviewing you, don't try to entertain him or her by telling outrageous stories or acting funny. Chances are, he or she won't be amused and will in most likelihood be annoyed. Simply act polite and answer his or her questions briefly and quickly. If you get lost in a technical or case question and do not get the feedback you expected, ask for feedback. "Am I doing this right?" "Am I on the right track?" It doesn't hurt to ask for feedback. Better yet, when you ask for feedback, try to flatter the interviewer at the same time: "Whoa, this is a really good, deep question. Frankly I'm lost and I wonder if I could use your help a little." I'll have more to say about answering technical and case questions later on.

What if you have the lucky draw of the day and run into an interviewer who's just, to put it mildly, uncooperative? He or she may seem to be trying to give you a hard time. But like the case with the super-friendly interviewer, what *seems* to be may not be. True, the person could just be a sadist and take great pleasure at seeing you sweat in pain. Or he or she could be having a hard time at work – for instance, the bonus number had just been announced and it just ain't good for the interviewer – and needed some way to let off some steam. Or it could just be acting. The interviewer might act hostile to see how you perform under pressure and in front of a belligerent "client." (In a way the interviewer is your client, as you try to sell him or her your labor skills.) An interview conducted in an atmosphere of duress can be nerve-wracking and harmful to your self esteem. But face it: on Wall Street there are many, many rude people. Your boss, your boss's boss, your client, your client's boss, your coworker, etc. As a quant you'll need to deal with them, so it's natural for an interviewer (who may not be a jerk himself or herself) to see if you are mature enough to handle such stressful encounters. Your strategy at handling such an interviewer? Think positive thoughts. Tell yourself that the interviewer is just pretending to be nasty (regardless of whether he or she is a truly nasty person). Tell yourself that the interview will be over soon. Tell yourself that you are doing fine. Tell yourself that anyone who's so nasty won't go to heaven when they die – and besides, the interviewer will be dead 50 years from now, likely before your time is up. Keep these positive thoughts flowing, and try not to become distressed or distracted by the person's attitude or behavior. Now, if you perceive his or her behavior to be unbecoming of a professional – e.g., if the person yells at you at the top of his or her lung, uses profanities liberally, or makes lewd or lascivious remarks that make you feel uncomfortable – you should be brave enough to tell him or her so, with the undertone that you may report this unprofessional behavior to his or her superior afterwards. I suggest you practice making such veiled threats before you go to any interview, but only use them when an interviewer is truly offensive in some way and refuses to back down when you protest.

(Side note: The past few years have seen a dramatic increase in how Wall Street firms deal with harassment, thanks in part to some high-profile lawsuits. Harassment in the workplace – and in the interview room – is defined as creating a hostile or intimidating environment through pressure and/or unwelcome remark or behavior. Of course, what's considered "hostile" or "intimidating" or "unwelcome" is difficult to define; unless a person is overtly racist, sexist or homophobic, for instance, it's difficult to determine what's unwelcome or reasonable. Nonetheless, Wall Street firms as a whole have become increasingly sensitive to what their employees say or do to one another. I think this is a welcome development, especially for women and ethnic minorities. If you hear something that you believe is harassment and you can substantiate your claim – e.g., recalling verbatim what was said between you and the interviewer – you should bring it to the attention of the department head. And do it immediately after the harassing interview. If the department head dismisses your concern, you should point out the gravity of the situation, and may want to follow up with a prompt written protest, cc'ing it to the company's general counsel [the chief in-house lawyer] and the headhunter. Again, I want to emphasize that you do this *only* if you are truly offended and can substantiate your claim that you are harassed. I don't want to encourage my readers to start suing prospective employers for feeling slighted in some way. Besides, there's absolutely no guarantee you'll win if you do file a lawsuit. And don't count on this as a way to get a job or plan for your early retirement!)

In the rest of this chapter, I will give you lots of tips on how to handle a quant interview. I'll start by discussing how you should use the scheduling of interviews to your greatest advantage.

Scheduling an Interview

"What? Are you implying by the section heading that I have controls over the scheduling of my interviews?" your curious mind may be asking.

To some extent, the answer is yes. Almost all potential employers give you a choice on when you want to meet them. For on-site interviews (which take place on the employer's premise), the choice of day is usually flexible within a range of dates. On the other hand, the employer may or may not let you pick your own starting time on the interview day; for example, many daylong interviews run the full day, so unless you have extraordinary circumstances, you'll be asked to show up at the office at a certain time. Phone interviews and interviews at career fairs (such as the one on the sideline of the annual ASSA meeting I discussed extensively in the previous chapter) usually do not allow you to choose the day, but often do allow you a degree of freedom in terms of picking a time of day.

How much freedom you are given in choice of day and/or time is up to the employer, but can usually be negotiated. For example, let's say you go to the ASSA career fair and have three interviews lined up on the same date. You can always tell each of the three firms that you are busy at certain time of the day and ask them to accommodate a time when you are not busy (and presumably when you feel you are at your best). Few employers will say no – if you ask early enough. (That is, don't wait till the last minute to ask for a scheduling change! That would seem rude, arrogant and/or uncaring, and could well put you in the "unfavorable candidates" pool before you even meet with the potential employer.)

How you schedule your interviews is important. The basic strategy, which is also the rule, is simple: schedule first the interviews for positions that you are the least interested in. That way, you can give yourself some real-world practice before you step into a job interview that's important to you. In effect, you are using the first interviewer or interviewers as guinea pigs for your own advantage.

Actually, the corollary of this rule is not quite true. You should not – let me repeat for emphasis, should *not* – schedule the most important interviews for last. The reason is after several rounds of interviews, you may be too tired. Your speech may have started to slur and your thought process may have started to slow down. This is especially true if you have a lot of interviews with different employers lined up on the same day at a job fair. Instead, you should place the important interviews – for the jobs that you really want – in the middle of the pack.

So the sequence of optimal interview scheduling should be like this: first, one or two interviews for positions you don't care much about, to test the waters and practice your interview skills in front of real interviewers; second, the important interviews, for positions that you truly desire; last, the interviews for positions that you don't feel strongly about. Please note that this optimal scheduling strategy applies equally to phone and in-person interviews. The bottom line is, if you have any wiggle room at all at controlling an interview's time and day, use that flexibility to your greatest advantage.

But what if you haven't lined up any interviews yet but expect to get at least one? You can still strategize along the same line. Submit your résumé early to places that you can afford to practice your interview skills at. Hopefully, these places will respond first, before the firms that you truly want to join. That way, you have a good chance at getting a practice interview.

Regardless of how you schedule out your interviews, you must still treat each and every one of them with equal seriousness. Don't leave the impression that you're just practicing, even if that's exactly what you are doing! Trust me, many interviewers are very good at telling whether you are just using them as guinea pigs. This is especially easy to tell if the candidate is at his or her very first job interviews of the season and acts as if he or she is not enthusiastic about the position. At interviews, always exude a strong interest in the position and put your full attention forward. Do not ever try to treat the interviewer as a fool. If he or she is already a Wall Street quant, chances are good that he or she is just as smart as you, if not smarter.

Before Interview Time

Regardless of whether it's over the phone or in person, you must treat the upcoming interview with utmost seriousness – especially if you are truly interested in the job. If the interview is to be the very first quant interview in your life, you should do a mock interview to practice your presentation skills in a setting similar to an actual interview. If you are in school, check with your school's career service office and sign up for a mock interview if you haven't done so. If you are already out of school (e.g., you're looking for a career change), ask your spouse or a good friend to give you a mock interview. Ask him or her to go over your résumé and dig into your background with you, pretending he or she is a potential employer. If the he or she is a quantitative type of person, be sure to ask him or her to prepare some technical questions.

You might think a mock interview is "stupid." After all, it's not the real thing, and if you do it with a friend, it just seems weird. But trust me, any practice is better than no practice. Obviously, if the mock interview is conducted with a career service officer at your school, that's the best approach since these people know how to conduct mock interviews – and you may be lucky and run into one that has knowledge of quant interviews. But even with a friend, you may be surprised at the usefulness. For instance, your friend might catch something unusual or unclear on your résumé. He or she might ask questions that you thought were easy but turn out to require quite a bit of explanation. He or she might have constructive criticism of your speech habit, your accent, or your body language – or even the way you dress. Doing a mock interview, at the very least, should give you some good preparation on questions related to your background and general qualifications.

The mock interview is especially important for those candidates whose command of English is less than ideal. In fact, if you speak with a heavy accent – you'll know you do when native English speakers frequently ask you to repeat what you just said or have trouble following you – I *highly* recommend that you seek the help of a professional speech therapist or speech coach. These are trained professionals who can identify the exact speech problems (accent, intonation, mispronunciation, etc.) in your spoken English skills, and can work with you to correct as many of them as possible. Do not put this off! Search for a speech coach or therapist in your area right now; you can browse your local papers, ask friends for referrals, or utilize a local services search site like Local Live (local.live.com). Many local universities and community colleges offer English classes taught by people who can help you improve your spoken English; you may even want to contact the instructor after class to see if he or she offers one-on-one speech coaching. If you do this and do your best to improve your communication skills, you'll find it one of the best investments (in money, time and effort) in your life.

Even if English is your native language, you may want to seek the help of a speech therapist or coach if your particular accent (e.g., southern U.S. or Australian) may be difficult for most other English speakers to understand, or if you have speech problems such as slurred speech, trailing tones or some type of speech impediment. You may have avoided facing this problem all your life, but now is the time to face it and deal with it. Ask a friend to comment on your speech pattern and habit. If there is anything less than acceptable about your way of speaking, be sure to seek help as soon as possible. I know it can be hard to admit the problem, let alone taking the necessary and arduous steps to address it – I have been there myself – but if you want to maximize your chances of getting a good job and succeeding in life, you need to take that painful step. Remember, any improvement, no matter how big or small, is way better than status quo.

Going through a job interview, especially a quant interview where the interviewer may ask very tough technical questions, can be a very stressful experience – in fact, it is for most of us mere mortals. I myself have gone through countless job interviews in my life but still find myself sweating and swooning when I walk into an important interview. It's just a human nature thing, given the significance of the situation. If you have the time, you may consider learning some self-calming skills. Tai chi (aka Taiji), Qigong (pronounced chee-gong), yoga, deep breathing exercises – whatever techniques that can help you calm yourself down. I find positive thinking, which I have alluded to a few times in previous sections, the best way to help me calm down. Slow, deep, controlled breathing also works for me, sometimes but not always though. Above all, the better prepared you are before you walk into a real interview, the more confident you will feel about yourself. And this usually translates into better interview results.

In addition to the mock interview, which gets your ready for questions related to your background and technical expertise, pre-interview preparation should also include doing some background check on the company, the department (or group) and the position. Chances are you've already done some homework on these; but now that you have an interview scheduled, it doesn't hurt to re-read some of the background materials. What exactly does the firm do? What area, department or practice is the position in? What specific tasks will the position entail and what prerequisites does the job description emphasize? Think all this preparation is unnecessary? You'll be surprised at how many candidates I have interviewed who came into the room totally ignorant of what business my company was in or what the position was all about. To me – and no doubt to many other interviewers – such ignorance spells disrespect: disrespect for my company, disrespect for the quant position, and disrespect for my time. The last thing I want to do as an interviewer is telling a candidate things about the company and position that were already clearly posted on the web. I enjoy offering candidates some details regarding the types of tools we use and the types of models we build; but spending time rehashing company and job descriptions is not my cup of tea – it's a complete waste of interview time.

Besides getting familiar with the company, the department (or group) and the position, you might also want to do some background search on your interviewers, if you have the list. Use a powerful Internet search engine like Live Search (search.live.com) to see if you can find any information on the person, such as his or her past publications. Remember the Dale Carnegie principle of making people like you? You want to encourage them to talk about *themselves.* By knowing something about the person, you can strike up a Dale Carnegie conversation and get the person to talk about his or her past academic and/or industry experiences, or about his or her peer-reviewed publications. Senior quants like to be flattered about their achievements. If they see that you know about their achievements – who doesn't want to be famous? – chances are they'll take a liking of you and that, my friend, gives your candidacy a powerful boost. Even if you hate flattering others, you might find things you have in common with him or her (e.g., you went to the same school, you studied under the same professor, you like the same sports teams, you lived in the same city once – but if you dated the same guy or girl, it's probably best to leave that one out!), and this gives you and the interviewer plenty to talk about during the interview – and it helps you relax, too. (A side benefit of stuffing an interview with informational chat is it might leave little time for the interviewer to ask you tough technical questions!)

General Tips for Handling Interviews

It should be amply clear now that quant interviews are not all alike. Despite the wide gamut of formats and venues and interviewer styles, though, there are some general tips that can help you handle an interview well. Some of the tips given here can be applicable to any job interview, not just a quant interview. Other tips are specific to Wall Street or quant interviews.

The first tip is simply be adequately prepared for an interview, be it a phone interview or a face-to-face one. This topic was discussed at length in the previous section. I just want to repeat here that you must *prepare, prepare and prepare!* Never, ever walk into an interview unprepared.

Groom and dress well for the in-person interview. Gentlemen, this means a clean haircut and nicely trimmed facial hair if you have any. It also means shirt, tie and suit, and those nice dress shoes you've been hiding since the senior prom. Ladies, this means a professional-looking hairdo, light and even make-up, and blouse and suit (skirt okay). A scarf is always a nice touch. Moderately heeled pumps are appropriate; avoid heels higher than three inches and avoid open-toe shoes. Everyone should remember that for a business interview, T-shirts, jeans, sneakers, flip-flops, and shorts are never acceptable.

Be sure to have had a good night's sleep and, in the morning, taken a shower and brushed your teeth thoroughly before heading to the interview. Bring chewing gum or another kind of breath freshener, too; after a couple interviews, you'll surely find yourself with a dry, smelly mouth. Real Wall Street quants may dress down or look haggard at work, but they expect to see freshly groomed candidates at job interviews.

If it's a phone interview and you plan to use a cell phone, make sure your phone is fully charged and has good signal strength. You may want to use a headset – but never use the speakerphone! (Using a speakerphone is the sure way of annoying the hell out of your interviewer and spelling the doom of your candidacy.) If possible, use a landline phone. Find a quiet place where you won't be interrupted and where you can feel comfortable and relaxed. Make sure there's no background noise such as that from a TV or stereo or crying baby. Get ready a few minutes before the phone interview time. You may want to use these few minutes to go over the things you will want to say. By the way, if you plan to use a book or computer for reference, e.g., during the technical questioning, make sure the other party won't be able to hear you flip through a book or type on a keyboard! If an interviewer finds out you are "cheating," he or she won't be happy about it at all.

For an onsite interview, or an offsite interview where you have an appointed time, it should be plenty obvious that you must arrive on time. In fact, you should arrive a few minutes early to familiarize yourself with the environment. Arriving early also gives you a chance to use the washroom if needed. If you drive or take public transportation to the interview site, leave home extra early to give yourself plenty of time to deal with traffic or delays. If you arrive at the interview site more than fifteen minutes before the interview time, you may want to hang out somewhere else (e.g., in a coffee shop) first, because showing up *too* early not only awards you no brownie point with the employer but may actually hurt your chance if the interviewer thinks you are too nervous or overly cautious. Five to ten minutes is a good amount of ahead time to report in and get familiar with the interview site. Feel free to ask where to get a cup of coffee or a glass of water – but only do so if you find an employee who's neither too busy nor hostile.

When you meet the interviewer for a face-to-face interview, try to initiate the greeting as well as the handshake. For greeting, a simple "Hi, Mr. Quanty! I'm William Candy." will suffice. Don't call the person "Dr. Quanty" unless you know for sure he or she has a doctorate. You don't need to say your last name; either way is fine. If the interviewer is a man, make the handshake firm (but never squeeze hard!). If the interviewer is a woman, the handshake should be full but gentle – no, a gentleman interviewee need not kiss the back of her hand. This handshake etiquette applies equally whether you are male or female. It's a good idea to practice with your friends beforehand. Should you find yourself so nervous as to have a sweaty palm, wipe it quickly and inconspicuously on your jacket or pants right before you offer your hand. In business etiquette, a firm handshake, signaling sincerity, is always a must. And don't forget to shake the interviewer's hand after the interview, regardless of how it went.

As you talk to the interviewer, it's vitally important that you maintain constant eye contact, meaning you look him or her in the eyes. A lot of quant candidates, coming from a background of constantly working with numbers and models and computers, dislike making eye contact. Instead, they would look down at the piece of paper in front of themselves or look up at the ceiling. An interview is not an interrogation (although it may feel like one at times). It's a one-on-one exchange of information and a chance for the interviewer and the interviewee to assess each other. A person who avoids eye contact inevitably leaves the impression of disrespect, immaturity and evasiveness. All three can negatively determine the outcome of the interview, so make sure you make eye contact.

Making eye contact, let me point out, is not the same as being aggressive in the Western culture. Making eye contact is a *good* behavior; it shows you respect the other person. It also shows you are paying attention to him or her – which is important in an interview setting. The only caveat here is you shouldn't stare. Good eye contact means *gently* looking into the other person's eyes, not staring hard as if you tried to devour him or her.

As you make eye contact, you should also smile from time to time. I'm not suggesting you maintain a continuous faux smile and look like a Cheshire cat. If you are the kind of person who likes to smile, do so liberally and naturally at the interview. If you are more of a serious type, force yourself to smile from time to time, for instance, every time either you or the interviewer finishes saying something. (Obviously, don't act like a robot!) It's more effective when you respond to the interviewer's talk with a smile and a nod. It's always better to smile too much than to not smile at all. I don't think any candidate should maintain a poker face at the interview table, because such a person would come across as cold, robotic or aloof, and few people feel comfortable working with someone who's cold or robotic or aloof.

An interview, phone or in-person, gives the potential employer a good chance to check out the candidate's communication skills. Hopefully, you followed my pre-interview advice in the previous section and did a couple of mock interviews (and worked with a speech coach if English is not your mother tongue). Come the real interview, make sure you speak clearly. While native English speakers seldom have trouble with pronunciation and grammar, they should still pay attention to their intonation, speed, as well as content. If your interviewer speaks American English but you grew up in Great Britain or Australia or another country where spoken English is quite different from American English, you need to make an effort at speaking in a "neutral" accent. To me, for instance, someone who speaks with a heavy Irish accent is no different from someone who has a heavy

Russian accent – I just can't understand either. Fortunately, native English speakers can emulate other English accents relatively easily, as long as they make a conscientious effort at doing it. (I devote an entire section later in this chapter to non-native English speakers.)

Speed of speech is important. If you are too fast or too slow, the interviewer will have trouble understanding you. As a general rule, as a candidate, it's better to speak slower than your usual speed (unless your usual speed is already quite slow). If you are unsure of what a "good" regular speed should be, turn on your TV to a news channel such as CNBC (for finance news) or MSNBC (for independent general news), and see how fast the professional broadcasters speak. If you manage to talk at a slightly slower pace than the news broadcasters, you'll go a long way in impressing your interviewers with your communication skills.

Regardless of your speech speed or accent or imperfect grammar, the most important aspect of speaking at an interview is, speak clearly. Do not rush words out of your mouth. If you are asked a question, think about the answer before you say it. When you say it, say it clearly and logically. Clear speech is a combination of all the aspects I've discussed before: accent, intonation, grammar, speed, the quality of your voice, plus the presence of logical thinking and expression. You need not be perfect in any particular aspect to be clear in your final speech. For instance, I've come across candidates who speak with heavy accents or who sound hoarse but who nonetheless come across as decent speakers. The key, again, is to think about what you're about to say and then say it in a logical and clear manner. If you're weak in this area, practice aplenty or seek the help of a professional speech coach.

While your oral communication skills will play an important role in determining your chances of success at interviews, your body language is important, too, when you have an in-person interview. Body language refers to the way you conduct yourself nonverbally. It encompasses a lot of aspects: how you sit, how you listen, how you maintain eye contact (see above), how you use your hands to aid your oral communication, etc. Here I'll talk about three major body language areas. (I already discussed maintaining eye contact and smiling earlier in this section.)

- How you sit at the interview table can leave a lasting impression on the interviewer. (Unfortunately, it's inevitable that it's the bad sitters who tend to leave such lasting impressions.) No, you need not sit stiffly upright like a German general, but you must sit properly and convey an air of professionalism, enthusiasm and respect for the interviewer. The "proper" way of sitting in an interview is: sit comfortably but upright in the chair with your butt covering the front 3/4 of the chair; lean slightly forward; place your forearms and hands on the table (as if holding your résumé or notepad, for example). Do not sit back in the chair as if you were enjoying a lazy afternoon conversation at a Starbucks. Do not cross your arms or legs (both signs of complacency and arrogance), although ladies should feel free to cross their feet at the ankles. And never put your feet up on the table! Feel free to move your upper body as you speak or when you need to change your posture for comfort, but do not overdo it. If you have a habit of tapping your fingers on the table or cracking those knuckles or playing with the pen, especially when nervous, watch out: they not only make you look too nervous or anxious, but likely annoy the hell out of the interviewer.

- How you listen to the interviewer not only reflects your ability to understand and absorb what others say, but conveys your attitude towards others. People who are egotistic and arrogant are poor listeners; they tend to dismiss what others have to say and only indulge in their own thoughts and talks. You absolutely don't want to come across as a bad listener. Maintain good eye contact and pay attention to every word the interviewer says. (Okay, probably not literally every word, but you should nonetheless try as you never know if something seemingly insignificant the interview is waxing lyrical about may come back as a question later.) Nod and say "yes" or "okay" or "good" frequently to show you are listening intently.

- How you properly use your hands for emphasis can make a difference in the impression you leave with the interviewer. Upfront I want to say that it's perfectly okay to use your hands to supplement your spoken words, but only when you wish to emphasize certain points. The best way to see the proper use of hand language is to watch panel discussions on news channels (i.e., not those reruns of Jerry Springer shows!). Pay attention to panel discussants who have class. See how they use their hands and body language to make their points. Whatever you do, avoid waving your arms wildly, and absolutely, positively no pounding on the table no matter how excited you get during the interview or how passionate you feel about your argument.

The key takeaway on proper body language is, use it minimally but when you do, use it effectively. Again, I recommend you watch TV news programs and roundtable talk shows to get an idea of how professional speakers use both spoken and body languages with maximum efficacy.

For employers, interviews give them a chance to make discoveries about the candidates: who the candidates are, what kind of personalities they have, and what skills (from technical to problem-solving to interpersonal) they possess. Part of this discovery process often involves asking tough questions. Interviewers ask difficult questions to probe holes on the candidate's résumé, to test the knowledge and/or stamina of the candidate, or to find out how the candidate performs under duress. One particular type of tough questioning involves probing holes in the candidate's background, such as a meaningless position or an unpublished paper. Or the interviewer could just bluntly ask, "What are your weaknesses?" When asked questions about your background that give you goose bumps, you should keep only one thing in mind: be forthcoming, be truthful. Never try to hide any deficiencies in your qualification, whether these deficiencies are evident in your résumé or are brought out in the course of the interview. It's always the case that the harder you try to hide something, the more conspicuous it becomes. What might have been a mere peccadillo could suddenly blow up into an egregious sin in the mind of the interviewer if you fail to tell the truth. The corollary of this rule is, don't sugarcoat those minor blemishes, either. Some interviewers probably don't mind a bit of sugarcoating on your part, but others will find any pretext objectionable and, again, may decide to exclude you from the job because you've been less than completely forthcoming.

Being forthcoming, however, doesn't mean you should volunteer information that may negatively impact your candidacy but which the interviewer doesn't already possess. For example, let's say you were let go from your last job really because you were not performing. But technically you were not fired, just let go. (Very few American employers actually fire people outright as doing so may bring lawsuits from the disgruntled employees – firing implies some kind of egregious wrongdoing on the part of the employee and a fired employee cannot collect any government benefits.) So if you are asked about the reason why you left the previous job, you should tell the interviewer that you were let go, e.g., as part of corporate restructuring. Do not volunteer the fact that you were deemed underperforming! Hiding this information is not telling a lie in most cases simply because whether someone was performing or not performing could be totally subjective. Plus, the definition of a lie is "an intentionally false statement" (according to the New Oxford American Dictionary inside my Sharp PW-E550 electronic dictionary). As long as you don't make a blatantly false statement, you are not lying, and you are not being dishonest.

In a later section, I will have more to say about the kinds of background questions you are likely to be asked, and the best ways to handle such questions.

Intelligent Questions to Ask

A job interview is a two-way exchange: the interviewer examines your qualification, and you, the candidate, find out if the job and the environment are right for you. This means you must ask questions during an interview, and you must ask the right questions. Never let an interview turn into a one-way street where only the interviewer gets to ask you questions. If the interviewer facing you is so garrulous as to dominate the interview, you should be assertive in the last five to ten minutes and tell him or her that you have some questions you'd like to ask. Be polite in doing so, but be assertive and show your confidence. For example, you can say "Pardon me, but I noticed that we are running out of time and I actually have some questions I'd like to ask of you before we finish the interview. Can I ask them now?" Repeat the request if the interviewer ignores you at first.

When you get to be the questioner, it's important you ask the right kind of questions. Yes, there are right questions and there are wrong questions to ask at quant job interviews. There are two basic guiding principles in asking questions as a job candidate: first, ask questions that can actually flatter the interviewer (remember our old friend Dale Carnegie?); second, ask questions that you really care about (except if the question is how much the job pays; see below).

With these in mind, let's see some examples of what to ask and what not to ask.

Questions that flatter the interviewer *and* show you care about the position include:

- "Could you tell me how you made the successful transition from an academic to an industry quant?" Or, "I find your experience inspiring, and I was wondering if you could tell me how you decided to work in this industry?" Or even just simply, "Could you talk a bit about your experience in this industry?" [This last question should only be directed at someone who looks like he or she has been in the industry for a while.] This kind of questioning gives the interviewer a chance to talk about himself or herself, something the vast majority of people enjoy doing. (In the very rare case where you run into a sociopath who hates to divulge anything about their background, you'll know it quickly and simply move on to questions that do not touch upon their past or present.)

- "Could you tell me about the kinds of projects you have done?" Again, this gives the interviewer a chance to chatter away about his or her favorite things, which hopefully will take up so much time that it leaves little time for him or her to ask you tough technical questions! It also shows you are interested in the specifics of the work his or her group is involved in.

- "I've heard that your group does cutting-edge empirical research in this field, and I was thinking whether you could maybe give me a rundown on how your group compares with your competitors." Hopefully the first part of what you just said is true! It can be true if, for example, the headhunter or a previous interviewer said it or *implied* it, or if you saw some claim along that line on the company's website. The second part of the question then shows that you care about the relative quality of the group and carries the subtle message that you want to join the best group on the Street, which is a good aspiration.

  A quick digression: ever noticed how many times you've come across the claim that "we are the leading firm in the industry"? Obviously, not everyone can be *the* leading firm in an industry (just like not everyone can be better than average). Well, it turns out that there are at least two ways around which companies work this claim: first, they can define "industry" however they want (e.g., a hedge fund may define the industry it's in as "absolutely positive returns enhanced by convertible arbitrage with a tinge of risk arbitrage"); and second, leading doesn't mean you are No. 1 – it simply means you are one of the best, but who's really doing the ranking? Like the many other industries, the world of finance teems with hyperboles.

- "What are the best things you like about your job?" This is a relatively generic question but nonetheless can be interpreted as flattering, especially if you sense that the interviewer indeed likes his or her job. (Obviously, don't ask this question if he or she has been volunteering negative information about his or her work or colleagues.)

- "As an ex-academic, what tips would you offer someone like me who really wants to work as a Wall Street quant?" Ask this question only if the interviewer seems friendly and supportive. When you do ask it, it can leave a lasting positive impression in the mind of the interviewer (assuming you didn't bomb some of his or her questions disastrously). It places the interviewer in the role of a tutor and can have a positive subliminal influence when he or she writes up that post-interview report on you.

One of the reasons you are at the interview is to find out if the job is right for you. To that end, the following questions will help you decide as well as sound intelligent to the interviewer:

- "Could you give me some details of the responsibilities of this position?" A good question that shows you care! The interviewer who's also the boss will surely be pleased with this question. Now, you might be wondering whether there's any value in asking this question, given you've seen the job posting which probably included a detailed list of job responsibilities. The answer is yes, there's value in asking this question – a lot of value, indeed. You can preface the question by saying something like "I read the job announcement and have a general understanding of the responsibilities, but would like to know more about them." By asking this question, you shows your maturity as a candidate who's eager to know what the job entails day-to-day.

- "Could you tell me what the career path is for this position?" Whereas the previous question concerns the mundane, this question demonstrates your farsightedness as well as self-confidence. By implying that you care about your career growth, you place yourself in a proactive role. Bosses in general like employees who are motivated and who care about their own future, because these employees are likely to work hard. This question also gives you additional bargaining power, so to speak, because it conveys the subtle message that you won't take a job simply for short-term gains.

- "How many people are there in your group and how are they divided in terms of projects or responsibilities?" The interview is a good opportunity for you to find out what the work environment is like. Hopefully you'll get a chance to walk around the floor and be introduced to key members of the group. A question like this, as well as related questions probing for details about the team, help you understand what it'll be like to be working here. They also leave the impression with the interviewer that you are a team player and care about the big environment.

- You should also ask questions about the job to which you genuinely want to know the answer. For example, if you don't like traveling, you should ask whether the job demands a lot of traveling (but don't tell the interviewer whether you want to travel or not – you never want to show your hand too early!). If you are afraid of dealing with strangers, you can ask whether the job involves a lot of face time with clients, again without leaving any hint on what your preference is. The one question that you should avoid asking is how much the job pays; see the second bullet point in the next list.

Stupid Questions to Ask

Even though a job interview is a two-way exchange process, the interviewer always has the upper hand in the sense that you want the job much more than he or she wants you – at least you never know if they really want you. Therefore, you must refrain from asking questions that can sound offensive or stupid to the interviewer. Before you post a question for the interviewer (or prepare your questions ahead of interview time), ask yourself: "If I were the interviewer, would I feel comfortable with, flattered by, or impressed by this question?"

Examples of "don't ask" questions are:

- Do not ask questions that probe the interviewer's personal life, except if it's something cultural that you two share. Never ask questions about the interviewer's marital status or sexual orientation. (If he or she mentions his or her kids with pride as part of the small talk, you can ask an innocuous question or two such as where the kids go to school or what they want to be when they grow up.) Never ask him or her about his political beliefs or religion. Never ask him or her how much he or she makes a year – that would be a sure question to get you a very bad post-interview rating! If you two are from the same country, you might ask him or her where he or she was born and grew up; but be aware that some people feel uncomfortable discussing their personal past. By the way, you should not be asked these questions by the interviewer, either; if you do get asked and feel uncomfortable, tell the interviewer so – and be sure to report this to the headhunter or recruiter after the interview so your refusal to answer personal questions will not be used against your candidacy.

- Do not ask how much you'll be paid. Wall Street people love money, and they love gossiping about how much *other people* get paid. But they loathe talking about their own compensations, and they loathe anyone who suggests they are in finance for the money. If you ask the boss how much the position will pay, he or she might question your motivation in seeking the job. If he or she thinks you are only motivated by money, that's quite a strike against you. If you ask an employee this question, he or she simply may not know the answer. In any case, he or she won't be happy thinking about how much *you* might be making relative to him or her. So this question is a sure loser, period.

- "I heard your firm got fined $30 billion by the SEC for illegal trading. What's your take on that?" Whoa, this really flatters the company and the interviewer, doesn't it? (Hope you noticed my sarcasm.) This question not only questions the legitimacy of the company but places the interviewer in an awkward spot. It may be a sore point with every employee, not something they want to discuss, and certainly not something they want to discuss with a job candidate. So steer clear of this question.

- "I heard the market is turning bearish and people in this industry may not have a job six months from now. What do you think?" If you are very concerned about job safety, Wall Street is not right for you. Besides, this question can really depress the interviewer – what if he or she is already worried about the prospect of losing his or her job? I don't think asking this will help your candidacy at all.

- "I heard your competitors are doing better and have fatter profits and bonuses. What do you think?" Again, avoid unflattering questions! If you have nothing positive to say about the company, the position you're interviewing for or the interviewer, don't say it!

- "Can you tell me my chances of getting this job?" This is just plain stupid to ask. Regardless of whether the interviewer is the decision maker, he or she will be reluctant to tell you how you rate against other candidates, even if he or she has an inkling. Chances are, he or she doesn't (e.g., they need to interview more candidates for comparison), and the question is not possible to answer. Either way, you end up looking immature and insecure, traits not desired in a Wall Street quant.

It's not possible to list all the potentially damaging questions you can ask of an interviewer. The simple thing to remember is: if a question is personal, negative or irrelevant to the context, refrain from asking! And never, ever talk about money at the interview!

More General Tips

There is one question that you'll want to ask – and in fact should ask – that may or may not be "kosher" with an interviewer. The question is "How many hours do you [or would I] work each day?" You want to find out what the lifestyle will be if you choose this job: how many hours you'll put in each day, whether you'll get a lunch break, if you'll need to work weekends, whether you can take two or three weeks off at a time, etc. It may be a "tricky" question to ask because the interviewer might turn out to be a martinet who believes in long hours of hard work and does not believe in taking lunch breaks or vacations. If he or she hears this question, he or she will immediately form a negative opinion of you. But if the interviewer is friendly and supportive, this will be a safe question to ask. Personally, I make sure I ask this question of at least one interviewer, because the answer to this question matters a great deal to me, because I really care about my lifestyle (especially now that I have a baby at home). I encourage you to ask this question at the interview, but only if the interviewer appears to be a nice enough person. (Another tricky aspect to this question is, the interviewer whom you did ask might simply lie! He or she may lie to conceal a sense of mockery. He or she may lie to entice you to take the job. Who knows.) If you don't find a good opportunity to ask the question at the interview, you can ask the headhunter or recruiter (if you are using one), or you can consider calling one of the more friendly interviewers and asking him or her in private.

After all that's been asked and answered, you need to close the interview on a positive note. Here's your chance to summarize your qualification and to make one last push for your candidacy. I'm not saying the interview should be closed with a "bang"; that's just difficult to do. But you can have an effective closing by highlighting your accomplishments so far, by emphasizing the core skills you have, and by letting the interviewer know how much you like the environment and want the job (even if that's not true!). If you bombed a technical question or two, do not bring them up. Always emphasize the positive – and secretly hope that no other candidate would get the same questions right, either!

As you shake the interviewer's hand, be sure to offer profuse thanks – and sneak in a flattering statement or two. Normal human beings like to be thanked and like to be flattered. Do try to be sincere in your thanks – practice beforehand if you need to. Also, be sure to ask for the interviewer's business card. It's not only a show of politeness and respect, but a good practice to send the interviewer an individualized thank-you note after you get home. The thank-you note should be very short but should thank the interviewer for his or her time as well as briefly highlight your qualification again. E-mail is perfectly okay and actually preferred in today's world. If you fail to send a thank-you note, you'll never know if the interviewer would hold that failure against you. Don't take that risk.

Tips for Short Interviews

There is no standard definition on short vs. long interviews. For our purpose here, let's just call interviews 30 minutes or less short and those over 30 minutes long. Oftentimes you'll find an interview scheduled for X minutes running over its allotted time. At the beginning of the interview, however, you don't know if that will be the case, so it's best to strategize according to the allotted time of each interview. (BTW, did you see the *ex ante* vs. *ex post* issue here? – you should if you want to become a quant!)

In short interviews, everything is "compressed" and you can easily find yourself short on time. This means you need to budget the limited amount of time wisely. As I've mentioned before, you want to leave at least five minutes, ideally ten, to ask the interviewer questions. This leaves the other 20 minutes or so for the interviewer to probe your background and probably test you on your specific quantitative knowledge. Trust me, those 20 minutes can go by very fast. The problem you face is really how to leave a lasting impression in the mind of the interviewer, so he or she will remember you when writing the post-interview summary.

First tip: be likeable. It's difficult for an interviewer to get a deep understanding of your qualification in 30 minutes or less, so first impression is all the more important for short interviews. If it's a phone interview, you need to sound polite and sound eager to answer the interviewer's questions. Exude a sense of confidence as well as strong interest in the position. For a face-to-face interview, maintain good eye contact and smile often; also be sure to exude a sense of confidence and interest. Don't forget to flatter the interviewer subtly at any chance you get: get him or her to talk about himself or herself; say how you aspire to be like him or her and how you'd feel honored to be working with him or her; etc.

Employers want smart and diligent employees, so as a candidate you want to come across as sharp-minded and willing to work hard. This is actually easier to accomplish during a short interview than a long one, because your answers will *have to* be concise and focused, which helps your cause. Too many times I've sat through an hour-long interview (as the interviewer) and at the end of the 60 minutes, I've forgotten what the candidate had told me at the beginning of the 60 minutes. If you can give precise, punchy answers to the interviewer's questions, you'll leave a strong impression as someone with a razor-sharp mind.

I think every candidate should pray that they be asked to talk about a paper they wrote or a research project they completed, for this question gives the candidate a great opportunity to use up as much time as possible and leave little time in a short interview for technical or case questions. Consider this a guerilla tactic: seize the opportunity and drag the interview into *your* comfort zone. This tactic is appropriate for short interviews (with longer ones, you can't possibly use most of the interview time to talk about one paper or project). You should know your paper or project inside out. Pepper your talk with intriguing points, such as "I found previous literature was completely wrong on this topic," which will cause the interviewer to want to know more. In fact, you might even want to make some deliberate (but harmless) mistakes, to allow the interviewer to point them out, which in turn allows you to talk and talk and talk. For instance, when you say "I was modeling interest rates and used OLS," most quants would recognize that you had a heteroskedasticity problem there; when they point it out, you go in for the kill and talk at length about how you accounted for that and was still able to use OLS or a variant thereof. Carrying out this tactic effectively requires some practice and requires your knowing your stuff really well, so do a mock interview or two with a knowledgeable friend where your friend asks you to describe your work in-depth and tries to probe every little detail.

If you are given a difficult technical question, work through it as fast as you can, but make sure you don't lose precious time on any particular step. Appeal to the interviewer for help if you can't solve something in more than a minute. Above all, if the interviewer offers you a hint, don't refuse it – if you do, you end up sounding stubborn and hostile. Given the limited amount of time you have, if you don't know the answer right away, it's unlikely you'll be able to solve the problem quickly. Your strategy is to avoid getting stuck for the remainder of the interview time and ending up feeling utterly defeated and upset. Trust me, if you end the interview with a technical question you can't answer, that'll be the only thing the interviewer remembers about you when he or she writes up the post-interview report.

Tips for Long Interviews

Long interviews are really a candidate's nightmare: they can cover a lot of ground (especially where the candidate doesn't want to tread), they can be a chance for the interviewer to wear down the candidate, they can be exhausting and confusing.

Unless the interviewer is a narcissist who sees the interview as a chance to flatter himself or herself, you'll likely face technical questions during a long interview. So the best way to prepare for long interviews is to know your stuff well, the stuff here being all those skills your résumé says you possess and the quantitative education your résumé says you undertook. If your résumé says you are a proficient SQL programmer, you can bet that someone will ask you a SQL question, so make sure you didn't forget all the important features of SQL. If your résumé claims you know option pricing theory inside out, well, make sure you can indeed explain every intricate detail of the pricing models, at least Black-Scholes. (That's why I emphasized in Chapter Two that your résumé must be truthful and substantiatable.)

The long interview can be tiring, both mentally and physically. I myself find any interview over 45 minutes long exhausting, whether I'm the interviewer or the interviewee. As the candidate, you need to constantly remind yourself to keep up the appearances. Don't forget to maintain adequate and friendly eye contact. Don't forget to flash those ingratiating smiles. Don't forget to sound enthusiastic and confident throughout the 45 or 60 minutes. Use positive thoughts – "the interview is really going well"; "I'm doing great"; "the questions are easy"; "the interviewer is an ugly idiot and if he can be a quant, anybody can be a quant" – to help yourself maintain that adrenaline rush and keep your mind sharp. If you feel a little fatigued, get a sip of the water you brought into the interview room. You can also move your body around subtly and slowly to relax those muscles.

For long interviews, the closing is especially important, because by the time the interview ends, the interviewer (and possibly you) may have forgotten what was said in the first half. (But remember: people *never* forget negative comments or gestures!) Use the closing to buttress your candidacy. Highlight your key accomplishments. Express your strong interest in the group and the job. If it suits your personality, slip in a flattery for the interviewer. Like you, he or she is tired, and any refreshment in the way of helpful reminders about your qualification – and flattery – will be quite welcome.

Handling Background Questions

Background questions form the backbone of the informational interview. These questions give the interviewer an opportunity to get details regarding the candidate's experience, education and skills. They also give the candidate an opportunity to corroborate his or her résumé. Almost every job interview starts off with background questions (after any exchange of pleasantries). Answering them right is of paramount importance, because if you should come across as evasive or unsure about your own background, your candidacy is likely doomed.

Background questions can potentially cover everything on your résumé – and may even go beyond your résumé. Earlier I mentioned that the interviewer cannot ask you questions related to your personal life or creed, such as your religious belief, sexual orientation, political affiliation, or favorite sports team (although this latter could be part of the small talk at the beginning of the interview). They can ask you questions about where you grew up or what books you like to read, although I find such questions rare at quant interviews. If any question is not related to the position or your qualification as a candidate, you can decline to answer. If any such question encroaches upon your privacy and makes you feel uncomfortable, you should report it to the recruiter or headhunter after the interview. Hopefully they'll do something to ensure that your refusal to answer privacy-invading questions will not be counted as a strike against your candidacy. (But frankly speaking, there's little you or they can do if the interviewer turns negative on you because of your reluctance to answer such questions, unless he or she writes something like "the candidate refused to answer my question about his view on religion" in the post-interview report, which people never do.)

Now that we know what questions should not be asked by interviewers, let's look at some of the questions they can, and will, ask.

Most interviewers start the conversation by asking you to describe yourself. The generic way of asking this is "Tell me about yourself." Answering this question is quite an art. There's no right or wrong way to answer this question. What you want to achieve in your answer is highlight your qualifications. You want to convince the interviewer you have a strong quantitative background and the right mix of analytical and technical aptitude for the position at hand. You want to praise yourself yet you also want to avoid sounding arrogant. The answer must also be substantive, not empty.

A good way to answer this "describe yourself" question is to start by highlighting your most recent accomplishment or experience, proceed to describing some of the other important things you have done or learned, and end your answer by mentioning again your most recent accomplishment or experience. Here's a fictitious example:

"I'm currently a fourth-year Ph.D. student in finance at Top Rank University. I just completed my dissertation which consists of three chapters. One of the chapters is my job market paper, and in this paper, I came up with a novel model to study the forecastability of the short-term volatility in naked credit derivatives traded over the counter. This paper has been well received at various seminars and I've submitted it to the *Journal of Finance* for publication. I'll describe my model in detail. [Give some details here – more if the interviewer shows interest and less if he or she does not.] My other two dissertation chapters cover financing uncertainty and mutual fund performance issues. [Describe briefly those two papers.] As you can see, my research topics have been diverse. In addition to my own papers, I have worked extensively as a research assistant for Professors Ford and O'Brien in my department; in fact, I co-authored a published paper with Prof. Ford on the pervasiveness of moral hazard in the hedge fund industry. I also taught various courses in economics and finance, and was voted the best teacher last two semesters. My research experience has given me a wide exposure to research methodologies in finance and econometrics, and I have gained practical experience using SAS, Matlab and Excel. I'm particularly proud of my job market paper as the modeling technique has never been attempted before."

Because the question itself is open-ended, you can structure the answer however you want. As long as you can impress the interviewer with your experience or knowledge, you've achieved your goals. Now, I want to emphasize that impressing the interviewer doesn't mean you brag, exaggerate or lie. It means highlighting your accomplishments – a well-received paper (even if unpublished), a teaching award, an A+ in a difficult math class, specific project completions in your current or previous job, etc. All these (and more) are accomplishments. Your job at the interview is to bring out the best in you – your best quant skills, your best quant experience, your best quant education, etc. In other words, you embellish important items from your résumé – but never lie or exaggerate.

You'll be surprised at how many interviewees I have met who did not know their own accomplishments. Not to sound too clichéd, but I do believe everyone who reads this book has achievements they can be proud of. You don't have to go to a top-ranked school or win an award to consider yourself achieved in some way. All you need to do is, before the first interview, looking carefully into your own life experience and education and pick out the three things that truly make you proud of yourself. Hopefully these things highlight your analytical or quantitative aptitude. But if none of them does, you should still practice talking about them and using them to convince the interviewer that you are a capable person. For instance, you can talk about your dependability, your industriousness, your determination, your leadership ability, etc. The bane of answering the "describe yourself" question is simply either not knowing what you have done so far in life, or not being able to articulate why what you have done matters to your candidacy.

When asked to describe yourself, should you talk about your personal life, such as where you grew up or what hobbies you might have? My own preference is to stay away from such topics, because if you start talking about them, that might signal to the interviewer that he or she has the green light to ask you such questions later. I would not dip my toes into such a gray area. And if you started the whole talk about your personal life, you would have less of a justification to complain later if you found a question "intrusive." So, my recommendation is to steer clear of mentioning personal things. That said, if you have some hobby that you think boosts your candidacy, or if you just have an irresistible itch to talk about the town where you spent your childhood (especially you are sure that's the same town where the interviewer came from), I won't put a gun to your head and stop you. But, please, whatever you talk about, avoid the following topics: sex (or your love life), politics, religion, and animal fur.

Speaking of hobbies, many interviewers do ask this question. This is one of those legitimate personal questions, so you should answer it. The key is to use the answer to your advantage. That means hobbies like surfing the Internet, playing video games, partying out with friends, etc. must be left out of the answer; they would add no value to the interview and, worse, they could cost you serious brownie points. (Trust me, few employers like to hear that a candidate has an Internet addiction or gets inebriated every weekend.) Another big no-no answer is "work," as in "I have no hobbies because I'm wholly dedicated to work." That's BS, period (even if true!). Don't expect any interviewer to take that answer seriously. (Besides, the interviewer in all likelihood won't be inclined to vote for a workaholic who, upon joining, would make everyone else on the team look like slackers!) So just don't say something like that. Remember, you want to be truthful as well as reasonable in your answering.

Proactive hobbies, on the other hand, must be mentioned (even if you are not asked!). "Power hobbies" such as solving crossword, Sudoku or other puzzles (if you mention this, just be aware that you might be asked to solve one on the spot!); playing chess, Go, bridge, or poker; and blogging on interesting, non-political topics are likely to earn some degree of respect from the interviewer. Other innocent hobbies such as philately (stamp collecting), music instrument playing or singing, wine tasting, reviewing electronic gadgets on websites like Amazon.com, etc. are perfectly okay to mention to an interviewer interested in learning whether you have interests outside of work.

As part of the routine background check, the interviewer will likely ask you to describe in detail one of your previous jobs, your thesis or dissertation, and/or something else from your résumé. Remember, this kind of question concerns a specific item on your résumé, so make sure your answer is relevant *only* to that item. The same two cardinal rules apply here: one, highlight and emphasize your accomplishments (what goals or impacts you achieved, what skills you mastered, what knowledge you acquired, and so on); two, refrain from talking too much and disclosing unflattering information about yourself.

Let's look at an example. Say last summer you had an internship analyzing traffic pattern data for your local DMV office. You started from scratch and built a complete system collecting and analyzing the tons of data that had been sent to the DMV. You learned SQL and gained database experience in the project. What should you emphasize in your answer? First, the fact that the DMV had nothing in place whatsoever before you arrived. Second, how you designed the system (including the background research you performed). Third, how you implemented the system in SQL – and how you overcame database construction and performance problems. Last, the positive impact the system had on the DMV's efficiency or traffic improvement. Even though that project had nothing to do with quantitative finance, your problem-solving experience and database knowledge from the internship put you at a distinct advantage over others – and your job at answering the question was simply to let the interviewer know about this. Plus, it successfully highlights a concrete achievement. One stone, many birds.

As you answer the question, always remind yourself to focus on the positive. If there was something negative about the topic – for example, you didn't really complete that traffic analysis system in time last summer – don't shy away from it (otherwise it would arouse the interviewer's suspicion) but be clear about why it happened what you did to rectify the situation. To continue with our example: you didn't complete the project in time, because the DMV is a vast, complex bureaucracy and to get the project off the ground took you much more time than you had expected. Then you had to go back to school at the end of the summer. State these facts. You are not giving excuses here; you are simply stating the facts. Then you mention that you *offered* to work part-time at the DMV to finish the project (assuming that's indeed what you did). Notice the word "offered" here. Even if you never went back (and would never go back for a million bucks), saying you offered your service is good enough to put a positive ending to this story. (Besides, who's going to check whether you offered or not?)

While it took me two long paragraphs to give you this example, in practice your answer is likely to be more concise and compact. You simply state the important facts: one; two; three; ….

Then you summarize what knowledge or skills you gained from the experience. If – and only if – the interviewer shows interest in more detail, you can take your time to fill him or her in on some of the less important details, such as which SQL system you chose, how you went about setting it up, what kind of model you used to analyze the data, what modeling issues you ran into and how you resolved them, what issues arose when interpreting the analytical results, etc.

Dealing With Difficult Questions

So far, so good. But what if the interviewer starts picking on you and asking tough questions about your background? We know that is bound to happen with some, if not most, interviewers. Good news here is, most quant people are relatively friendly, so you'll less likely face tough questions on your background than your friends who go for investment banking or management consulting interviews. But still, if you go to enough interviews, you *will* run into someone who's bent on breaking you down with tough questions. They may do so either out of habit, out of a bad mood on a bad hair day, out of a dislike of you, or out of curiosity to see how you handle stressful situations. Of course, what their true intentions might be doesn't really matter to you. You'll feel your heart leaping up and down like a bunny on a roasting pan, and you know you must answer the question and answer it with aplomb and dignity.

Those last two words here are the key: aplomb and dignity. What they translate into in practice is: answer the tough question truthfully, politely, and confidently. Remain calm. Don't get antsy. Think positive thoughts that help you maintain your poise. Thoughts like "Man, this guy is a real jerk, and he's ugly" or "I'm smarter than this ass and I can answer the question" can help you gain self-confidence as you contemplate the response, even though they may sound silly. (That's why you should not say them out aloud! And never display an expression of disdain on your face!) I find it helpful to adjust my sitting posture by straightening my spine and lifting my chin. This both injects some extra adrenaline into my blood stream, which puts me in an active mode and allows me to focus more, and makes me look more confident. The last thing you want to do is seem intimidated by the tough question and behave as if you were looking for a way to escape. Remember, Wall Street quants deal with tough problems and tough people all the time, so *not* shying away from stressful situation is a necessary trait to possess as a Wall Street quant. If you want to be a quant, you have to start behaving like one.

The truth is, it's only human nature to feel uneasy when asked a tough question. Your job is to turn that negative feeling into positive action and words. I know, I know, I've started sounding like a bullshitting psychologist or motivational speaker, but there's really no other way to put it. The interview can be like a battleground. While the interviewer is not necessarily your enemy, you have to show him or her your strength. Otherwise, he or she won't respect you and won't recommend you for the job.

All right. Enough of the general talk. Here's a hypothetical but specific example.

Let's say that you, like many people, have changed jobs often in the past. Say in the last three years you had four different jobs, one after another. That opens you up to some tough questioning. The interviewer may ask you why you changed jobs so often. A tougher version would follow up with a secondary question on whether that reflects a fickle personality or perhaps serious immaturity. Or perhaps you get bored easily. The interviewer may then state his or her objection to your qualification for the position: if you are hired, you probably won't stay for long (given your capricious past), so why should they hire you in the first place? (Hiring and training new employees are very expensive to firms.)

Before you read on, put this book down for a minute. Image you are facing a hostile interviewer – in fact, he is not only hostile, he is cynical about you. This is someone who obviously doesn't want you to be on his team – and he doesn't hide that feeling at all. How would you answer this question? Put down the book now and think about your possible response. Then come back. (Take a well-deserved break, too, if you so desire.)

Welcome back. Was the question difficult for you? If you said no, I think you lied. This question gets asked all the time because, as I said, many people do change jobs often. And you know what? There's no perfect answer to this question. No matter what you say and how truthful and sincere you are, your answer simply may fail to please the questioner. But there are some points to keep in mind in proffering a believable and convincing explanation as to why you changed jobs so often in the past.

The first angle of attack is to focus on the jobs themselves. There's no denying that you changed jobs four times in the last three years. (By the way, there's no point telling the interviewer that it was *really* three-and-a-half years or three years and 10 months. That would make you sound argumentative, petty and evasive.) But there must have been something with the jobs that forced you to leave after a short time, right? For example, maybe the first two jobs were with small companies that folded under unprofitability. Maybe on your third job you had a difficult boss. (Warning: don't try to be a smart ass here by insinuating that the interviewer is in some way like that difficult boss!) Maybe your fourth (and current) job lacks challenge. Whatever negative things you can say about the jobs themselves, say them. But don't emphasize negative things about your ex-bosses or ex-coworkers, because the interviewer might take your complaints about other people as a sign that you are a chronic kvetch, someone who doesn't play well in a team environment. That would have been a fatal assessment, so when you say negative things about the jobs or the ex-bosses, tread carefully and try to focus on objective descriptions. And be extra careful not to be so carried away in your story-telling that you start pounding on the table or peppering your speech with invective. Keep your message precise and short; usually one negative sentence about each job is sufficient to convey the message that you left the jobs because there were problems beyond your control.

The second angle of attack is to emphasize the (unfortunate) misalignment of your interest with the previous jobs. Here, the factors that made you change your job didn't just come from the previous jobs themselves, but also from what you were looking for in a job. I think it's totally legitimate for someone to leave a job when he or she finds out that it's not fulfilling. Of course, what is fulfilling and what is not is difficult to define – and you'll do well in your answer if you focus on the intellectual development aspect of a job. So, you may not want to say something like "I left my third job after six months because I wasn't getting paid enough." Instead, something along the line of "I left my third job because I was given work more befitting of a data entry clerk than a quant professional" or "I was never able to leverage my analytical and quantitative abilities on my previous jobs" or "those jobs were totally lacking in challenges or a clearly defined career path" is more interesting and sympathy-arousing. Back up your general answer with some specific examples.

The third angle of attack is to acknowledge you might have been a little immature in the past and thus picked the wrong jobs, but you have learned a great deal from the experience and have come to know exactly what kind of job you want. This is an example of the growth story: it shows the interviewer that you have grown in some aspect of development. Many quants themselves were once lost in life and explored other options before coming to work on Wall Street; in fact, many are still searching for professional happiness (and the meaning of life). So this way of answering may generate enough sympathy (and empathy) from the interviewer to satisfy him or her. Close your answer by saying something like "That's why during my current job search, I'm being extra careful to make sure that the new job will be both intellectually challenging and well-aligned with my quant interest, so I can build the quant career I've always wanted to have." See how I climaxed the response with a positive forward-looking statement? I bet you that most interviewers will be impressed with this response – assuming you delivered your lines with heart-felt sincerity (i.e., no faking or acting!).

The fourth angle attack is, I believe, a bit less credible than the previous three: it invokes non-work-related circumstances beyond your control. A primary example is changes in your personal life that necessitated the job switches. For instance, you might have gotten married on the first job and needed to move to a different city. Maybe on your second job one of your parents developed needs for special care and you felt obliged to move back to your hometown. Then on your third job you had a baby and needed to find a better-paying position. If personal stories like these apply to you, by all means tell the interviewer so – but be sure to deliver the message with utmost sincerity. In fact, you may even have wanted to bring some evidence along to buttress your answer and to show that you were not making the stories up. Unless the personal circumstances were compelling, I doubt the interviewer would readily buy them. Therefore, if you could use one of the previous three approaches, try that first.

Of course, you can always use more than one of the four answers I provided here, although I see no need to. The key aspect of your answer should be to focus on the future: how those four jobs in three years were just a temporary stage of your life and you now know better and are in fact working hard to establish a truly fulfilling and lasting career.

In the limited space we have here, I can't possibly list every hostile or difficult question you may come across, but here's a sample list that may get you started preparing for such questions:

- "Why did/do you change jobs so often?" or "You have a job now, so why are you looking for a new one?" I already discussed possible approaches to this question; see above.

- "You have a strong background, but I don't see anything in your skill set that adds value to our team." or "What do you have to offer us in terms of knowledge and skills?" This question sure puts you on the spot. It questions whether you'll deserve that big fat paycheck. It tries to shake your confidence in yourself. In answering this question, it's not enough to rehash what's already in your résumé or what you've already said earlier in the interview – and definitely don't try to recite a laundry list of your skills. Your answer, instead, should focus on the fit between your background and the job requirements. The reason you answered the job posting is because you felt you have something to offer, right? And the fact *they* picked you for an interview means they must have seen something fitting in your background, right? Now is the time to highlight the match between you and the job. If the job requirement says "modeling experience" and you analyzed traffic patterns in the past, well, that *is* modeling experience, isn't it? Emphasize that. Pick out a couple job requirements and match them with a couple skills you have. Remember, this question is likely a ruse: since your résumé passed the initial screening round, it must be because the hiring manager felt you had something to offer.

- "Wall Street is all about taking risks. Your résumé indicates you've taken the traditional route of education, summer internships, and now a full-time job. So you haven't taken any risks in your life, have you?" or "What kind of risks have you taken in life and how did you manage those risks?" To be honest, I find these questions very difficult to answer – because I was asked them and I fit that "traditional geek" mold! The questioner is basically saying you have grown up in a green house and therefore you may not be ready for the harsh reality of Wall Street, for the dog-eat-dog atmosphere of a money-driven industry. What you need to do here is to think back carefully and recall any activity that involved some risk. Now, the usual warning applies here: don't mention anything stupid or less than responsible. If, in your wild teenage years, you experimented with drugs or drove while intoxicated, leave those out! (The last thing an employer wants is a drug addict or drunk driver.) Focus on intellectual risks you might have taken. For example, trading stocks involves risk (the risk of losing your principal), and if you ever traded or invested in stocks – either on your own or for friends and family – mention that and describe how you tried to maximize your gains and minimize your losses. This answer will work particularly well with a trading desk interviewer, for obvious reasons. Activities such as rock climbing, playing poker, getting into a new field (e.g., you were an English major in college and then went to grad school to study economics), and moving to a new country to continue your education, all involve taking risks. And don't forget any research projects you started on your own initiative: as with any new business, a new research project involves risks as well, because your success is never ensured at the beginning. If you look back at things you have done and think carefully about whether each activity had some degree of uncertainty, you'll discover the many risks you've already taken in life. (A couple bonus examples: marriage and kids – those involve big risks!)

- "You went to a mediocre school. Why?" or "Why weren't you able to get into Harvard (or MIT or whatever Ivy League school)?" Ouch! You've got to hate the interviewer who asks this question! It's like rubbing salt on an old wound. Honestly, now is the time to think about whether you want to work for or with a jerk like this. On the other hand, maybe he or she is just toying with your emotions to see how you act under duress. So you still need to answer the question satisfactorily. Let's see. You didn't go to Harvard either because you never applied there, or you did but didn't get in. If the former, it was probably because you didn't want to go to Harvard, because you found the school you eventually enrolled in offering exactly what you were looking for, or because you never thought you could get into Harvard. If you applied but didn't get in, that must have been due to the stupidity or short-sightedness of the admissions committee, or due to racial and national quotas at the school (we all know such quotas exist), or due to the fact you weren't up to their standards. This question is actually easier to answer than it sounds. You just give the inquirer the straight facts. What you must do is spin it in a positive manner. For example, you can say how you are so very glad that you enrolled in your school because you met the best professors and fellow students there, because the program offered the best education you could dream of, and because you loved the town or city. (Here you can exaggerate a little even if in reality you didn't really love the school or town.) A believable pretext is to say your boyfriend or girlfriend got into the same school and you two wanted to be together. (Yes, even geeky quants can be mellowed down by such lovebird stories.) The key is to exude confidence and maturity in your response – and to sound believable. Never tinge your answer with an apologetic tone. You have nothing to apologize for. You have nothing to be ashamed of. You are an accomplished person in many ways, and many, many graduates produced by Harvard and other Ivy League schools are mediocre or worse in the real world.

- "I see you dropped out of the Ph.D. program after a year. Why? Does that make you a quitter?" This question is similar in spirit to the first question on this list. The approach is similar: focus on the mismatch between your interest and the Ph.D. program you enrolled in. Talk about how you realized you didn't want to become an academic, therefore getting a Ph.D. would have been an overkill. (By the way, this is really true.) Talk about your dismay at discovering that it was taking an average of seven or eight years for the students in your Ph.D. program to graduate (this would arouse some degree of sympathy from the quant interviewer). You may want to avoid complaining about the professors, as the interviewer might know or admire one of your professors, but if your advisor really gave you a hard time, you can mention it but do not dwell on it. If the interviewer is a Ph.D., you need to tread extra carefully so as not to put down the value of a Ph.D. in general.

- "I think you are overqualified for this job. Don't you think you'll get bored here easily?" or "You have a Ph.D. but this position really only needs someone with a master's." Okay, you may feel flattered by the statement, but it's anything but flattery. The interviewer may be taking a jab at your bookwormish background, or he or she may be expressing some skepticism on your qualification as a whole. So how do you counter this objection? First, thank him or her for the "overqualified" remark; be sincere in your acknowledgement, not sarcastic. Then, point out that you *might* have been a little overqualified in some area but, overall, you have a lot to learn from the position. Plus, your "over-qualification" may allow you to contribute more to the position than any other candidate. Tell the interviewer that by hiring you, they are effectively hiring two people for the price of one! Reiterate your strong interest in the position, and briefly list the why's. In short, you want to reassure the interviewer that you want this job and will perform well on the job.

- "From your résumé I don't see you have any time series [or fixed income pricing, or panel data, or C++, or Excel, or whatever] experience. We use time series here all the time. Don't you think that puts you at a disadvantage?" This is exactly the flip of the previous question. The interviewer is implying you are not quite qualified for the position. Whether that's an intentional insult or unintentional slip is immaterial. He or she has doubts about your candidacy. You must dispel these doubts. Start by admitting you are not a perfect candidate. Without sounding defensive or apologetic, tell the interviewer why you had the deficiency. For example, if you can't program in C++, just say "I have never programmed in C++ because I've never had a chance to do it." Follow up immediately by emphasizing what you *can* do: "But I have done a lot of programming in Matlab, S-Plus and SAS, and I'm confident that I have the ability to master any programming language and analytical tool quickly. In fact, if you hire me I promise you that I'll have mastered C++ by the time I start working here." See the seamless positive spin you've just put on the whole thing and the confident forward-looking statement that reveals you as a capable person? That's the spirit here: de-emphasize the negative, emphasize the positive and look to the future. I hope you see that this has been my central message all along.

- "I spoke to your ex-boss and he told me you were a complete
  jerk who never did the work as asked and was not getting along
  with other coworkers. Can you explain?" I have never heard
  this being asked in a real interview but you just never know
  (especially if you really didn't get along with your ex-boss).
  Take the high road; don't badmouth your ex-boss. Instead,
  offer examples that show you were always a good worker.

When you get a chance, check this book's website for more sample
questions.

If there's a "silver bullet" for tackling difficult background
questions, it is this: know your strengths and weaknesses well, very
well. There's no other way around it. When you know yourself well,
you can always come up with ideas to put your best foot forward no
matter what question you get asked. Of course, practice makes it
perfect; be sure to practice how to think on your foot – it's a skill that
will literally save your day many, many times over.

Answering Technical Questions

By technical questions I refer to questions that test specific subject
knowledge and analytical skills of the candidate. The word "technical"
here doesn't necessarily mean only IT (programming), but
encompasses all things related to modeling know-how: from theory to
empirical techniques to programming aptitude.

Technical questions can cover a wide range of subjects, from
quantitative disciplines like mathematics and statistics to specific
topics in economics and finance to programming. Depending on the
interviewer, you may be given no technical questions at all, one or two
short ones, one or two long ones, or a large number of short ones.

Short technical questions usually ask you to define some
concepts from a quantitative or technical subject area, or to solve a
quick problem. Concepts you may be tested on can be drawn from any
discipline you claim you are familiar with. So, if you say you know
finance, you may be asked to describe and explain CAPM, Black-
Scholes, APT, mean-variance optimization, etc. If you claim to know
panel data techniques, you may be asked to explain the difference
between fixed effect and random effect. If you position yourself as an
empirical modeling guru, you may be asked about Monte Carlo,
bootstrapping, etc. For programmers, questions covering the difference

between procedural programming and objected-oriented programming, hashes, arrays, data structures, etc. can be asked. There are simply too many possible questions to list here. Bottom line: if you claim you know something, be prepared to be tested on it.

Long technical questions not only test your claimed knowledge of some specific area, but usually involve a more advanced concept or longer problem to solve. For example, if you claim to be an expert in econometrics, you may be asked to explain in detail when and how to use the IV (instrumental variable) technique, or when to use logit vs. probit. If your résumé screams "finance expert," you could be called on to explain the pros and cons of CAPM vs. APT or what the shape of the yield curve says about the economy at large. Then, since you want to be a quant, you could be asked to solve a real math, stat or programming problem.

There usually isn't much you can do the night before the interview to prepare for such in-depth technical questions – although you can power-read through some of the books I recommend in Chapter 7. The only way to ace technical interviews is knowing your stuff well, period. (A recurring theme in this chapter, isn't it?) This also goes back to what I preached in Chapter 2: whatever you put down on your résumé, make sure you can back it up with concrete evidence, such as displaying the said skill or knowledge at interview time!

As a general rule, as you get ready for your interviews, you might want to spend most of your time reviewing quantitative materials; subject matters like finance and programming should take a backseat. The reason is twofold: one, quants are hired to do quantitative analysis and may not come into contact with a lot of finance; two, whereas financial concepts can be easily learned and programming skills easily picked up, solid analytical aptitude takes a long time to hone. This last observation means that between a candidate who knows little finance but possesses unusually strong quant skills and one who has read every finance book but has no experience in quantitative analysis, the employer will likely pick the former for the quant job.

When you do get asked technical questions, take a deep breath and let your quant geek self take over. If it's a question familiar to you, don't rush into offering an answer. Think carefully over your answer even if you are 1,000% sure of its correctness. This measured pace serves two purposes: first, it allows you a chance to double-check your answer and to watch out for any "traps" in the question; second, it takes time away from the rest of the interviewer so, hopefully, the interviewer won't get a chance to ask more tough questions! So, you can say something like "Let me think about the answer for a minute" and then proceed to think about it for an appropriate amount of time. At this point, it would be really helpful if you brought a pen and notepad along, both as a thought-organizing tactic and as a self-calming technique.

With long questions, you need to learn two techniques in answering them: one, you need to learn to think out aloud (see the case questions section below for more information on thinking out aloud); two, you need to know when you get stuck. By thinking out aloud, you not only show the interviewer how you approach the problem, but also get him or her involved in the problem-solving process, which in turn can give you some valuable feedback and help as you struggle along with coming up with the answer. If you do get stuck, you should immediately ask for help. Simply state that "I think I'm stuck. Could you give me some help here?" Most questioners will give you some hint.

Some of the technical questions you may be asked include:

- *Quantitative:* How do you estimate panel data? When do you use GLS vs. OLS? What's Ito's Lemma and why is it important? How do you deal with sample selection bias? If random variable A's variance is x and B's variance is y, what's the variance of A+B (or A-B or A*B)? Given some sample data, how do you infer the population's distribution? You randomly draw three numbers of ten, what's the number of possible combinations you can get? What are the odds that two people on my team of 20 have the same birth month and day? How do you test or prove causality? Under what circumstances would you use non-parametric methods? What steps are involved in a Monte Carlo analysis? What is Brownian motion? How do you test stationarity? How do you estimate unbalanced panel data? What's the sum of $1+a+a^2+a^3+...$? What is co-integration? Given any data sample, how do you detect outliers?

- *Finance:* How is the CAPM derived? How is Black-Scholes derived? What are the major criticisms of the mean-variance optimization approach? What's the difference between a forward contract and a futures contract? When I do bond pricing today, what discount rate should I use? What are large caps, mid caps and small caps, and why do we care about dividing stocks into cap groups? What are the major assumptions behind the dividend pricing model? Tell me why people use swaps, and give me an example of a swap. When interest rate goes up, what happens to bond prices – and why? Right now the yield curve is inverted, what does that mean and what does it imply? Do you agree that stock prices follow a random walk? What does a company's P/E tell us?

- *Economics:* In game theory, what's a Nash equilibrium and why is it an important concept? When a country such as the United States runs a huge current account deficit, how does that impact the country's economy? When inflation rises, what happens to asset prices? What is moral hazard and what can firms do to prevent or discourage it? How does an economic agent decide how much insurance to take on? What happens to a country's exchange rate when its inflation doubles? How does unemployment rate affect interest rates? What's the difference between GDP and GNP (and which measure does the United States use)?

- *Computational:* What are the three (or four) most fundamental concepts in OOP? How do you sort 100 million data values in the quickest way? How do you find the median of 5 billion unsorted numbers quickly? In [insert statistical package here], how do you read in an Excel file? I need to do OLS in Excel, what are the two ways of doing it? I have some [insert language] code here and there's a bug in it, can you identify it and then suggest a fix? In SQL, what's the difference between an inner join and an outer join? If my program causes a core dump, what does that mean and how can the core dump help me?

I hope these examples give you a flavor of the wide range of technical questions that can be asked at quant interviews. Unfortunately, the possibilities of questioning are endless. Now you know why I said the only way to prepare adequately for such questions is to know your stuff well – particularly the stuff you put down on your résumé. There's just no substitute for that.

Handling Case Questions

Ah, case questions – the particularly sudorific part of a quant interview! Nothing can be more horrifying than being given a tough case question that you must answer in minutes. The experience, especially for beginners, can be overwhelming.

Well, first the good news. Case questions are actually not common at quant interviews. These questions are more often asked at management consulting and corporate finance (investment banking) interviews. Management consultants, in particular, love to indulge in such questions, because they think of themselves as problem-solving gods. Case questions, after all, serve the purpose of testing a candidate's critical thinking and problem-solving skills: how he or she processes the information given, asks the right questions needed to understand the situation thoroughly, analyzes the important issues involved, and identifies potential solutions.

But since Wall Street quants solve problems all the time, some quant interviewers do ask case questions. By probing the problem-solving skills of a candidate, an experienced interviewer can tell the bookworm types apart from the ones who can think independently and logically. Most employers look for candidates who are more than a human calculator. It is said, for example, that many Ph.D.s suffer from the "can see the trees, but can't see the forest" syndrome, i.e., they possess the technical know-how to apply sophisticated modeling techniques, but often fail to ask the big-picture question: is this or that technique appropriate or valid in the current context. The ideal quant candidates can think for themselves instead of requiring someone to hold their hands. The ideal candidates can actively identify and solve problems, instead of needing to be told what to do all the time. Case questions, while not a perfect stethoscope of problem-solving health, can reveal whether a candidate thinks actively and critically. (Critical thinking means always asking the right questions and seeking out the relevant answers.)

Now, good news again. Case questions often do not have a right or wrong answer – or, at least, interviewers who ask such questions are usually not looking for the right or wrong answer. Instead, they want to see *how* you think, not what particular end solution you come up with. This open-endedness is what distinguishes a case question from a long technical question (the latter always has a "correct" answer). This also has a very important ramification for how you approach case questions: you must focus on the thought process itself, not on whether your answer is correct or wrong.

In practice, this means you should employ the "think aloud" strategy in tackling case questions. This strategy is taught to management consulting and investment banking interview candidates. It's very simple: every step throughout the answering process, you talk out aloud what you are thinking. Here are the details (I'll give a sample case question later):

As you are given the case question, jot down the important facts about the case. (You brought a pen and notepad, didn't you?) You need to be very focused and process the information you are given actively. What are the important keywords coming out of the interviewer's mouth? What are the known facts and what are the unknowns? What problem am I being asked to solve? Etc. If there's anything you don't understand during the questioning phase, don't hesitate to ask the interviewer for clarification. Asking questions when you are being given the case also allows you some extra time in digesting the information.

After the interviewer finishes giving you the case, you should quickly review the important facts – aloud. This means you should read out a few of the important facts you were given. But don't read back everything! Just a few select facts, to show the interviewer that you understood the important points of the case as well as what you were asked. Hopefully, if you missed an important fact or two, the interviewer would step in and remind you of those facts. This is the benefit of turning the case question session into a two-way street process; and you can only do that by thinking out aloud.

You should also summarize, aloud, what the problem or goal is in this case. Even if it's a Sudoku puzzle, for example, you should say something like "obviously, the goal here is to fill the small squares so unique digits appear in each row, column and 3x3 box," so the interviewer knows you truly understand what you are supposed to do.

Now, begin solving the problem. Every problem requires two major steps: identifying the issues, and coming up with solutions to these issues. Whether it's a specific modeling question or a brainteaser puzzle, these two steps are usually necessary.

So the first thing you do is saying out aloud "okay, here are some of the issues we face here," and then proceed to listing the issues. It just doesn't hurt, even if the issues are obvious. Please note that issues are more than the facts you are given. They are deeper in the problem-solving process. For instance, if you are asked to construct a specific econometric model for some sample data (bond prices, stock trading volumes, interest rate volatilities, whatever), the issues include what kind of distribution the population might have, what problems – such as missing data or dirty data – the sample itself may have, what candidate econometric techniques would do the job and whether their theoretical assumptions fit this situation, and what kind of computing power would be required to model the data adequately. As another example, if you are told that "our volatility forecasting model used to work beautifully but stopped working two years ago and now just gives nonsensical results" and asked to troubleshoot the situation, you should recognize all the potential problems that can break an empirical model, from dirty data to bugs in some new code to a drastically different investment environment to sabotage by a disgruntled employee. I want to emphasize that your job at the interview is not to cover all possible bases, but to identify some of the *relevant* issues. Oftentimes, if you can list two or three most critical issues, you are already way ahead of the curve.

(Digression: how do you become apt at identifying issues in a case question? First, you need to know your stuff well. Second, some practical experience would really help in this regard.)

After you list the issues out aloud (and be sure to write them down on paper as well), you need to solve them. There may be only one issue, or there may be myriad issues. If the latter, identify the most important ones – and convey your thought to the interviewer. He or she may approve or disapprove your approach; use that feedback to help yourself move along. Now you see why it's important to think out aloud: it keeps your interviewer informed of your progress, and it allows him or her to give you feedback – be sure to take that feedback!

Each problem-solving process may be iterative: you try one solution; if it doesn't work (e.g., the interviewer tells you it's wrong), you try another solution. By telling the interviewer the approach you are taking in coming up with the solution – e.g., "with this Sudoku I'll first scan the rows and columns for numbers that appear twice and see if I can fill the third into a square," or "to get rid of the endogeneity I'll use an instrumental variable" – you show you are thinking actively. As mentioned before, a subtle yet powerful effect of thinking aloud is you turn the problem solving itself into a collaborative effort, with the interviewer acting as your senior partner (since he or she knows the answer). Thus, you also prove your teamwork ability. One stone, two (or is it three?) birds.

If you have friends who are management consultants or who are seeking management consulting positions, you may have heard the phrase "outside-the-box thinking" (or "outside-the-box solution") thrown around a few times. Outside-the-box thinking refers to creative problem-solving approaches that try to break out of the traditional bounds of the situation, or that try a radically different approach than what's been done before. For example, an outside-of-the-box solution for a company that's been losing money for years and is trying to get back to profitability may simply be shutting down and exiting the business altogether; after all, why should a company without a raison d'être be allowed to continue depleting resources?

Indeed, most innovations in our society occurred precisely because someone was able to think outside the box. There's no doubt that creativity and originality play an important role in finance. However, my view (as someone who's worked both in management consulting and finance) is that most people are not good at thinking outside of the box, and interview time may not be the best time to try to be wildly creative. In other words, don't use a job interview as the time to show off your creativity or originality. Most interviewers (quant or non-quant) lack the humor or vision to appreciate your unconventional approach, and if your answer ends up completely befuddling the interviewer (even though you thought it was utterly ingenious), you may as well kiss the job good-bye. During job interviews, you want to be lucid and to-the-point.

Indeed, some candidates fail to grasp the true meaning of outside-the-box thinking. For instance, there was this time when I asked a candidate how our team could solve a particular problem. Her response? "Hire a consultant." She evidently thought her response was outside the box – and she was probably trying to sound cute – but, to me, it was quite stupid and inappropriate in the context of our interview. It was either a sign of her immaturity or an indication of her trying to hide the fact she didn't know the answer or even what I had been asking. Either way, such answers should probably not be offered up for admiration at a job interview.

To sum up, case questions test how your solve problems, not whether you can come up with the right or wrong answer. As in real life, many case problems simply do not have a definitive solution. What's important is the methodology you employ to approach these problems and find the most efficient solutions – or know when there's simply no solution. Thinking aloud at a case interview allows your interviewer to see that you are a thinker.

It's time we took a look at some sample case questions.

Broadly speaking, there are two types of case questions. In no particular order, the first type involves using quant skills to solve a fairly "big" problem; you can think of these questions as extended versions of technical questions (the line of distinction can be blurred here); in fact, you have seen a couple of examples earlier when I discussed thinking out aloud. The second type of case questions are brainteasers, puzzles that test your general logical reasoning without resorting to technical skills. In either type, the word *case* refers to the fact that the question concerns some kind of situation – a modeling situation, or a puzzling situation.

To illustrate how to approach case questions with a technical bent, I'll give a detailed example. Then I'll list some sample case questions in the context of quant modeling and make general remarks; check the book's website (`www.quantcareer.com`) for details on how to answer these questions.

"Our client has asked us to put together a balanced portfolio that can withstand significant downturns in the market. How would you assemble such a portfolio?" The interviewer might stop right here and now the ball is in your court. Or he or she might offer some additional information such as *"The portfolio can be composed of any stocks and bonds, and the client may be willing to consider other asset classes."*

Obviously, to answer this question you must know what an investment portfolio is; if not, you might want to offer to pass on this question, stating frankly that none of the terms in the question makes sense to you (and hoping the interviewer will be nice to you and forgive your ignorance in this area). Let's assume this degenerate case doesn't apply to you and you do know some portfolio theory. We need to use the thinking aloud approach, remember? So the first thing you do is rephrase the question out aloud, "Ok, the client wants a balanced portfolio of bonds and stocks and possibly other assets like commodities, real estate or hedge funds, right? [The interviewer nods in agreement. Good. Now take a breath and continue.] The client seems averse to market downturn risks, so our goal is to design a portfolio that minimizes such risks." While this rephrasing may seem superfluous, it does serve the important purpose of confirming to your interviewer that you understood the question. After all, the last thing an interviewer wants is not knowing whether the candidate even understood what the question was asking. Take away that feeling of uncertainty in the interviewer. Keep him or her informed of your every thought regarding the problem at hand.

Next, you should ask for more information that can help you better understand the context and solve the problem. For example, if the interviewer had been terse and hadn't told you what the portfolio might contain, you should ask: "Could you tell me if this portfolio can have stocks, bonds, or other types of assets?" Another piece of information missing here is how market downturns are to be measured; in other words, what's our benchmark? And what exactly is this "market" the client refers to? Be sure to ask. Can you spot yet another thing you can, and should, ask the interviewer to clarify? It's the word "balanced." Different people define it differently, even when they all talk in the context of a portfolio. So make sure you and the interviewer are on the same page regarding every detail. You might also want to inquire as to what this client is and what other investments the client already has. If you forget to ask for important information at the beginning and realize it later, don't panic. You can ask questions any time. The vital point here is: don't be afraid to ask questions – relevant questions, that is.

Assuming now you know what type of client you are dealing with here, what kind of market downturn he wants to avoid, what asset classes are permissible in the portfolio (including whether the assets should be domestic only or global), the next step is spelling out the issues we face and trying to deal with those issues. You may have no clue what kind of portfolio you need to build. You may have some inkling but can't be sure if you are on the right track. It doesn't matter. Remember: it's the *thought process* that counts, not the answer to the question *per se*. In other words, it's how you answer the question, not what you offer up as the solution.

Thinking out aloud, you proceed as follows (note how I mix the identification of issues and potential solutions all in one swoop here): first, since the client dislikes market downturns, the portfolio should have as little risk in terms of exposure to the market as possible (again, you need to ask the interviewer what "the market" means in this context); second, we need to find out if the client will be happy with a cash-heavy portfolio, i.e., one that consists mostly of money market and short-term Treasury instruments which are safe but low-yielding; third, assuming the client wants more than just cash in his portfolio (i.e., he wants some equity exposure so he can get some higher returns, too), the balanced portfolio needs to be tilted heavily toward safe assets (bonds, cash, income-generating stocks) but will probably contain a small percentage of growth stocks or commodities or hedge funds; finally, to put together the portfolio, we need to make some assumptions concerning the asset returns and risks and run some kind of optimization algorithm to produce the asset weights. With the last step, you need not give the technical details unless you are further asked to do so. Many case interviewers aren't necessarily interested in the final technical details; they are interested in how you arrive at the step where readily available technical techniques can be applied.

If you are wondering why I didn't offer a complete solution to the question, you are missing the point. You have to remember that with case questions (as opposed to specific technical questions such as how to carry out a portfolio optimization or what to do in case of heteroskedasticity) you are tested on your problem-solving methodology, not on the correctness of your solution. Re-read this section from the beginning if you still aren't clear on this.

Here are some more examples of case questions; check the book's website (`www.quantcareer.com`) for even more samples that will be regularly updated.

- "We need a way to understand where our trading costs come from. How would you help us find out?" This is a cost attribution question. You need to find out from the interviewer what assets are traded, where they are traded (e.g., public exchanges, over-the-counter, or private arrangements), how costs are currently measured, and (most important) whether current cost measures include implicit transaction costs such as price impact or market drift.

- "We have been approached by a few statistical arbitrage hedge funds. We have never invested in stat arb funds before, and we aren't sure if they add any value to our current portfolios. How would you find out?" If you don't know what statistical arbitrage is, ask. (Remember, an honest person who's not afraid to say "I don't know" is way better than someone who tries to BS his way out of something he doesn't know.) In fact, you don't really need to know how stat arb works to recognize what this questions asks is how you compare the portfolios' performance before vs. after adding in stat arb strategies. You probably need to do some kind of comparative analysis. Don't forget to inquire about the big picture, e.g., what the firm is already investing in.

- "Our daily work relies heavily on processing large amounts of data, which are currently stored in text files across a dozen different servers. Do you have any suggestions on how we can optimize our data files?" This example illustrates an IT type of case question. It may seem odd that a quant candidate would be asked a question like this, but, remember, the question tests your ability to think, not your solution *per se*. Besides, quants may be called upon to don many hats, especially at smaller firms, so it's not unusual for us quants to have to know databases and data warehouses inside out. In answering this question, you should find out what kind of data the group works with, and then suggest a few data-centric solutions such as utilizing a dedicated high-speed database server.

- "Currently we trade only stock options, but we are interested in branching out into other liquid assets. How would you propose we proceed?" This question combines business sense with financial market knowledge. You should focus on the value add concept: how does a particular asset or class of assets add value to what the firm or team is already doing. In particular, what are the risks and rewards? Do the potential marginal returns offset the marginal risks? Is core competence an issue here? List two or three examples of possible new asset classes to trade and analyze them in as much detail as you can. There's probably no need to try to come up with an exhaustive list unless the interviewer signals so to you.

- "We need to forecast volatility as accurately as possible. Can you think of a few ways of achieving this?" To answer this question you need to consider how volatility is measured as well as which financial econometric models, such as ARCH/GARCH, may be appropriate or whether non-statistical methods like historical volatility or implied volatility would work. Analyze each method in detail and weigh its pros and cons. Get as much contextual information as you can before offering potential recommendations.

By the way, some candidates may wonder whether any original ideas they come up with during an interview may be "stolen" by the interviewer and/or his or her firm. The chances of this happening are quite remote. After all, it's very unlikely you'll come up with a completely original solution to a case problem. But if you feel your solution is quite innovative and potentially profitable, you may want to think about how much of an answer you want to let out. In other words, I wouldn't be concerned about this possibility, but I'd be on the watch-out for a genuine "Eureka!" idea that could turn me into a rich guy.

I mentioned that the second type of case questions are brainteasers. These serve purely as IQ tests to probe your logical reasoning ability. The end of the exercise is not necessarily to solve a puzzle correctly – although doing so would be very nice – but to demonstrate your reasoning skills. If you want to solve a puzzle as much as you can, be sure to pay attention to all the background information the interviewer gives you and ask as many questions as you can to extract additional assumptions from the interviewer. Brainteasers sometimes do require outside-the-box thinking; oftentimes, what's obvious can be safely assumed to be a trap. Don't take every piece of information at face value; think over carefully why that information is given. Remember, brainteasers are usually short, which means pretty much every word carries an important meaning. Also analyze closely the way the assumptions are given. The best way to become a good puzzle solver is to simply get a few puzzle books and practice.

Will you ever get asked brainteaser questions? I think so. I have been asked many times at quant interviews (and not to mention at management consulting interviews). If you have little time between now and the interview, I'd suggest you beef up your technical knowledge as much as you can first. Becoming adept at solving brainteasers does take practice (or a very high IQ).

Here are a few sample brainteaser-type case questions:

- "Why are manhole covers round (instead of square or diamond or whatever other shape)?" This was supposedly invented by someone at Microsoft as an interview question, and is popular on the interview circuit. Can you figure out the answer? (Hint: why wouldn't a square or diamond shape work?)

- "I have 12 gold coins, one of which is fake and weighs slightly differently than the others. I don't know if the fake is heavier or lighter. I have a balance scale. What's the minimum number of weighings I need to carry out in order to find out which coin is the fake?" You need some outside-the-box thinking to get this right. If you start with the obvious approach of putting six coins on each side of the scale, it won't work. The answer to this question is three; an alternative version of the question therefore asks you "how do you find out the fake in no more than three weighings?"

- "How many hamburgers are eaten in the United States each day?" Whoa, where did this come from? Similar questions can ask you to figure out how many PCs are sold each day or how many people work on Wall Street. You need to perform a top-down or bottom-up back-of-the-envelope estimation. How many people are there in the United States? How many eat burgers on a given day? You get the idea.

- "I have two water containers, one five-gallon and the other three-gallon. How do I get exactly four gallons of water?" Isn't this puzzle featured in a popular action movie? Anyway, you'll have to do a few pourings to get the right answer.

- "A man dies and his soul comes to two unmarked gates, each guarded by an angel. The gates look exactly the same as do the angels. The man knows one gate leads to Heaven and the other to Hell, but he doesn't know which gate leads to Heaven. The man also knows that the angel who guards the Heaven gate always tells the truth while the one guarding the Hell gate always lies. He gets to ask exactly one question, but he can ask only one of the two angels. Obviously the guy wants to enter Heaven. So what's the one question he should ask in order to pick out the correct date?" The answer is quite convoluted, but the way to approach it is to first try out some (obvious) questions that won't work, and gradually deduce the right answer.

The Don'ts of Interviewing

The following is a list of don'ts at an interview. Avoid these interview no-nos at all cost. Most of these apply to the in-person kind of interview, but some are relevant to phone interviews as well. Yes, this list is long; it's because it represents a compendium of the various mistakes I've personally seen committed by real job candidates. While I don't suggest you memorize this list, you should go through the items carefully and ask yourself, and ask the friends who help you with your mock interviews, whether any of the items applies to you. You'll go far by avoiding any of these common mistakes, since each of them can be the real deal breaker.

- *Don't be late.* If you are late for an interview, the interviewer will likely be pissed at both your sloppiness and disrespect and the fact you are wasting his or her time.

- *Don't show up in casual wear.* You'd think that everyone would dress up for a business-oriented interview, but you'd be surprised at the occasional candidate who walks in dressed in a Hawaiian shirt or flip-flops. Unless your religion forbids it, you should wear a Western suit and leather shoes.

- *Don't forget to bring a copy of your résumé.* Many interviewers forget to print out a copy of your résumé, so it'll be handy if you brought a copy yourself. After all, it's your résumé, and don't go anywhere without it.

- *Don't forget to make eye contact and smile.* I have emphasized the importance of these two behaviors, and you must practice them to perfection before going into your first interview. Someone who refuses to look the interviewer in the eye leaves the impression that he or she is arrogant or has something to hide. In fact, it's frustrating to talk to someone who doesn't look at you. You are never sure if they are listening to you or care about what you say (or if you have a big zit on your face that's scaring them). For an interviewer, such frustrations will not translate into a positive impression of the interviewee.

- *Don't forget your tableside manners.* If you are taken to lunch, don't let your guard down. It's advisable that you avoid having an alcoholic drink even if offered. (Even a beer, coupled with nervousness, can impair your ability to work through some complicated math in the afternoon.) If you are from a non-Western culture, you must remember that in the West, people chew with their mouths closed and chew quietly. They also avoid talking and chewing at the same time. Now, I'm not saying you should sit stiffly like a robot or act gingerly like a Japanese geisha, but observing good tableside manners is important. Practice beforehand if you think you are lacking in this area.

- *Don't argue with the interviewer.* Intentionally or not, the interviewer might engage you in a controversial topic, such as politics, sports, or the merit of some famous theorem or model. For example, the interviewer might ask you for your opinion on the validity of CAPM, or the real-world applicability of GARCH. He or she might tell you that you are wrong. He or she might do this either because he or she wanted to test your ability to defend your opinions under pressure, or because he or she truly thinks you are wrong, or because he or she is a cocky jerk. (Remember, many quants are geeks who lack social grace – how they passed *their* interviews is everyone's guess.) If you are sure of your answer, you should politely defend yourself – and defend yourself you must. (In other words, don't act like a wuss in front of an authoritative figure.) Of course, if you are wrong or unsure, admit it. Never get into a shouting match with the interviewer. Put yourself in his or her shoes: if you were interviewing a job candidate and he, the job seeker, gets into a shouting match with you, the decision maker, how would you feel?

- *Don't look or act arrogant.* Next to the lying interviewee (see below), I really dislike, and flunk, the one who acts as if he were God himself. Let's check the facts, shall we? You are at the interview because you are looking for a job. Check. You are looking for a job because you need a job. Check. (You wouldn't need a job if you had won the Powerball, for instance.) So you are in no position to be arrogant. Besides, the guy sitting across the table from you already has a job – the kind of job you dream about – and you're just trying to be like him! So no matter what kind of person you are in real life, look and act humble in front of an interviewer. Be polite and respectful. And never put your feet up on the desk!

- *Don't be too aggressive.* This don't is related, but different, from the previous two. In a sense, it encapsulates the previous two, but it's more. It's okay to sell yourself hard, but overdoing it will surely backfire. For example, when an interviewer questions the validity of your last independent research project, you don't want to act hostile or condescending (the previous two don'ts). You also don't want to be aggressive in defending yourself. For example, if you start reciting a long list of literature that you think supports your case, or if you brag about your *other* research projects, or start gesturing wildly and/or pound on the table to make your points, you may come across as too aggressive, and the interviewer may not want someone aggressive on his or her team. You have to remember that quants are not salespeople. We are not supposed to be pushy. Yes, it's a stereotype, but it's generally true, and when it comes to dealing with non-aggressive people, it's always better to act like one of them.

- *Don't interrupt the interviewer.* Whether it's due to an aggressive personality, a case of near nervous breakdown, or a sense of self-righteousness, cutting the interviewer off in the middle of a sentence is a high offense. It's rude, it's disrespectful, and it's wrong. It doesn't matter if you do it because you actually want to sound eager or want to please the interviewer. To the interviewer, being interrupted mid-sentence is quite an insult. What you need to do instead is being a good listener: listen to what the interviewer is saying or asking, nod frequently (but not continuously!) to show you are listening, and let him or her finish talking before you offer your response.

- *Don't act clownish.* This admonition may seem amusing, but someday when you become an interviewer, you'll be surprised how many candidates would try to act like a comedian during interviews. They would try to crack a joke at the most inopportune time, or they would act funny as if in a desperate attempt to entertain you. Don't. Such behavior would make you look immature or "weird." Now, if you are a funny person by nature, you need to watch yourself closely and not get carried away when talking about your experience. A job interview is a business meeting, and as most quants are not necessarily funny people, being clownish just takes away precious points from your report card.

- *Don't ask stupid questions.* Okay, so what are stupid questions to ask of an interviewer? Anything that doesn't belong in a job interview. For example, while it's okay to ask the interviewer about his or her professional background and experience, it's not okay to ask about his or her marital status or sexual orientation. In other words, don't probe the interviewer's personal life. (The possible exception is when the interviewer asks you about these things first – that's a sign he or she tries to be casual with you, although he or she could also be nosy, and a lot of nosy people hate other people being nosy.) Stay away from questions that add no value to the discussion, such as "What does your company do?" (you should have done your homework). It's also bad if you ask about the pay during the first round; save that question for the headhunter or for the last round – better yet, don't ask it at all and just wait for the offer. Questions like "What hours do you work" and "How many vacations days do you get?" are usually okay (and, frankly, you *should* try to find out how many hours people work at the place), but I'd ask them only if the interviewer is genuinely friendly and ready to answer such questions without reservation.

- *Don't ramble or BS.* There are two general ways to BS during an interview. First, you go on and on about some trivial experience and attempt to exaggerate your qualifications. Second, you don't know the answer to a technical question but try to cover this fact up by talking about irrelevant point *ad nauseam.* I see both types all the time, especially the latter. Don't do it. If you have no clue about a question, be upfront and admit it. If you get stuck in your solution, don't feel ashamed; admit it. Remember, you're here at the interview because your résumé already attracted sufficient interest, so you don't need to exaggerate or make up stories. You simply cannot BS your way through an interview; people will notice and will note it in a negative way in their post-interview reports.

- *Don't overuse excuses.* If you don't know the answer to a question, it's best to just admit it and then move on. While it's okay to explain why you don't know something once or twice, don't end up offering nothing but excuses for your lack of knowledge. Nobody has the answer to every interview question. Besides, most interview questions probably aren't even relevant to what the job is really about. A corollary to this don't is, if you stumble on a question, don't start telling the interviewer what you do know. That's not what he or she asked, and telling him or her you know things totally not related to the question can be extremely annoying.

- *Don't put on an act.* Be business-like in your demeanor. Talk and conduct yourself in a natural manner (but don't forget to maintain eye contact and smile liberally). An interview is not a stage, so don't act as if you were in a play. Don't exaggerate your facial expressions or gestures. For example, if the interviewer tells you about an anti-social former colleague, you can nod and display an expression of sympathy, but don't fawn. If you are asked to describe a past job or project, do so in a calm, natural manner; don't try to recite a prepared script or wave your hands around like a mad man.

- *Don't talk too much.* Some candidates just can't stop talking. When asked to give a one-sentence question, they'll want to talk for ten minutes – and 99.9% of the time it's just BS. If you are asked a simple question, just offer the straightforward answer. Don't try to get smart and expand on the question and say things that weren't asked. For example, if you are asked why you are interested in the job, give the real reasons (other than the allure of the money, of course). Don't start talking about how you have successful quant friends or how you explored other opportunities but found them unappealing or how your mother called you last night to ask you what you had

had for dinner. If you have a tendency to talk too much and pad your answers with useless information, you should see a speech therapist to get this bad habit corrected. This don't is especially critical for phone interviews, because people have lower level of tolerance for long-winded speeches on the phone.

- *Don't read off index cards.* A few candidates are so concerned about the last two don'ts that they actually bring cue cards on which they have prepared anticipated Q&As to the interviews. Don't do this. Nothing looks more stupid than an interviewee's reading out prepared statements. Of course, it's perfectly okay to bring some prepared notes to the interview, but study them before you are seen by anyone from the company, and keep them hidden away throughout the interview.

- *Don't lie.* This is perhaps the biggest no-no of interviewing. Do not lie, period. If you do, either the interviewer will sense it and immediately strike you out, or the lie will come back to bite you later on (e.g., during interviewing with another employee from the same group, or even after you join the company). Nobody is perfect. In fact, if you had a perfect background, you probably wouldn't be looking for a job but would have already been highly sought after. If you never programmed in C#, tell the interviewer so; don't pretend you know it because the interviewer might actually test you on it! If you were fired from your last job, be frank about it and explain the circumstances. It's okay to sugarcoat the story a little, but don't tell an outright lie.

- *Finally, don't forget to send your interviewer a thank-you note.* Some people considered this practice passé, but it really is not. The post-interview thank-you note – which should be sent within a day of the interview – serves two important purposes: it shows your respect for the interview's time, and it reminds him or her of your qualifications. The note should be brief but should include references to the positive points from your interview, and it should highlight your qualifications. For example: "Dear Dr. Quanty: Thank you very much for taking time from your busy schedule yesterday to meet with me. It was my great pleasure meeting with a highly accomplished

Wall Street quant and learning so much from our discussion. In particular I enjoyed our talk about my dissertation research on the relationship between sub-atomic structures and financial market efficiency. I believe my expertise in advanced mathematical modeling and C++ programming make me a good fit for the job. Thank you again."

Taking a Break (Between Interviews)

When you go onsite for an all-day interview, you'll likely be able to take a brief break or two (in addition to the lunch break). Obviously, you'll need to use the restroom. More importantly, try to use a break to do some body stretching as well as mind refreshing.

If possible, take a walk outside, weather permitting. Some fresh air will help you clear your mind and prepare for the upcoming "battles." If you can't go outside, see if you can stroll around the office a little. Just don't be too conspicuous; and definitely don't act like a Mr. Bean's version of 007 or a stalker. Just relax and walk in a hallway away from the office and cubicles. Avoid talking to yourself (or talking on your cell phone via a Bluetooth headset) as you walk, or you'd look very strange and scary to passersby.

When you take a break, drink some water or tea or coffee as you like, but it's probably best not to eat anything. Bad breath from munching that bag of onion-flavored potato chips aside, food may make you drowsy and dull your "edge" – and you absolutely need every bit of concentration power you can muster. Remember, even though you'll be worn down toward the end of the interview day, to each interviewer his or her particular interview of you is new to him or her, so he or she will expect you to look and act fresh and alert. It's no easy task, no doubt, but if you care about the job, you need to put forth your best – in your answers and in your attitude.

A big no-no for an interview break is to make a personal phone call, unless it's genuinely urgent. A lot of interviewers I know do not look favorably upon candidates who spend their break time chatting away on the cell phone. Doing so would just make you look unprofessional – and who really wants to hire someone addicted to cell phone calls (or text-messaging)? Speaking of cell phones, be sure to leave them on silent – not vibrate, but total silent – before you walk into the first interview. And never check your cell phone for calls during an interview. If you did, you might as well kiss that lucrative job good-bye.

So whatever you do on that break, act professional and look professional. You never know if your future employer and/or coworkers might be watching your every move.

What to Do If Interview Not Going Well

It happens to all of us: we prepared well for an interview, we walk into one and five minutes later, we know it's turning into a disaster. Between feeling defensive and panicky, we desperately want to know what to do. Is there anything one can do to salvage an interview that's going badly?

The answer is, maybe. If the interview is going badly because the interviewer bombards you with difficult technical questions that you simply don't know how to answer, there's probably little you can do to reverse the situation. Your best bet is probably to give the questions your 110% (remember, think out *aloud*), and then gracefully acknowledge your ignorance. If the interviewer shows disappointment in your performance, too bad. You need to regain your composure and move on. Try to make up for the "deficiency" by emphasizing the things you do know, but don't BS. There's also a chance that no other candidate has ever been able to answer these same technical questions, or that the interviewer in fact doesn't really care whether you got them or not. (Remember, your inability to answer these questions doesn't necessarily mean you will be an incompetent quant.) Hopefully the later interviewers will be kinder to you.

If the interview is bombing because the interviewer is behaving like a brute and trying to intimidate you (e.g., with sarcastic questions about your background), you need to counter that. How you do this depends on your personality. If you are the aggressive, take-no-BS type like me, you can pointedly ask the interviewer why he or she is giving you a hard time. You can subtly insinuate whether he or she is treating you poorly because of your ethnic background or your accent. That will make them back off, fearing your complaining to the company's HR later that you were being discriminated against. If you are the non-aggressive type, you can do your best to remain polite and attempt to answer each question diplomatically.

A middle-of-road approach might be to pre-empt the interviewer by asking him or her questions at the first chance you get;

for instance, after you answer one of his or her questions, immediately follow up with a related question of your own. "How many people on your staff have Ph.D.s and how many of these Ph.D.s had practical, hands-on experience when they joined the team?" could be a counterattack question when the interviewer tries to interrogate you as to why you "only" have a master's. Of course, when you do this, you risk raising more animosity between the two of you, but you may be able to push back on an aggressive or hostile interviewer. Whichever approach you choose, the key is remembering to stay calm (always think positive thoughts, belittling your adversary *in your mind* if necessary), and to avoid any prolonged confrontation – and definitely no shouting match in the interview room, please.

If the interview is not going well because you are too nervous, you have to force yourself to calm down. Taking a deep breath or two can help. Sipping some water (but not caffeinated drinks) can also help. It's okay to tell the interviewer "Sorry, but I'm feeling really nervous because this is my first real interview" and then ask his or her permission for you to close your eyes for a few seconds. My own experience has been that, once I become a nervous wreck in the middle of an interview, it's extremely difficult for me to become calm for the remainder of the talk. It doesn't mean I don't try to relax; it just means that the best cure for in-interview nervous breakdown is to prevent it in the first place. That, in turn, means preparing well ahead of the interview time – and practice as much as possible.

If you feel physically sick in the middle of an interview and it's adversely affecting your performance, you need to make a judgment call as to what to do. On the one hand, you want to convey to the interviewer that you are not feeling well. On the other hand, you don't want to risk making him or her think you are looking for an excuse, a way out when you can't take the heat; besides, you never know if you'll get another interview opportunity at the same place again if you bolt for the door now. I think all interviewers always assume that no candidate will ever be genuinely ill during an interview. (One day, when you become an interviewer yourself, you'll know what I mean.) If you had not been feeling well before you went in for the interview, it would have been better to reschedule the entire interview for another time. When you are already at an interview, it's probably in your best interest to carry on. Now, I'm not saying you should persevere if you are genuinely sick and need medical attention. In that case – for instance, you are pale, running a fever or sweating profusely – tell the interviewer and find out if you can either take a break (and take some aspirin) or reschedule the rest of the interview. Otherwise, as long as you can hold up physically, it's probably best to continue with the interview – but you needn't be shy about asking for a break at the end of the ongoing session.

Regardless of how disastrous you think an interview was, don't forget two things. First, don't forget to shake the interviewer's hand at the end and offer thanks in a sincere tone. Second, don't forget to send him or her a thank-you note when you get home. You just never know whether your assessment of how the interview went is correct or not. I can say this because I have been there myself: at least twice in my life, I walked away from an interview thinking I had totally bombed, but only to be called back later with a job offer – and told that the tough interviewer was the one who really liked me. (Unfortunately, the converse case has also happened to me!) On Wall Street, people skills are often as important as technical skills. Always keep that in mind when you interact with your future employers and coworkers.

If You Speak English With an Accent

This special section is for those readers who speak English – the specific variety of English spoken in the country of your residence (or where you'd like to seek a job) – with a foreign accent. (I will assume, as I do in the rest of the book, that you're looking for a job in the United States.)

Language, written and spoken, is *the* tool for exchanging ideas. Someone who's not easily understood by others may find it difficult to be accepted. Good communication skills are especially important during job interviews, which are conducted in conversation as opposed to on paper or via e-mail. Successful candidates almost inevitably possess good communication skills.

If English is not your mother tongue and you speak with a heavy accent – or even if English is your mother tongue but your spoken English carries a heavy non-American accent – you may feel quite nervous about making yourself understood. This feeling is natural, and should not distress you too much. In fact, many quant positions do not emphasize superb oral communication skills – and often, what constitutes "good communication skills" really depends on the job requirements and the particular decision maker.

Wall Street quants work with quantitative models, and most types of quant jobs do not require quants to speak much in way of human languages throughout the working day. In other words, quants spend most of their time working in front of computer screens, not other people. Therefore, you do not need to be glib to be a quant.

When quants do talk, they usually talk in "quantspeak" and use a lot of technical terms. As long as you are conversant in "quantspeak" and can be understood by other quants, you'll be fine. You can gain skills in talking about quantitative topics by practicing at presentations, whether as a presenter or as a member of the audience.

Most quants on Wall Street are foreign-born, and I'll go out on a limb and say that most quants on Wall Street do not speak English (of any variety) as a first language. So when you go in for a quant interview, chances are you'll be meeting with people who don't speak English very well – possibly worse than yourself. Now, don't take this to mean they'll be sympathetic to your heavy foreign accent! A quant interviewer who speaks with a heavy Jamaican accent does not necessarily empathize with a candidate who has a thick Japanese accent. But many quant interviewers will tolerate your accent to some extent – probably to a greater extent than native English speakers. You still need to speak English *clearly* enough so people can understand you, but you don't need to worry about being accent-free (which is pretty much impossible for anyone who picks up English after age six or seven.)

The upshot is, if you speak with an accent, you should first find out if most people can understand you okay. For example, do your classmates or English-speaking friends have trouble understanding you? If few people complain about your accent, you should take comfort in the fact that your accent will not hamper your oral communication, and you should talk naturally at interviews – the only thing you might want to do is make yourself even more clear in speech. If people often ask you to repeat what you just said, or display puzzled looks whenever you talk, you know you should work on your accent. In this case, a professional speech coach or speech therapist is highly recommended. They'll analyze your speech characteristics and pinpoint the problematic areas (e.g., intonation, rhythm, speed, etc.). They'll then come up with solutions to help you overcome these speech hurdles.

For people whose first language is not English, accent is but one area where they face some hurdle. The other area is grammar, which includes sentence structures and word usage (as well as vocabulary, but that's relatively easier to improve by just memorizing a lot of words). You may have been told that your grammar is often incorrect or you use words incorrectly. My take on this is, don't worry too much. I have yet to come across a candidate whose English grammar is totally out of whack. As long as you get the basics right – and I bet you can already do that if you can read this book – you'll be fine. I do ask you to pay attention to two fundamental grammatical principles in English:

- Plurals. It's all too often to hear candidates say "I published three paper in top journal." That just sounds bad, period. Plurals are very important in English. If you can get them right, you're already halfway to speaking proper English. If your mother tongue does not use plurals – e.g., Chinese, Japanese and most other Asian languages – be sure to practice, practice, practice. It's "three dollars," not "three dollar." It's "ten persons," not "ten person." It's "two jobs," not "two job." And so on and so forth.
- Verb tense. There are different tenses in English to indicate actions or events that occurred in the past, are ongoing in the present, take place regularly, or will transpire sometime in the future. At the minimum, make sure you use the past tense for things past and use the present tense for other things. Avoid incorrect sentences such as "I take many finance course last semester" (should be "I *took* many finance courses last semester") and "My professor tell me I'm one of top student" (should be "My professor *tells* me [or told me] I'm one of the top students").

Of course, there are many grammatical areas that a non-native English speaker should pay attention to if he or she is interested in speaking well. I mention the above two basic principles because to a native English-speaker (and a non-native speaker who commands near-perfect English skills), these mistakes always stand out and sound at best comical and at worst sloppy and careless. So, as a job candidate, do whatever you need to do to avoid making such fundamental mistakes. If you manage to use plurals and past tense correctly almost all the time, you'll have boosted your chances very significantly.

Interviews That Are Not Interviews

This chapter will not be complete without mentioning that interviews are not the only way by which firms verify the qualifications of quant candidates. Because of the highly technical nature of a quant's job, it's not unusual for firms to test their candidates in other manners.

Some firms, including Credit Suisse and a few hedge funds, actually give out written exams to candidates who are expecting or already have a Ph.D. That's right: they make you sit down in a room with other candidates and take a test to be graded by their quant employees. The exams can cover fundamental mathematical concepts, economics, finance, econometrics/statistics, and other topics, depending on the firm. Your grade, like the SAT or the GRE, will be part of your application dossier and could play a heavy role in the hiring process.

If you are told that you need to sit in one of these exams, don't panic. After all, you've survived countless exams in your life so far, so what's another exam? Of course, you should prepare. First, ask the recruiter what the exam covers. Second, study. That's it. Nothing tricky about the whole thing. You just do your best come exam time, and hope for the best.

Another type of non-interview interview I've heard of is that some firms would invite candidates who survived the first round of interviews to some fun group event, say, a night out at the local bowling alley, a weekend at a ski resort or a trip to the local hotshot golf course. Candidates are told that the event is not an interview of any kind and they should relax and have some fun while getting to know some employees. Inevitably, some candidates let their guard down and drink themselves to utter stupor. Don't ever do that! Companies actually use these "fun events" to watch your behavior closely, to find out how well you handle work-related situations outside of the formal workplace. You must remember to conduct yourself well. After all, quants are highly educated Wall Street professionals. Don't do anything to stain that reputation.

Chapter Summary

This has been a very long chapter. There's no doubt that interviewing is the most stressful and exhausting part of a stressful and exhausting process – and you'll likely go through quite a number of interviews.

This long chapter gave you plenty of pointers and tips on how to prepare for and handle job interviews of different kinds. The single secret to acing any job interview is the prepare well beforehand; there's just no substitute for that. Treat each interview as a fresh battle, and you'll likely do well regardless of what personality the interviewer might possess.

EDUCATION: ARM YOURSELF WITH KNOWLEDGE

Chapter 5: Undergraduate Preparations

In this chapter:

This chapter is for readers who are still doing their undergraduate studies. If you are in college, you'll be looking for either a summer internship or a full-time junior position. Either way, you need to know the basic concepts and modeling techniques of quantitative finance. Sure, it's true that undergrads lack the advanced knowledge and practical experience required of most Wall Street quant jobs, but there are nonetheless plenty of opportunities for smart undergrads who are not afraid to work hard. In this chapter I will give you some guidance on what knowledge and skills you need to acquire, as well as where to obtain them.

Basic Concepts of Quantitative Finance

Quantitative finance, as its name implies, involves two disciplines: quantitative analysis and finance. It's all about the application of various quantitative methods in analyzing financial instruments. Let's look at the two areas in detail.

Broadly speaking, quantitative analysis uses tools from mathematics, statistics and econometrics (which is the economist's specialized version of statistics). The vast majority of the quant analysis practiced on Wall Street is empirical, meaning the analyst works with data. This is different from researchers who concern themselves with only theoretical aspects of research: they build abstract models and leave the testing with real data to others.

Doing empirical work, however, does not mean you need not know theory. After all, in any discipline theory forms the foundation and backbone of practical knowledge. I'm not here to engage in a pedantic discussion of whether a theory-driven research paradigm is the ideal one, or even the correct one. But because empirical quantitative techniques (regressions, forecasting, simulations, etc.) derive from theory, a quant must possess adequate theoretical knowledge to know when to use which tool.

For example, everyone knows OLS (ordinary least squares), right? It's a very simple regression model and can even be implemented easily in Microsoft Excel. But are you aware of the underlying assumptions of the OLS model? In other words, what conditions about the data must be met before we can confidently use OLS knowing the results we get are sound? You must know those assumptions, because a violation of any one of them invalidates an OLS analysis. Better yet, if you know the entire theory behind OLS – from the optimization it attempts to achieve to the derivation of parameter estimates (and what these estimates signify) – you'll be able to use OLS correctly and know when to use a different model when OLS is inappropriate.

Of course, as a summer intern or junior quant, you'll usually be told precisely what model to use. Your job is often simply to run the relevant data through a given model and then report the results to the boss. But as you gain more experience, you'll be expected to contribute to the modeling part of the process. If you want to build a successful career in quant finance, you'll need to be able to both explain the nuts and bolts of a model (from theory to empirics) and offer insight into its construction, implementation and interpretation. A real quant does not blindly apply the same technique to every situation. He or she thinks about the big picture, understands the theoretical issues, and offers specific and appropriate empirical solutions to these issues.

Think all this talk about the importance of knowing the theory is just BS? Well, think again. As a modeler, you may be called upon to explain intricate details of the model – and the audience could well be a highly skeptical client who has a strong quant background. What would you expect this client to say during your presentation? He or she will surely ask a lot of tough technical questions, such as what assumptions you made, why you made them, how you dealt with certain estimation issues (e.g., endogeneity, heteroskedasticity, sample selection bias, etc.). If you don't know theory, you'll likely have no clue what the client is asking, let alone how to respond.

Therefore, as an undergraduate, it's important that you not only start taking as many math, stats and econometrics classes as you can, but also pay attention to the ideas behind everything you learn. When you learn OLS, don't just be content with knowing how to do it in Excel or memorizing the formulas. Instead, focus on the big picture: where does OLS come from, what does it really do to the data, what assumptions are needed to make OLS estimates valid, why do we use R^2 and t-statistics (and what's the difference between them), etc. You may think of these questions as advanced knowledge, but they are not. They are quite fundamental, and they are easy to understand. All that requires is an inquisitive mind – which, incidentally, is a characteristic trait of a good Wall Street quant.

In the next section I will list the classes you should take and do well in if you set your sight on a quant job on Wall Street. Now, let's turn out attention to the other discipline: finance.

Finance, in our context, is the study of financial assets. (Refer to Chapter 1 for details on what financial assets are.) Specifically, finance is concerned with the fair pricing of these assets. For example, what's the fair price of a share of IBM's stock? What's the fair aggregate value of a company about to go IPO? What's the correct price of a company's corporate bond when the company is about to go bankrupt? Given the similarity of Intel and AMD, is there an intimately linked relationship between the two companies and, if so, how do we find and quantify this relationship? The job of every Wall Street financial professional, from traders to equity analysts to credit officers to investment bankers, is to help figure out the fair prices of assets.

Why is it important to know the fair prices of assets? There are at least two reasons. First, nobody wants to pay more than the fair price or sell less than the fair price. Second, in the long term (but nobody really knows how long is long term), assets tend to trade around their fair prices, so people who can predict these fair prices stand to make a lot of money.

So, whether you want to be an equity trader, an options analyst, a portfolio manager, or a derivatives researcher, you'll be dealing with the pricing of assets. Think this sounds boring? Actually it's not.

There are literally hundreds of different *kinds* of financial assets, each with its own characteristics, and there are hundreds of markets where these assets trade, so even a small portion of this big asset pricing pie can be overwhelmingly complex for a sophisticated quant.

As you embark on the journey towards a successful career in quant finance, you first need to think about if there's anything in particular you'd like to work with. For instance, you might have felt an affinity to all things equity: stocks, stock indices, stock options, stock index futures, stock mutual funds, private equity, etc. Or you might be only interested in working with options. If this fits your description, you should focus your studies on the topics that interest you, in addition to acquiring a solid footing in quantitative analysis.

Most undergraduates aspiring to be quants likely aren't sure what they want to do. In fact, many want to try everything, to explore. The good news is Wall Street is full of opportunities for young people. There's no need to worry about competitors in the job market who already know what they want to work on; chances are, their percepts are incorrect and they will change their interests at some point. So you are not at a disadvantage wanting to be a generalist, starting with a clean slate. Just be aware that once you find your first quant job and stay there for a few years, your future career is likely to be influenced by what you did on that first job. This is mostly due to the increased specialization on Wall Street. For example, if you worked for a credit analysis group first job out of college, you'll likely find future offers in that area while people in equity or commodities may express little interest in your skills. Of course, if you possess really strong quantitative skills, you may be able to attract employers in other fields who are willing to bet on your ability to transfer those skills into their fields with ease.

Quant Opportunities for Undergrads

The advantage – the beauty, indeed – of being an undergraduate is that you have many options open to you in terms of what you can do as a junior quant. A Ph.D. in finance, in comparison, is *expected* to know certain advanced topics and add immediate value to the quant team. An undergraduate can afford to know a bit of everything and to learn along the way. People will be more forgiving of your mistakes – as long as you catch them in time (i.e., before sending results to an important client or finalizing a model as a released product) and also you show an ability to learn from your mistakes.

Because the typical undergrad is not yet well-versed in modeling techniques, he or she tends to be given data-intensive jobs at the beginning of the career. Here are some of the tasks a junior quant is often asked to do:

- Conduct background material search via the Internet. The first phase of any modeling project is to see what's already been done – and in finance, almost no stone is left untouched, so there's bound to be something that has already been written on any imaginable topic. In academic circles this is known as "literature search," where literature refers to past writings (usually those published in academic and/or trade journals) on the relevant topic(s). The junior quant can be expected to mine the Internet and other resources to find such information. For example, you might be asked to search for past journal articles on equity trading cost optimization; your job, then, is to find as many such articles as you can, so a senior quant will read them. The first few times you do this, you'll be told exactly what key words or phrases to look for. As you gain experience (something master's and Ph.D. students learn in grad school), you'll be able to figure out on your own where and what to look.

- Verify basic mathematics in the model. If the model has some mathematical formulas, you may be asked to double-check some of them for correctness. Obviously, how much you're asked to do depends on your math skills. Sometimes, regardless of your actual math knowledge, you may be asked to check for typos. When I was a senior quant at a major global investment bank, for instance, I often asked the junior folks to double-check my Word-typed formulas for subscript and superscript consistency as well as whether my transcribed parameter values were correct vis-à-vis the original output files. (A boring task for anyone, but somebody's got to do it – at least twice!)

- Help collect data. Wall Street differs fundamentally from Ivory Tower academia in that, to Wall Street professionals, real-world results are more important than theoretical elegance. In other words, people care about what a model means in terms of profits, not whether it involves some magnificent and ingenious math. That's why Wall Street quants work with data all the time: to test an idea, to develop a model, to enhance an existing product, to make money. In Wall Street finance, data are like gold mines, and the job of quants is to dig these mines for gold. As a junior quant, you don't necessarily have all the skills to efficiently dig for the gold yet, but you will be called upon to acquire the data (from different vendors, for example), to place the data in the team's computing environment, and possibly to help clean the data as well. (Cleaning the data means identifying erroneous values and deleting them.)

- Get involved in testing and debugging the model. As a model is subject to empirical testing, you'll be asked to help monitor the process and collect results. You'll also be engaged in identifying problematic areas (e.g., a forecast value that's way off the charts) and may be asked to help track down the sources of these problems. As a specific example, consider a portfolio optimization model implemented in Excel (i.e., via the Solver facility). The portfolio's characteristics depends on the inputs to its components, e.g., returns, volatilities and correlations. You may be asked to manually try out different sets of such inputs to see what the portfolio would look like under various assumptions. Or you may be asked to write a simple VBA program to automate this process. You may also be asked to chart the more interesting cases. As you can see, the number of things you can do is endless. (Now you know why we Wall Street quants work long hours!)

- Assist in putting together product presentation. Hopefully the model you were testing had good results worthy of presenting to people from other groups in the firm. Or maybe your boss thinks it's good enough to be shown to clients or even submitted to a journal for publication. You'll be asked to help put together the presentation, whether it's purely marketing BS or serious research literature. Your task will likely require you to leverage your PowerPoint or Word skills to create an attractive, coherent presentation.

There's no denying that much of what a junior quant does falls into the "boring" category. Before you start having second thoughts about working as a junior Wall Street quant – you probably dreamed of a fast-paced, high-octane working life, didn't you? – you should know that, first of all, most jobs are boring (unless you feel absolutely passionate about what you do), and second, junior positions in any industry (even in movie-making!) are boring and often little more than menial. Indeed, don't be surprised to find yourself being asked to fetch coffee or lunch for the senior guys, especially if you work on a trading desk. The good thing about Wall Street, though, is that it's largely a meritocracy, and if you're willing to work hard and be proactive in seeking out "challenges," you'll likely find a pleased boss and the door to a path paved with gold slowly opening up in front of you (as always, your stars also need to be aligned in your favor for good things to happen, regardless of your abilities or diligence – remember, there are no sure things in finance).

Must-Take Courses in College

Unless you are already in the last semester of your undergraduate life (in which case you should skip ahead to the next two chapters), you can, and should, choose classes that enhance your educational background and prepare yourself for a future in Wall Street quant. The first thing to keep in mind is that Wall Street recruiters like to see candidates who take on challenges and grow. What this means in plain English is twofold: first, you need to take some advanced classes; second, you need to take harder classes as you go through college. If you take a graduate-level calculus class in your sophomore year (and do well), great. If you then take a graduate-level real analysis class in your junior or senior year, even better. Wall Street recruiters believe that people who constantly push themselves to work harder are the ones who can contribute to their firms' growth and succeed – to a large degree, this belief is correct. So if you want to be a Wall Street quant, start working like one now.

As you pick and choose the courses to take, also remember to cover all your bases, i.e., get exposure to all the subjects that a quant needs to be knowledgeable about. This means you need to take courses in mathematics, statistics, economics, econometrics (which is distinct from general statistics), finance, and computer science.

In addition, if you get some exposure to other quant-driven disciplines such as physics and engineering, you may put yourself at an advantage over many other candidates. Engineering, in particular, can give you sound training in practical problem solving, which, as we saw in Chapter 4, is an important skill for quants who wish to be successful.

So what are the courses you should take? Let's look at the must-cover subject areas one-by-one. I present them in order of progressive education, so the earlier topics and courses help you prepare for later ones.

- *Mathematics:* Calculus and linear algebra are the must-take courses. They form the foundation for everything else that follows. Take at least two of each if you can; graduate-level coursework is even better – and pretty much a must in today's highly competitive environment. Numerical analysis and other advanced classes can not only make your résumé shine but give you some solid grounding in analytical methods.

- *Statistics:* Probability theory forms the foundation of statistics and this should be the first stat-related course you take. (Please note that some purists object to categorizing probability theory together with statistics.) Your college may not offer a separate probability theory course but instead combines it with basic statistics; that's fine. In any case, a basic course in statistics is a must-take. I'd probably take no more than two stat classes and save the time for the other disciplines, especially since econometrics (discussed below) will give you more relevant training in statistical analysis (as apposite to applications in economics and finance).

- *Economics:* An introductory class that touches on topics in both microeconomics and macroeconomics is necessary and should be sufficient for most undergraduates. Taking an intermediate-level microeconomic course, especially one geared toward mathematically inclined students, would expose you to useful analytical methodologies. Additional coursework in international finance (really a macroeconomics course as opposed to what we call finance in this book) could be beneficial, especially if you want to work in a global environment.

- *Econometrics:* Econometrics courses are usually offered by the economics department. Take at least one econometrics class to see how statistical concepts like regressions and hypothesis testing are adapted for economics and finance. If your school offers a separate time series course, take it, as time series models are heavily used on Wall Street. Make sure you learn to use at least one popular statistical programming package such as SAS, Matlab, SPSS, Stata, or S-Plus (or its open-source equivalent, R).

- *Finance:* Undergraduate finance courses are usually offered by the economics department. For future quants, a course on the basic concepts of investment theory is an absolute must. Courses that deal with specific topics such as options and futures or fixed income can be taken to get more in-depth exposure. If a financial modeling course is available – it's usually taught at the graduate level – do your best to take it; it'll give you invaluable exposure to analytical topics for the career you've chosen for yourself.

- *Computer science:* An introductory computer science course taught in C++ is the best, although some colleges now use C# or Java to teach CS 101. (C and Pascal are too ancient, too passé.) The important thing to learn are the object oriented programming (OOP) paradigm and algorithm design and implementation. If time allows, an additional course in advanced concepts in algorithms will be very beneficial as you gain insight into how to translate thoughts and solutions into languages computers can understand. If your college offers a course in Excel – especially if the course provides applications in economics and finance – take it. Excel, despite not being a "real" quant tool, is immensely useful in a quant's everyday life, and proficient Excel skills are highly valued everywhere in today's business world, including Wall Street.

I want to mention that, the long list of courses I recommend you taking notwithstanding, I am a firm believer in a well-rounded undergraduate education. I myself went to a liberal arts college (Harvard) and took fascinating courses in English literature, psychology, fine arts, classical music, etc., in addition to all the quant coursework (I skipped on computer science because I had done a lot of real-world programming since high school). I encourage you to do so, too. As we say in finance, you need to hedge yourself, just in case it turns out that quant finance is not what you really want to do at all.

Job Now, or Grad School First?

A question many brainy undergrads ask themselves is, should I get a full-time job now, or should I go to grad school and get more education first? This is a really good question – and, alas, there's no right or wrong answer. (Wouldn't the world have been wonderful if every meaningful question had a "yes" or "no" answer?)

What you should do after college, for the most part, depends on your interest and long-term goals. If you have always liked learning things in a controlled environment like that offered in a university, I think it's better if you go to grad school first and learn as much as you can while you are young and hungry for advanced knowledge. Even though you can also learn stuff while working full-time, the learning will occur in bits and pieces which may not quench your thirst for extensive knowledge.

If you have been itching to get out of school and make some real money, the answer is simple: go with what your heart feels and get a job now. If you forced yourself into grad school, you'd probably be green with envy, and burdened with regrets, when you hear about your college friends' making six figures while you barely survive on a grad student's shoestring budget.

If your long-term goal is to become a serious quant and stay involved in research – remember, not everyone wants to be a manager – then grad-school-first is the sensible approach. If your long-term goal is to rise up the corporate ladder and become an executive of some sort, then either path is okay.

Some undergrads feel they want to get a Ph.D., but aren't sure if spending five or six years in grad school is worth the time or effort. As someone who went through a top-ranked Ph.D. program myself, I advise strongly that you think twice or thrice before committing yourself to a Ph.D. program. (And when you do commit, please follow through with your plan – way too many Ph.D. students drop out already!) Ph.D. studies are intellectually challenging and gratifying, but there's high uncertainty as to whether you will ever get the doctorate degree, often for reasons beyond your control. For instance, even if you would never consider dropping out, you may end up with an uncooperative advisor who refuses to let you graduate. In fact, many Ph.D. advisors at top-ranked schools frown upon students who want to go to the industry (as opposed to academia) after graduating. You just need to be aware of all the rewards and risks of pursuing a Ph.D. before you commit five or six years of your life to doing it. Talk to a Ph.D. student or two to get some idea as to what it is like to study for a Ph.D.

Still can't decide what to do? Maybe you should consult your professors, your parents, your friends, you mentors, or others whose opinions you value. (A fortune-teller may help, too!) In the end, if you are equally torn between the two paths, try flipping a coin and let Fate decide for you. But I don't really recommend that approach.

Chapter Summary

This chapter has given the undergraduate reader some tips on what he or she can do to maximize his or her college education in terms of preparing for a career in quantitative finance.

Chapter 6: Graduate Studies

In this chapter:

If you are a graduate student – pursuing a master's, Ph.D. or any other advanced degree – this chapter is for you. Because of their advanced trainings, graduate students face completely different employer expectations than undergrads. For example, whereas undergrads are usually given a guiding hand in performing their quant duties, at least in the first few months, new employees with graduate degrees are expected to get up to speed and start contributing to the firm almost immediately from the start.

You should not feel intimated by this high expectation from an employer. Chances are, your advanced education will have prepared you well for quant work by the time you start your employment. As long as you are willing to work hard and to learn actively on the job, you'll do just fine.

In the previous chapter, I devoted a section to the basic concepts of quantitative finance. If you are completely new to finance, you should read that section starting on page 169. From this point on, I assume you are familiar with the fundamentals of quantitative analysis as well as possess some rudimentary knowledge of economics and finance (e.g., you know what the supply-and-demand curves are and what the difference between stocks and bonds is).

Quant Opportunities for Grad Degree Holders

In Wall Street finance, opportunities truly abound for folks with advanced degrees. Graduate-level training imparts in you not only in-depth topical knowledge, but practical analytical skills that make you a better modeler.

The types of work done by quants with graduate degrees span the entire gamut of finance, from stocks to fixed income to derivatives, from big one-stop-shop banks to niche hedge funds, from high-level strategy designs to day-to-day implementations, from front-office sales and trading to back-office post-trade analysis.

What separates an advanced degree holder and an undergrad is mainly two-dimensional. First, a person with a graduate degree is expected to possess enough knowledge and analytical aptitude to understand the context of a model and contribute to ensuring its overall validity and relevancy. (Undergrads can afford to just follow orders on what calculations to perform without worrying about whether those calculations make any sense in the context.) Second, an advanced degree holder is expected to be more mature, both intellectually and personally, and to be able to lead instead of simply following in some aspects of the research process. For instance, you may be called upon to be in charge of testing the model or interpreting its results or recommending additional parameters or options for inclusion.

A concrete example will serve to illustrate the difference between a senior quant (usually one with an advanced degree or one who has a lot of quant experience under the belt) and a junior quant. Let's say the project is to forecast the intraday volatility of some financial instrument (stocks, bonds, convertibles, whatever). A senior quant, in this situation, is expected to decide or recommend one or two particular modeling approaches. For instance, can we use a simple time series model such as MA or AR? Or do we need to implement a "sophisticated" model like GARCH? Even more fundamentally, how do we measure intraday volatility? The senior quant either makes the call on each of these modeling questions, or at least contributes to the final decision to be made by the big boss. In essence, the senior quant designs the modeling approach. Come actual model building time, the senior quant also directs the implementation: deciding what data to use, working out the details of actually constructing the variables needed, making calls on the appropriate time lags in a time series framework, determining ways to test the forecasting power of the model, and interpreting the modeling results.

The junior quant, in comparison, writes the actual programs that read and transform data as needed (a process sometimes known as LET – load, extract and transform), converts formulas to programming code, runs and monitors the program executions, and compiles results for the senior analyst to interpret. Oftentimes junior quants are encouraged to do more than just write and run programs, but in the end, the senior quant is responsible for the final form of the model.

Now, does having an advanced degree (Master's or Ph.D.) automatically mean you'll be working as a senior quant? Hardly. Whether you are hired into a senior or junior position depends significantly on your modeling experience and finance knowledge. If you graduated from a degree program that gave you extensive exposure to both skill sets – such as one of the quantitative finance programs to be discussed in the next section, or a Ph.D. in economics or finance – you'll likely qualify for a senior position. If you lack vital analytical skills and cannot yet make independent decisions, you'll start as a junior quant, even if you have a double-Ph.D. in mathematics and physics.

Some employers only hire people with advanced degrees. At such places, some quants have to perform the relatively menial tasks often delegated to an undergraduate quant. If the place is democratic, everybody shares in such unglamorous duties. If the place is more hierarchical, then newcomers or those with "lesser" degrees may have to shoulder most of these chores. I point this out to prepare you for the possibility that, in the beginning of your quant career, you may be doing a lot of extremely boring and seemingly meaningless tasks – even if you are hired as a senior quant.

Quant-Oriented Graduate Programs

If you are considering enrolling in a quant-oriented graduate program – for example, you may be an undergrad pondering on going to grad school after commencement, or you may already be matriculated in a graduate program but also be thinking about switching into a different program or getting an additional advanced degree – you may be wondering which programs you should look into.

First of all, you need to consider whether you want to get a master's or Ph.D. (See the next section for a detailed discussion.) Let's assume you have already made that decision.

If your goal is to get a quant-oriented master's degree, you can choose from general-purpose master's programs or specialized programs. In the former camp are the traditional academic disciplines such as mathematics, applied mathematics, statistics, economics, econometrics, and finance. Please note that I leave out computer science, because computer knowledge (including programming skills) is secondary in the career of a quant – computers are tools, not a replacement for analytical competence. Specialized programs are a relatively recent phenomenon and cater expressly to people who desire advanced training related to quantitative finance. They go by such names as quantitative finance, mathematical finance, financial mathematics, financial engineering and analytical finance. It seems that most top business schools now offer this popular route, as running such programs is immensely profitable to the schools (in terms of both current tuition fees and future alumni donations).

If you have a choice, I recommend trying for one of the specialized master's programs first. Here are why:

- They provide training that is relevant to your future career as a Wall Street quant. General-purpose programs usually include courses that are fundamental to the discipline but not too pertinent to Wall Street finance. For example, in economics, coursework in micro and macro theories as well as labor economics is often required. None of these topics applies directly to your job as a Wall Street quant, although some of the modeling approaches you learn can be helpful. Specialized quant finance programs go straight to the heart of the field and allow you to learn only what you will need to work as a competent quant.
- They give comprehensive coverage of the various areas of quantitative finance. Because specialized programs skip over non-relevant materials, they can devote more time to covering all those nuts-and-bolts details in quantitative finance. Many even include computer training to get you familiar with using Excel and programming in a popular language. The end benefit is you get a well-rounded education that touches on every aspect of quant work.

- They are often taught by industry veterans, who can potentially act as your contacts when you look for a job. Remember how I emphasized the importance of establishing helpful contacts back in Chapter 3? Specialized programs are probably some of the best places to do this. Because the course materials are real world-centric, schools usually employ part-time instructors who have full-time Wall Street experience to teach their courses. This is especially true in financial centers like New York, Boston and Chicago. As long as your city or town has a few financial firms or is close to a city with financial firms, you can count on the local finance program being taught by a few practicing professionals. Utilize your instructors to build your job search contact database. In addition, your classmates will be both your competitors and comrades come job hunting time, and you can obtain helpful information from them.

- Because of the close associations between specialized programs and the industry, students in these program often get internship positions. These part-time jobs often act as the jumping boards for full-time jobs after graduation. Furthermore, such close links between programs and the industry give the students ready access to job information on Wall Street. Some of the top schools, for instance, have dedicated career service staff for their quantitative finance programs who can provide immensely valuable services to the students.

As you can see, I'm biased towards specialized programs in quantitative or mathematical finance if you are interested in a master's degree. I just think these programs give you more bang for the buck, so to speak. Of course, they are very expensive – they are among the most profitable curricula at the schools that offer them – and admissions are extremely competitive. But if acquiring a solid foundation – and getting a good taste – of quantitative finance is your goal, as it should be, nothing beats the values of these programs.

What about an MBA, you might ask. In particular, is there any value in getting a finance MBA? The answer is a "maybe" with a tilt toward "no." On the yes side, a finance MBA gives you broad exposure to various topics in finance that are not quantitative in nature; for instance, you'll take classes in corporate finance (investment banking) as well as learn the intricate details of how capital markets and international finance work. But this emphasis on broad exposure as well as a general lack of quant emphasis also means you won't learn much in the way of modeling. Finance MBA programs simply do not include sufficient quantitative training in their typical two-year curricula. If your career goal is to become an investment banker or non-quant trader or corporate executive, then an MBA can give you a worthwhile education – but then, you have been reading the wrong book! For people bent on working as quants – the audience of this book – an MBA is not of much merit since the skill set of an MBA is quite different from that required of a quant. The one exception to this view is, if you already possess strong analytical skills (e.g., you already have an advanced degree in a quantitative discipline) and want to be well grounded in general finance, then an MBA can provide you a strong leg up in launching and thriving in a Wall Street career.

If you are interested in a Ph.D., proceed to the next section for which programs to look out for.

Ph.D. vs. Master's

You already know that the two major graduate degrees relevant to a quant career are a master's or a Ph.D. (Some schools offer a Doctor of Science degree in certain quantitative disciplines) In this section I discuss the pros and cons of each.

A master's program usually takes one to two years. Like in college, your time is devoted to taking classes taught by professors or instructors. Toward the end of the program, you are usually required to write a master's thesis concurrent with your coursework. In order to graduate, you need to pass all your classes as well as the thesis screening.

A Ph.D., on the other hand, is a research degree. You take classes in the first two or two-and-a-half years and devote the rest of your time to full-time research (after you pass a set of qualifying exams). On average, a Ph.D. in economics or finance (or a similar discipline) takes five to six years to complete. Your training culminates in your Ph.D. dissertation, which in economics and finance usually consists of two or three independently produced research papers that may or may not relate to one another. In order to graduate, you must successfully defend your dissertation in front of a committee of professors and scholars; in some cases, your defense will be held in front of the entire department.

Master's and Ph.D. programs aim at producing different types of graduates. A master's degree holder has gained some advanced knowledge on the subject of study. Coupled with independent reading and thesis research, he or she has developed enough practical analytical skills to carry out various modeling tasks on his or her own. A Ph.D., on the other hand, is trained to be an academic researcher who not only possesses a deeper body of knowledge about the subject matter but can think independently and creatively. Please note that there isn't necessarily a correlation between having a Ph.D. or a master's and getting hired as a senior or junior quant. Both degree holders are expected to play senior roles at some point in their careers – although the roles may differ; for example, a senior quant with a master's may focus on model implementation details and be empowered to make decisions on those details, whereas a Ph.D. senior quant may focus on researching new modeling frameworks as well as directing the overall structure of a model.

At this point I want to dispel the myth that in quant finance, a Ph.D. is necessarily better than a master's. In terms of the intrinsic value of the degree, Ph.D. training does provide more in-depth exposure, but it's also often heavy on theory ("academic fluff") and light on practical skills ("real-world substance"). In terms of personal quality, many Ph.D.s never turn out to be the creative and independent thinkers they were trained to be and fail to leverage their research experience fully. This, in part, is due to the nature of working in a pragmatic industry such as finance, where a rocket scientist will be treated worse than the janitor if he or she can't contribute to the bottom line of the firm. (Remember, the rocket scientist is being paid many times more than the janitor.) Ph.D. graduates should hold no illusion that Wall Street is a haven for intellectuals: it's only a haven if you can use your brain power to make money for your employer; otherwise, it's quite a cruel place to be (highly stressful, super-competitive, intoxicatingly money-crazy).

As finance becomes more and more sophisticated quantitatively, the demand for Ph.D. quants has been increasingly steadily. In the world of quant research (as opposed to trading), a Ph.D. is increasingly a prerequisite for moving up the corporate ladder. The fact that many Ph.D.s have made successful transitions to the industry encourages firms to utilize their expertise and independent research abilities in more aspects of finance and to hire more Ph.D.s. into their ranks. The upshot is, if you have a Ph.D. and plan to stay in research, your degree will grant you a golden ticket to a lucrative career in quant research. Otherwise – if you want to be a trader or product manager, for example – a Ph.D. does not necessarily enjoy career advantages over a master's.

Compared to the Ph.D., the master's degree does have one major disadvantage: it's all too common. Even the top-ranked schools churn out scores after scores of master's graduates each year. (Because master's students usually pay for their education whereas Ph.D. students often get full financial support, master's program are lucrative for the universities.) While I wouldn't call this a "dime a dozen" situation at all – I truly believe in the value of a quality master's education – you should keep this in mind if you have just a master's degree or plan to get one. This is also why, in the previous section, I highly recommended one of the specialized quantitative programs to readers who are interested in obtaining a master's – they are less common and therefore offer an aura of uniqueness when it comes to job search time.

Getting a Ph.D., on the other hand, carries more risk as well as opportunity cost than getting a master's. It'll take far longer to graduate – and there's no guarantee that you'll ever graduate if your advisor turns out to be a slave driver interested in usurping the cheap labor of his Ph.D. students or a martinet who won't let a student graduate unless his or her dissertation is "perfect." The drop-out rate among Ph.D. students is high – and for a good reason. In addition, Ph.D. programs (especially in economics and finance) aim to create young professors, and those students who openly talk about going into the industry after graduation are often frowned upon if not hostilely treated.

So, master's or Ph.D.? Here's the answer for you… Drumroll, please… Alas, it depends! It depends on your academic interest, on your time frame (when you want to get a job), on your career goal, and on your personality. If you have any desire of becoming an academic (e.g., a professor), then going for a Ph.D. is your choice, even if eventually you drop that plan and go to Wall Street instead. Otherwise – which I suspect is the case of most readers of this chapter – you need to ask yourself whether committing yourself to five or six years of studying while enjoying no guarantee of obtaining the Ph.D. degree is worthwhile. Of course, Ph.D. students do enjoy financial support, which can be substantial if the program is offered by a business school, as well as a lifestyle that is nothing short of pleasurable or even idyllic. (For example, I really enjoyed the uncountable lazy afternoons when I sat at a sidewalk café near Washington Square in Manhattan and chatted for hours on politics and the dotcom craze with my buddies.)

Must-Take Courses in Grad School

Regardless of the graduate program you are currently (or will be) enrolled in, there are some courses you must take in order to prepare yourself adequately for future quant work on Wall Street.

If you have had no or little exposure to any one of the disciplines in quantitative finance – mathematics, statistics, economics, econometrics (which is distinct from general statistics), finance, and computer science – you must take an introductory course or two at the undergraduate level. If that's the case, refer to the course list in the previous chapter starting on page 175. After you've taken the introductory courses, you can proceed to enrolling in advanced classes for in-depth education.

The graduate-level courses in each of the disciplines which you should take include:

- *Mathematics:* A course or two in calculus are a must, because calculus is the foundation to understanding everything else quantitative. Further coursework in applied mathematics such as linear algebra, differential equations and computation mathematics should be undertaken as well, especially if time allows. These challenging courses not only give you a sound applied mathematical foundation but make you stand out via the résumé – employers always want to hire people who conquer difficulties. If your school offers an operations research course that appeals to you, you may want to check it out and acquire some knowledge about applied optimization.

- *Statistics:* There's probably not much you need to take in this area – I recommend you spend as much time instead on econometrics (including time series), which is the specialized branch of statistics that deals with economics and finance. But if you really, really want to take an advanced stat class, consider one that includes survival analysis (a topic that's not covered in econometrics but increasingly relevant in empirical finance).

- *Economics:* Even though my Ph.D. is in econ, I actually don't think you need to take more than one graduate-level course in this area. Finance has branched out from economics enough to be quite different, so your time would be better spent taking finance classes. One economics class worth taking (but, truth be told, not absolutely necessary) is stochastic processes as applied to economics; be forewarned, though, that it's going to be one tough class, but the benefit is that it gives you exposure to stochastic methods, which are often talked about if not actually used in finance.

- *Econometrics:* Econometrics courses are important for the future Wall Street quant, as quant work is all about implementing empirical models that utilize econometric techniques one way or another. Take as many econometrics classes as you can, and be sure to cover non-linear models, non-parametric methods and that all-important time series. If possible, enroll in classes that are empirical rather than theoretical; while you can learn the theory on your own, you want to maximize your hands-on time in class. Learn as many statistical packages – S-Plus (or its open-source equivalent R), Stata, RATS, SAS, Matlab, etc. – as you can. If you plan to work as a research assistant (RA), find RA work that involves using one of these packages – and try to learn as much about that package as you can.

- *Finance:* Your goal in taking any graduate-level finance courses is to hone your quantitative analytical skills. Continuous-time finance, while extremely challenging (and overly theoretical IMHO), offers you an opportunity to explore some of the most advanced concepts in finance; it also impresses readers of your résumé. (Remember, though, that come interview time you must be well prepared to demonstrate what you learned in class!) If your school offers them, be sure to enroll in a few seminars that focus on quantitative aspects of finance.

- *Computer science:* An algorithm-heavy course (at either the undergrad or grad level) would be helpful for two reasons: one, it teaches you how to think logically, not only at programming time but in general, as algorithms are all about solving problems efficiently; two, most Wall Street quants are lousy programmers, which means those who have a background in algorithms enjoy a tangible competitive advantage.

Given the increasingly competitive landscape in quantitative finance, if you want to travel far, you must arm yourself with as much quant education as possible. I've given you a list of courses that will prepare you well for the battles and journey ahead; I hope you do take my advice to heart and get into the habit of challenging yourself to the fullest if you haven't been doing so already.

For quant-oriented books outside your classes that are worth reading, check out the next chapter.

Chapter Summary

There's little doubt that graduate studies are intellectually satisfying. Part of the reason has to do with the way undergraduate education works in the United States: college students learn the basics but learn a lot, while in-depth topical knowledge is left to graduate-level education. As a grad student, you can use your time to not only satisfy your own intellectual curiosity, but gain the status of a believable quantitative analyst. I want to emphasize that graduate coursework in advanced quant topics is not a "paper tiger" that's only meant to impress others, but can – and should – give you real knowledge you can leverage when you interview for quant positions and become a quant someday.

Chapter 7: Self-Education

In this chapter:

The last two chapters were devoted to helping undergrad and grad students get the "right" kind of education for the quant job search process. The goal of this chapter is twofold: first, to provide self-education information to readers who are no longer in school and not interested in going back to school; second, to recommend books that all readers can read in order to acquire or enhance quant knowledge on their own. Sure, the books listed in this short chapter won't necessarily make you an enlightened quant, but they'll help you acquire or enhance knowledge and skills requisite of Wall Street quants and make you a stronger candidate, regardless of whether you are in or out of school.

In the previous two chapters I mentioned the disciplines that make up what we call quantitative finance. I'll repeat the list here in case you skipped over those two chapters. The disciplines are:

- Mathematics
- Statistics
- Economics
- Econometrics

- Finance
- Computer science

Later on in the chapter I'll devote separate sections to these disciplines. In each section I'll give you a list of books to read and study. But first, to satisfy your impatient intellectual curiosity and thirst for quant finance knowledge, I'll give you a list of "must-read" books.

Power Reading List for the Impatient

The books recommended in this section are must-reads because they cover exactly the kind of quantitative knowledge you need to know if you want to become a Wall Street quant. Each is written specifically for future quants (as well as working ones) and covers a wide range of topics in its subject area. Each book can be used both as a teaching text and as a reference. I find them indispensable in my everyday work as a quant.

In addition, if you have an interviewing coming up, cramming through one of these books can help you get ready for technical questions. Of course, I hope you'll have gained a solid foundation through careful studies, not cramming, by the time you go to an interview. But let's face it: it's impossible for anyone to thoroughly understand and remember everything in quantitative finance, so it'll be good to have a few nice reference books to consult.

Most of these power-read books, however, do require some prior knowledge in mathematics and/or statistics. If you haven't done *any* coursework in these two subjects, consider taking a class or two, or read the books I recommend later in this chapter. Then come back and read these books.

You can buy these books from Amazon.com, BN.com as well as many other bookstores. The Amazon.com links included here point you to the latest U.S. edition as of this writing; they allow you to find the exact books quickly. The price after each link is for a fresh new copy of the book bought on Amazon.com. I highly recommend you buy these books new since they'll be useful to you for a long time to come, even after you become a quant. You can also find more recommended readings on this book's website at

www.quantcareer.com.

Analysis of Financial Time Series, by Ruey S. Tsay
Amazon link:
www.amazon.com/exec/obidos/ASIN/0471690740/pd_bk-20
(~$92)

Tsay is a professor of econometrics and statistics at the University of
Chicago business school and a specialist in analyzing high-frequency
data and applying MCMC methods. His book on financial econometric
modeling has become quite popular among quants and is now in its
2nd edition. The emphasis of the book is on time series analysis of
financial data, from ARCH/GARCH type of models to microstructure
models to extreme value analysis. Other important topics covered
include PCA, multivariate volatility models, MCMC methods, Kalman
filter, and more. This book is very comprehensive in its coverage. The
best thing about it is it's tilted toward application rather than theory.
To that end, the author includes actual computer code segments (for
SCA, RATS or S-Plus) to show you how to implement many of the
estimation techniques. As long as you have a good math background,
you'll find the book accessible and easy to follow. I highly
recommend this book, even if you don't think you'll be dealing with
time series a lot (which, by the way, may be a bit unrealistic as every
field of quantitative finance uses time series). In short, **if there is one
single book on quantitative financial modeling you want to read,
this is the book.** Yes, it's that good.

Options, Futures and Other Derivatives, by John C. Hull
Amazon link:
www.amazon.com/exec/obidos/ASIN/0131499084/pd_bk-20
(~$159)

Hull, a finance professor at the University of Toronto, has written two
popular textbooks on options, futures and derivatives. One is called
Fundamentals of Futures and Options (Amazon link:
www.amazon.com/exec/obidos/ASIN/0131445650/pd_bk-20,
~$151) and is aimed at casual undergraduates. The other book is
Options, Future and Other Derivatives, which is the textbook many
mathematical finance programs use, and it also has a large audience
among Wall Street practitioners. It's written for graduate students as
well as working quants, and contains comprehensive coverage of
topics related to financial derivatives with a fair amount of math that's

nonetheless accessible to readers without special knowledge of advanced math topics such as stochastic processes. If there's one book on options and other derivatives that you want to read, this is it.

Fixed Income Mathematics, by Frank Fabozzi, et al.
Amazon link:
`www.amazon.com/exec/obidos/ASIN/007146073X/pd_bk-20`
(~$57)

Fabozzi is the Frank Sinatra of financial modeling books, as he has churned out over a dozen such books, often co-authored with others. His specialty is fixed income, although he has also published books on other assets (see below for his book on equity modeling). This book is his signature work and offers quant-oriented coverage on a dizzying array of fixed income valuation topics, from pricing of various types of bonds to credit risk analysis to MBS structuring. The beauty of this book is it includes both mathematical pricing and valuation models as well as statistical models, the latter often omitted in fixed income books. If you have set your heart on a quant career in fixed income, this is definitely a must-read book.

Financial Modeling of the Equity Market, by Frank J. Fabozzi, et al.
Amazon link:
`www.amazon.com/exec/obidos/ASIN/0471699004/pd_bk-20`
(~$50)

This book is the latest by the prolific writer Fabozzi (see above), and focuses on quantitative modeling of equity products and portfolios. There's only one short chapter on predicting stock returns; rather, the focus of the book is on risk and cost models as applied to the equity market. In fact, much of the book's quantitative content is rather generic, but the authors do manage to provide an equity backdrop for the discussions. Because I work with equity, I find the book quite helpful, and feel comfortable recommending it to folks interested in this subject.

Self-Education for the Aspiring Quant

The sections that follow give you my recommended reading lists for the various disciplines that make up quantitative finance. These are by no means the only books you can read, but, IMHO, they are the best books to read for their respective subject areas. These books I recommend are not only authoritative and comprehensive, but readily accessible to most people who are smart and inspired to work hard, regardless of whether they have a prior quantitative background or not.

Some readers of this book may wonder whether they really need to read books or whether they can acquire all the relevant knowledge by surfing the Web. My answer is, you should read, and study, the books I recommend below. The reason is simple: even though the Internet is a huge library, a lot of quantitative finance stuff is scattered around, and a lot of the stuff you find is inaccurate, incomplete or misleading – and 99% of the time it's written by someone who can't write in good English. By buying books recommended here, at least you'll take comfort in the assurance that the stuff you study will be accurate and practical, plus the convenience of having these ready-to-use references which save you time and effort in the long run. Obviously you don't need to buy every book listed below, just those that interest you.

For each recommended book, an Amazon.com link is included for your convenience so you can see the latest edition quickly. The inclusion of Amazon.com links here does not constitute an endorsement of that website, although personally I have had very positive experience buying things from them. And I recommend you get your own fresh, new copy of each book you want to buy (Amazon.com price given here for each recommended book), because these books can be used both for teaching purposes and for future reference when you start working as a quant. You can be assured that you'll be using them for many years to come. If you study these books diligently and thoroughly, the return from them will far exceed the costs.

Mathematics

You already know that mathematics is the foundation of everything quant. While not as widely used as statistics and econometrics, mathematical modeling techniques are popular among fixed income researchers as well as derivatives analysts. As I mentioned previously in Chapter 5 (page 171), Wall Street finance is all about asset pricing, one way or another. Mathematics is heavily employed when historical data is not available or reliable, or when the researcher sees the need to come up with a new approach.

What you may not already know is that *applied* mathematics is what's relevant in quant finance. While it's nice to tout your advanced theoretical math knowledge around, Wall Street employers mostly care about what you can do, practically, with your math knowledge. For example, a few years ago people who were string theorists were hotly pursued by Wall Street firms. But after it turned out that few people were true string theorists and that even those who were failed to bring much to the bottom lines of their employers, Wall Street learned a lesson and started emphasizing applied knowledge.

This is actually good news for you. After all, theoretical mathematics is much more difficult to learn than applied mathematics; whereas the former is all about abstract concepts and proofs, the latter is about applications and adopts a data-centric mindset like statistics and econometrics. Applied math is also less boring, although that's not to say studying it is a walk in the park. You still need to apply yourself arduously when you learn the advanced topics.

So, what math do you need to know? Here are *some* examples of the topics you should know well:

- *Calculus:* Derivatives and integrals, limits, implicit functions

- *Optimization:* Kuhn-Tucker conditions, envelope theorems, concave programming

- *Linear algebra:* Matrix and vector manipulations, Euclidean spaces, linear dependence and independence

- *Differential equations:* first- and second-order differential equations, eigenvalues

While you can read up on the abovementioned topics separately, there are books that cover them all from the perspectives of economists and financial analysts. One such book is *Mathematics for Economists* by Simon and Blume (Amazon link: www.amazon.com/exec/obidos/ ASIN/0393957330/pd_bk-20, ~$132). This book is chosen by many master's and Ph.D. programs in economics and finance as an introductory graduate-level math textbook. It's written for students who do not already possess a strong math background (although, truth be told, if you have had little or no exposure to math you may find this book difficult to digest), with application examples in economics and finance. You'll find detailed treatment of the topics mentioned above.

Statistics

Statistics encompasses a wide range of data analysis topics, from probability theory to statistical distributions to regression analysis to hypothesis testing. There's also something called the Bayesian approach which offers an alternative set of techniques that perform statistical analysis differently from the "traditional" way – it's almost like Austrian economics vs. traditional economics.

Because I believe you should focus your attention on econometrics, that special branch of statistics which deals with economics and finance, you should spend most of your reading time on that subject instead of pure statistics. The only exception is learning the fundamentals of probability theory and statistical distributions; I have yet to come across an econometrics book that offers a good exposition on these topics – and understanding these fundamental concepts is crucial to obtaining solid knowledge in statistics/econometrics. The general statistics book I recommend is *Introduction to Mathematical Statistics* by Hogg, et al. (Amazon link: www.amazon.com/exec/obidos/ASIN/0130085073/pd_bk-20, ~$121), an oft-used textbook in graduate economics and finance programs. It's one of the more readable textbooks on this subject, and gives you a solid grounding in the essential knowledge needed to understand more advanced econometric concepts. After you study it, move on to econometrics books (see page 200).

Economics

As finance has spun off more or less completely from economics as a discipline, economics itself is not as important a subject area for the Wall Street quant as it used to be. However, there are economics books that are of interest to anyone working on Wall Street, and one particular book (recommended below) is a must-read for anyone interested in the economic principles behind trading, exchanges and financial markets.

As you may already know, economics comprises of two sub-fields: macroeconomics and microeconomics. If you are interested in how interest rate policy affects the economy or why traders who deal with global financial instruments watch exchange rates with utmost vigilance, you may want to read up on macroeconomics, which studies the overall workings of national economies. Microeconomics, on the other hand, concerns itself with the behavior of agents. Game theory, for example, is usually associated with microeconomics because it's concerned with what individual economic agents – firms, consumers, etc. – do under specific conditions.

For quants, there are regrettably few worthwhile economics books to read. One exception is a microeconomic book on market microstructure (i.e., how financial markets work) written by Larry Harris of USC: *Trading and Exchanges* (Amazon link: www.amazon.com/exec/obidos/ASIN/0195144708/pd_bk-20, ~$66), which has an extensive, in-depth discussion on the economic principles of financial trading and markets. The treatment is non-quantitative, but the book is very accessible even to those without a finance background. I highly recommend this book for would-be quants, so they can gain a solid understanding of the context of their work.

If you absolutely feel the need to study general economics, consider the classic undergraduate-level textbook *Economics: Principles and Policy* by Baumol and Blinder, two venerable academic economists (Amazon link: www.amazon.com/exec/obidos/ASIN/0324221134/pd_bk-20, ~$155). Again, I think you should read an economics textbook like this only if you have plenty of spare time to kill; otherwise, complete your other self-education first.

Econometrics

Econometrics, including time series analysis, is heavily employed in the analysis of historical financial data and in forecasting. Its applications can be found everywhere in quantitative finance, from volatility forecasting to asset pricing to performance attribution. It's probably safe to say that every quant will use econometric methods at least some of the time. For quants who work in data mining areas such as statistical arbitrage, convertible arbitrage, volatility arbitrage, pattern-based forecasting, etc., econometrics is *the* weapon in their lines of work.

Econometrics originated in economic applications of general statistics. As economics and finance became increasingly sophisticated disciplines in their own right, econometricians have developed specialized techniques for confronting estimation issues specific to economic and financial data. For example, economic and financial data often exhibit non-constant variance in the error term in a regression model; this behavior is called heteroskedasticity (alternatively spelled as heteroscedasticity), and was first studied extensively by econometricians. Econometrics, however, is not isolated from developments in general statistics and other offshoot disciplines of statistics. An example is the increasing use of survival analysis, first developed by biostatisticians and now often employed in finance to make predictions such as the probability of a limit order getting executed and the probability of an option getting exercised before expiration.

Econometrics can be roughly divided into three major areas: microeconometrics (also known as cross-sectional modeling), time series analysis (occasionally called macroeconometrics), and panel data modeling. Some less-used topics include non-parametric methods and Bayesian techniques. Monte Carlo methods, popular among quants, cut across the entire topical spectrum of econometrics. I recommend you become proficient with the three main areas first, before attempting any further education.

Microeconometrics is concerned mainly with cross-sectional analysis, that is, statistical relationships among members from a data group. For example, the group may be the stock market where the members are the individual stocks, and the relationship we study may be how differences in P/E affect the stocks' prices. Microeconometrics practitioners also spend a lot of time trying to understand what happens when crucial assumptions are violated; for example, what happens to parameter estimates when a significant independent variable is omitted or when there's endogeneity in the system. For financial economists, the most important microeconometric models include discrete-choice models (e.g.., logit and probit), truncated sample models (e.g., Tobit), and linear models.

Time series analysis involves the relationship between a data variable and one or more of its lagged values (plus possibly other variables). The introduction of the lagged value or values brings on some special modeling issues which in turn necessitates some special techniques, and that's the subject of study in time series. For financial quants, the poster child of macroeconometrics is GARCH and its related models, which are heavily employed in modeling asset volatility. You can bet that if you are asked a question on time series at an interview, it'll likely be about GARCH. (So if you claim to be a time series expert, know GARCH and its cousins well!)

Panel data consists of observations across individual members of a group (e.g., stocks) as well as across time. Panel data modeling aims to estimate the parameter values efficiently. (The term efficiency carries a special meaning in statistics; a discussion is unfortunately beyond the scope of this book.) In finance, you often come across panel data when you need to analyze multiple securities (or asset classes) over different time periods.

For a practical introduction to econometrics as practiced in finance, consider Chris Brooks's *Introductory Econometrics for Finance* (Amazon link: www.amazon.com/exec/obidos/ASIN/ 052179367X/pd_bk-20, ~$37). While it does not cover every financial econometrics topic under the sun, it serves as a good first course in this important topic. For example, it even devotes a chapter on selecting the right econometric software for use. Its accessibility makes it a good read for those who are not yet familiar with econometrics. Another plus about the book is it's quite affordable (at least it is so on Amazon).

If you are interested in a more academic approach to studying econometrics, you may be interested in NYU professor William H. Greene's *Econometric Analysis* (Amazon link for current edition: www.amazon.com/exec/obidos/ASIN/0130661899/pd_bk-20, ~$157 – upcoming new edition for fall 2007: www.amazon.com/ exec/obidos/ASIN/0135132452/pd_bk-20, ~$160). Greene's book is the standard econometrics text in most graduate economics programs, and it also serves well as a reference. Its key feature is a right mix of theory and application, and the book can be used often when you need to figure out how to implement a model or how to explain why a model should be chosen. As a textbook it's expensive, but you can find good deals on Amazon and other websites, including poorly-printed "international editions" originally sold in India.

Last but not least, Ruey S. Tsay's *Analysis of Financial Time Series* (Amazon link: www.amazon.com/exec/obidos/ASIN/ 0471690740/pd_bk-20, ~$92) makes a great introductory and reference read for time series modeling in finance. As I mentioned previously on page 195, if there's just one book on financial econometrics you want to read, Tsay's book fits the bill.

Finance

Interestingly, a lot of Wall Street quant positions do not require much finance knowledge. I actually know fairly successful quants who know very little finance beyond the one or two concepts they come into immediate contact with in their everyday work. Still, instead of guessing whether you'll ever need finance knowledge when you get the job, it's important to learn the fundamental financial concepts, not the least because you may be asked finance questions at interviews.

The one general investment finance book I recommend is the modestly titled *Investments* by Bodie, et al. (Amazon link: www.amazon.com/exec/obidos/ASIN/007331465X/pd_bk-20, ~$152). This popular textbook, recently updated, serves up a respectable introduction to the many important concepts (such as CAPM, APT, portfolio theory, fixed income pricing, derivatives valuation, etc.) in finance. One may say the book lacks depth – its target audience are undergrads and early graduate students – but there's no denying that if you have no prior exposure to concepts in finance, this is a good place to start.

Quantitative finance often deals with pricing of financial derivatives. Hull's book (Amazon link: www.amazon.com/exec/obidos/ASIN/0131499084/pd_bk-20, ~$159), which I recommended earlier on page 195, gives a comprehensive and accessible treatment on important topics related to derivative modeling. A lot of job candidates pride themselves in the fact that they have read Hull's book. Well, I don't think reading the book (or any book) alone turns a non-quant into a quant, but Hull's volume does dispense a good education on its covered topics.

For specifics of fixed income and equity modeling, consider the two Fabozzi books I recommended earlier on page 196.

Many would-be quants are intrigued by hedge funds, that part of the financial industry that perennially gets heavy coverage in the business media because of their fast growth (in terms of both assets under management, or AUM, and the number of hedge funds), their tendency to cloak themselves in secrecy, and their exaggerated boom-or-bust nature. If you count yourself among those curious as to what exactly hedge funds do to make (or lose) money, a book worth reading is *Investment Strategies of Hedge Funds* by Filippo Stefanini (Amazon link: www.amazon.com/exec/obidos/ASIN/0470026278/

pd_bk-20, ~$50), which unlike other hedge fund books is written as a reference on strategies hedge funds employ. It's not a quantitative read but can be quite an eye opener.

Computer Science

This section is going to be long because there is not a single title on the market that covers all the computer skills a quant needs to possess. Instead, you must tackle each area of computer knowledge individually.

While you can pick up some programming skills by studying econometrics and using statistical analysis packages like Matlab or SAS, you won't become a competent programmer until you read a good programming book and learn not only the syntax of a programming language but the way a good programmer thinks and writes code.

You may not think highly of programming or programmers (also known as "developers" on Wall Street). Well, if I ask you to count the number of American billionaires who began their careers as computer programmers, would that help change your attitude toward programming? I hope so. In fact, Wall Street quants find themselves programming all the time. Model implementation means writing computer code to read in and analyze data or to simulate real-world phenomena. As the amount of data quants deal with explodes exponentially each year, the art of programming becomes all the more important. Indeed, there are now a lot of "mini quants" on Wall Street who are a hybrid between a traditional quant and a programmer; they have some basic quant modeling skills, and they spend most of their time writing programs. A (traditional) quant who does not possess adequate programming skills will necessarily find his or her opportunities limited – unless he or she doesn't plan to stay in a research role for long.

The first order of business is to learn a real programming language – real as opposed to statistics-oriented packages like Matlab, Stata or SAS. As object-oriented programming (OOP) languages such as C++ and C# become increasingly popular on Wall Street, and as more and more model implementations are done using these languages, it's a good idea to get acquainted with at least one of them. The old C ("ANSI C") is being phased out more or less, so your focus should be on C++, C# or Java. For C++, a good book to learn from is

C++ Primer Plus by Stephen Prata (Amazon link: www.amazon.com/exec/obidos/ASIN/0672326973/pd_bk-20, ~$35). Its 1,000-plus pages are packed with detailed information about the language and lots of code examples.

Because empirical modeling in finance involves working with data – large amounts of data – many quant shops also use a data-processing language such as Perl or Python for text-based (ASCII) data files and SQL (pronounced "sequel") for database access. SQL, in particular, is a very useful language to learn, as few people on Wall Street know SQL but it's gaining fast in popularity. You can put in some time on Perl or Python if you are so inclined; my feeling is that as long as you are proficient in C++ or one of its offshoots, you can pick up Perl and Python pretty quickly.

To learn SQL, consider *Learning SQL* by Alan Beaulieu (Amazon link: www.amazon.com/exec/obidos/ASIN/1600330525/pd_bk-20, ~$35). For Perl programming, I highly recommend *Sams Teach Yourself Perl in 21 Days* by Lemay, et al. (Amazon link: www.amazon.com/exec/obidos/ASIN/0672320355/pd_bk-20, ~$30); its emphasis on hands-on Perl coding makes the language easy to learn. If you want to learn Python, *Beginning Python: From Novice to Professional* by Magnus Lie Hetland (Amazon link: www.amazon.com/exec/obidos/ASIN/159059519X/pd_bk-20, ~$28) will be a good place to start.

Being a good programmer is much more than just knowing the syntax of some programming language. You need to think like a computer, and that means knowing something about algorithms. For each programming problem, there are usually many different ways to write the code, but only one particular way is the most efficient from the perspective of computer resource (CPU, memory, storage, etc.) utilization; and this is what algorithms are all about: finding the most efficient way to solve a problem via computer programming. For instance, if I give you a dataset containing 1.3 billion unsorted numbers (say, the annual income of every individual in China or India) and ask you to find the median in the shortest amount of time possible, how would you do it? Sorting 1.3 billion numbers is no easy task even with "traditional" sorting algorithms such as quick sort. Hopefully, after doing some reading on algorithms, you'll be able to solve this problem. (Hint: you do not really need a completely sorted list of the 1.3 billion numbers, but you do need to break down the 1.3 billion data points into smaller chunks and still sort only the chunk that contains the population median.) A good introductory book on the subject is *Beginning Algorithms* by Harris and Ross (Amazon link: `www.amazon.com/exec/obidos/ASIN/0764596748/pd_bk-20`, ~$26).

So far I've been talking about programming skills. What about general IT knowledge? First of all, you should be familiar with Microsoft Windows. Most Wall Street firms have standardized on Windows XP Professional, with some firms still relying on the older Windows 2000. Eventually firms will move over to Windows Vista, the latest version of Windows, but that's not likely to happen before 2009. Second, knowledge of the Microsoft Office suite, particularly Excel, is helpful for most quant positions and required for some. Apropos Office, you may also want to look into learning some VBA (Visual Basic for Applications, a mini programming language for writing Office macros); VBA is very easy to learn and can not only enhance your candidacy but make your Office life a lot easier later on. Third, quite a few firms still employ UNIX servers for data-intensive tasks, so basic UNIX skills can be helpful and make you stand out among the job candidates. If you want to go fancy on UNIX, learn one of the shell programming languages or Perl. As to the question which text editor, vi or emacs, you should learn on UNIX, I'm rather agnostic, and I encourage to find a friend who already knows one of them and learn from him or her. (In case you are curious, I use vi, but that's mainly because when I started using UNIX 20 years ago, emacs was still crude whereas vi was much easier to learn as well as more user-friendly.)

Here are the books that help you pick up the general computing skills mentioned in the previous paragraph:

- *Windows XP:* Wow, you must have been hiding under some rock in Utah if you don't already know how to use Windows! Oh, well, in case you do need to pick up basic Windows skills, check out the excellently produced, beginner-oriented *Microsoft Windows XP Step by Step* (Amazon link: `www.amazon.com/exec/obidos/ASIN/0735621144/pd_bk-20`, ~$20).

  What about Windows Vista, the latest (and greatest) version of Windows? My take is Vista won't become ubiquitous in the business world until 2009 at the earliest, and since it's based on Windows XP, your XP skills will prepare you well for the future Vista days.

- *Microsoft Office:* The programs you should know are Excel, Word and PowerPoint. It would also be nice to know Outlook, the e-mail program Wall Street firms have migrated to or are in the middle of migrating to. Most firms now use Office 2003; an en masse move to the newer Office 2007 is unlikely to occur anytime soon as that version features a drastically different user interface which will take a significant amount of time for users of all previous versions of Office to adjust to. A good beginner's guide is *Office 2003 Simplified* by Sherry W. Kinkoph (Amazon link: `www.amazon.com/exec/obidos/ASIN/0764599593/pd_bk-20`, ~$19).

  By the way, if you don't already have Office installed on your PC, you can download a trial version of Office 2003 (the version I recommend, *not* Office 2007) on Microsoft's website, or get the ~$130 Microsoft Office Student and Teacher Edition 2003 (Amazon link: `www.amazon.com/exec/obidos/ASIN/B0000C0XT1/pd_bk-20`), which allows you to install the software on up to three PCs (a really great deal!).

  There's a book called *Advanced Modelling in Finance Using Excel and VBA* British authors Jackson and Staunton (Amazon link: `www.amazon.com/exec/obidos/ASIN/0471499226/pd_bk-20`, ~$60), which combines Excel learning with financial modeling. It doesn't attempt to treat either subject in-depth, but can be useful when you need to know exactly how to do something specific in Excel.

- *VBA:* Visual Basic for Applications is useful and fun to learn. You can pick up some basic VBA knowledge from the abovementioned *Advanced Modelling in Finance Using Excel and VBA* (Amazon link: `www.amazon.com/exec/obidos/ASIN/0471499226/pd_bk-20`, ~$60). For more in-depth learning – especially if you want to use VBA across the entire Office suite, not just in Excel – check out *Mastering VBA* by Guy Hart-David (Amazon link: `www.amazon.com/exec/obidos/ASIN/0782144365/pd_bk-20`, ~$26). If you have Office on your computer, you already have access to VBA.

- *UNIX:* Almost 40-years-old, UNIX is still widely used by quants, especially those into hardcore programming. A good introductory-yet-comprehensive book is *Unix for the Impatient* by Abrahams and Larson (Amazon link: `www.amazon.com/exec/obidos/ASIN/0201419793/pd_bk-20`, ~$54). If you are good with tinkering with computers, you can install Linux on your PC to practice. Do keep in mind that each flavor of UNIX and Linux can differ significantly in command syntax, so you'll need some adjustment when your employer uses a different version of UNIX or Linux than the one you are accustomed to.

- *UNIX shell programming:* The standard book is the aptly titled *Unix Shell Programming* by Kochan and Wood (Amazon link: `www.amazon.com/exec/obidos/ASIN/0672324903/pd_bk-20`, $23). For Perl, which is related to shell programming, check out the book I recommended earlier, *Sams Teach Yourself Perl in 21 Days* (Amazon link: `www.amazon.com/exec/obidos/ASIN/0672320355/pd_bk-20`, ~$30), for a quick yet effective introduction.

To CFA or Not to CFA

I'm often asked the question by would-be quants: should I enroll in the CFA program?

In case you didn't know, CFA stands for Chartered Financial Analyst. It's a certificate title bestowed on folks who have met educational and experience requirements established by an organization called the CFA Institute (website: `www.cfainstitute.org`) and passed all three levels of the CFA exam. One common misconception among people considering getting the CFA title is that they can become a CFA once they pass all three exams. Not so easy! You'll still need to meet the education and experience requirements; for example, you must have a certain number of years working in an approved industry and in an approved capacity in order to qualify for the title (or charter, as the CFA Institute calls it). You'll also need the sponsorship of an existing CFA before you become one yourself; this, I suppose, lends an air of exclusivity to the title.

The CFA is largely a buy-side phenomenon; few people on the sell side care about the title, let alone go for it. In particular, the CFA is popular among people who work in asset management such as mutual funds. The three CFA exams – and the necessary preparations for these exams – cover a wide range of topics in finance, but the emphasis is far from the kind of quantitative analysis (mathematical and statistical modeling) we have been talking about in this book. In fact, you'll spend a lot of time on things like reading corporate earnings statements and basic accounting, topics that aren't pertinent to a typical Wall Street quant's work. The positive aspect of this broad exposure, of course, is you may leverage your CFA in getting into non-quant areas of Wall Street finance, particularly on the buy side.

Some people look at the CFA as an alternative to getting a master's degree. I think that's a fair view – but only for non-quants. Readers aspiring to be quants should enroll in a quantitative analysis-heavy graduate program. Still, if you (a future quant, I presume) are interested in getting into the buy side, getting a CFA, or enrolling in the CFA program, can be advantageous, especially if you are getting or already have an advanced degree.

So, if you are 100% sure you'll only go to the sell side (e.g., becoming a trader or analyst on a prop desk), you can safely skip the CFA. Also, if you already have an economics or finance Ph.D. , or have a master's degree in mathematical finance, you don't really need the CFA, either. If you are contemplating a serious career on the buy side, you should definitely start the CFA program as soon as possible – especially if you don't know for sure whether you'll want to work as a quant forever. If you can't decide between the buy side and the sell side, consider enrolling in the program anyway; the costs – for the studying materials and the exams – aren't prohibitively high (and may be tax-deductible – consult your tax advisor), and becoming a CFA (or just passing the exams) can never be disadvantageous.

(Caveat to the last statement: once you get on the CFA track, many potential employers expect you to finish it. Quitting would look bad, if only in the short term.)

Chapter Summary

This chapter has shown you how to acquire quantitative knowledge on your own. All the books recommended here, of course, can be used to supplement your in-school education. It's important for me to emphasize here that as you read the modeling books, make sure you understand the big picture: what problem is the model trying to solve, what are the crucial assumptions, and what data inputs would you need to implement the model. Just passively reading a bunch of books doesn't make you a quant; if you find opportunities to practice what you've learned – doing the exercises in the books certainly counts – you'll find yourself a well-educated future quant.

EXPERIENCE: ACQUIRE REAL-WORLD SKILLS

Chapter 8: Working While in School

In this chapter:

No matter how much book- or class-based education you get, it cannot substitute for real-world experience – relevant real-world experience, that is. This is not to say education is not important. But what you learn from reading a few quantitative analysis books or taking a quantitative class is quite different from how things are actually done "on the street." For example, in everyday quant work, dealing with data, from collecting to cleaning to exporting, occupies an enormous amount of time, whereas in class, you are usually handed a small and clean dataset to practice with. A candidate with practical experience inevitably looks stronger in the eyes of potential employers than one with similar education but no experience in the real-world of quantitative analysis.

If you are in school, this chapter discusses what kinds of practical experience you should acquire and how you can do it. For those readers who are already working full-time in an industry outside of quant finance, please proceed to the next chapter.

You can gain practical quant experience in several ways:

- You can stay in academia and either work as a research assistant for an economics or finance professor or carry out your own quant research projects (in addition to what you are required to do, e.g., Ph.D. dissertation research). Either way, your experience should give you ample exposure to empirical research methodologies.

- You can find a part-time job with a financial firm. Since you are also attending classes, this means the firm must be located nearby, for example, in the same city or town.

- You can find a full-time summer job with a financial firm. This gives you much more flexibility in choosing where you want to work and thus opens up more opportunities. Many Wall Street firms also have systematic summer internship programs whereas they may not have many part-time positions available.

In order of preference, I'd recommend a full-time summer position first. If for some reason you can't work full-time in the summer, consider a summer-time or academic-year part-time position – assuming there are such opportunities in your locale. Doing academic projects alone has a lot of limitations, chief among them the usually narrow focus of such a project. This constrains both the topics and the methodologies you'll be exposed to. Therefore, I highly recommend a "real" job if possible.

Here I should point out that some Ph.D. programs go to extraordinary lengths to discourage their Ph.D. students from working in the industry, either during school or after graduation. If you are in such a Ph.D. program, you should talk to a trusted advisor or your fellow students first. You may not want to jeopardize your chances of graduating successfully and obtaining your Ph.D. within the timeframe you had set in mind. (On the other hand, if you are unsure of whether to continue with your Ph.D. education or quit midway through, a summer internship or part-time job may just be the perfect opportunity to help you make that decision.)

Quant Internships

By internships, I refer to part-time and summer positions regardless of whether the actual position is called an internship position – after all, when you get such a position you are essentially a trainee trying to gain experience, which is the definition of an intern. Most internships are paid, although your local financial companies may only have a few unpaid positions. Whether getting paid on an internship is important depends on your own perspective on life as well as on how much actual work you'll be expected to put in.

The kind of work you'll perform and the type of experience you'll gain vary greatly among firms as well as among specific departments (e.g., equity vs. fixed income, agency desk vs. prop trading desk). If you are an undergraduate, you'll likely be asked to carry out some of the more mundane duties of a junior quant – such as entering data into a database or spreadsheet or writing simple programs to read in data. If you are a graduate student, you'll be more or less treated like a part-time junior quant (even when you work full-time in the summer); this means you'll be involved at a higher level than an undergraduate intern, but your involvement will likely focus on short-term projects rather than long-term tasks. Some firms – many trading desks in particular – may be wary of "letting out the secret" (trade secret) to temporary workers such as interns. Remember, your goal is to acquire practical experience, and an internship will give you ample exposure to what Wall Street quants do and how they do it. That exposure (together with the money, I suppose) should more than compensate for any "hardship" you might have to overcome as you get your first taste of high finance.

Chances are, there is just as much, if not more, competition for internship positions as there is for regular quant jobs. This is especially true with regard to the major Wall Street firms in New York. These firms have quite a few summer and academic-year internships available, but the number of applicants is usually several times the number of positions. There are two things to keep in mind as you embark on the journey to finding an internship job.

First, start early. More so than with regular positions, firms tend to be considerably positive about internship candidates who apply early. This is so, I think, because firms see all interns as more or less the same. In other words, whereas a full-time quant is expected to be highly competent and contribute to the firm's bottom line, an intern is still looked upon as a "kid" who is not expected to contribute much but who is in the market for experience. Wall Street firms are very happy to accommodate the ambitions of these "kids" – their youthfulness may have reminded many a senior Wall Street quant of their own intern days – and those who show early enthusiasm are looked upon favorably. So, once you decide you want to be a Wall Street quant, get your internship search going as soon as possible.

Second, remember that internship positions are usually unadvertised. Because interns are not seen, and usually not treated, as regular employees, internships are rarely announced or posted. In fact, many such positions are created on the spot, or whenever a manager sees it fit to hire an intern. (The amount of money involved in recruiting an intern is miniscule compared to that for recruiting a full-timer.) Many internship positions are rewarded to applicants who come in through contacts or cold calling. Contacts, in particular, are very important for finding and getting an internship position. If you know anyone who works in finance, lobby them to find you an internship position. Your school's career office can also be helpful in hooking you up with a Wall Street person.

Many Wall Street firms also participate in various programs that recruit interns who fit certain characteristics, such as being ethnic minority, being female or having some special kind of background. If you are non-white, you should be aware that some programs designed to bring minorities to Wall Street define minority groups to be only black, Hispanic or Native American (so-called "underrepresented minorities"). Before you apply to any such minority-only programs, be sure to check whether you qualify. To find these programs, contact your school's career services office.

In general, the most straightforward way to finding internship positions is to simply write to the firms you are interested in and ask them whether they are interested in hiring an intern. Because you are essentially cold-calling, your cover letter must be crafted carefully. It should contain two important points. First, it should reflect your enthusiasm for working in finance and eagerness for learning the trade. Second, it should tell the reader your qualifications. The qualifications are more than academic skills, though. Employers usually like to hire interns who are easy-going (the "interns are kids" psychology), so candidates who exude a high sense of collegiality will usually get ahead. In the letter, give a brief, real example from your life to show the employer that you'll make a good intern who will be liked by everyone else on the team. Of course, everything in your cover letter and in your résumé must be absolutely truthful. The last thing you want to do is lie about your background – because all liars find their pants on fire sooner or later. (Remember, interns working in the financial industry go through extensive background checks just like full-time employees, as mandated by Federal law.)

Interviewing for an internship is very similar to interviewing for a full-time quant position. The only key difference is intern interviews are shorter. For example, when you are brought on-site, instead of meeting with 8-10 people from the team, you'll probably talk to two or three, including the boss. Whereas hiring a full-timer often takes some degree of consensus, decisions on interns are usually made by just the boss. You'll still need to impress everyone else that you come into contact with at the interview, though, because you don't want one person to dislike you so much that he or she will do everything to sabotage your chances.

Interns aren't expected to be knowledgeable or skillful – although those who already know a few things about quantitative modeling will be more likely to land a job. (But then, your chances at landing an internship position also depend on whom you know, more so than with regard to regular full-time positions.) What employers look for in an intern are:

- *Enthusiasm:* Bosses like interns who are energetic and work hard on the job.

- *Intellectual curiosity:* Interns should exhibit an eagerness to learn, to excel. They should not be afraid to ask questions.

- *Maturity:* Despite being seen as "kids," interns are nonetheless expected to be able to follow all the rules of being a Wall Street professional, such as showing up for work every day and taking responsibility for their work.

- *Adequate computer skills:* As quant interns are often employed in the performance of "dirty work" (such as data collection and cleaning), computer skills are highly valued by employers. Some firms require strong Excel knowledge, while others demand proficient programming skills.

- *Obedience:* Employers don't want to hire young interns who turn out to be clones of Dennis the Menace (remember him?). They want docile interns who dutifully follow orders.

You may have heard horror stories about Wall Street interns who spend an entire summer fetching coffee and pizza for traders or xeroxing paperwork. The fact is, quant interns won't be engaged in such low-level tasks. They are hired to help with modeling work and that's where they'll be put to work. Of course, given their lack of analytical experience, quant interns usually spend most of their time writing programs that are part of the overall model implementation process or otherwise doing tasks that don't fit the quantitative label.

To some extent, an intern is like an apprentice: you perform the most basic tasks (which may include, but will definitely be far more than, fetching coffee for others), and you learn the tricks of the trade by observing and learning. Let me repeat it again: your goal of working as an intern is to find out what it is like to be a quant as well as to gain practical skills. These intern skills will mainly be in programming and conducting background research, both of which are essential ingredients of a quant modeling process.

An internship also serves as a self-discovery tool. After three months of working 13 hours a day and not having lunch breaks, you may decide that a career on Wall Street is not for you. After toiling through thousands lines of C++ code that does nothing more than reading in some stupid data and manipulating them into forms of suspicious value, you may decide working as a quant is too boring for the one life you've got to live. After seeing all the questionable shortcuts taken in the modeling process, you may decide Wall Street research is little more than voodoo art. In fact, many trading desk interns leave their positions totally unimpressed with the quality of work and life, or even disgusted with the permeating vulgarity among traders. A Wall Street career is not for everybody. It's better to find out early on, when you are young and have no long-term attachments, rather than later in your career.

You may find it advantageous to get internship experience in different quant research areas. For example, one summer you may work in equity research, the next summer you may work in derivatives trading. Or you may spend half a year part-timing in portfolio management and another six months part-timing in trading strategies. The possibilities and opportunities are endless, and I encourage you to explore as much as you like. More so than junior quants, a quant intern can afford to dabble in many different areas until he or she finds something to the liking.

If, at any time during your internship, you find yourself abused or harassed or hazed, you should bring this up with the group manager or the HR contact. Even if you aren't sure of your judgment – for instance, you feel that a coworker is hitting on you in an unwelcome way but you aren't sure of it because he seems subtle and/or sophisticated in his approach – you should bring this to the attention of HR. Of course, talking to a friend or a trusted coworker first can also be helpful. The last decade has seen remarkable progress on Wall Street toward taking employees' complaints seriously, thanks in part to high-profile lawsuits brought by employees who felt they had been harassed or abused. Every person, including interns, deserves respect. Unfortunately, a lot of Wall Street high rollers (or those who think they are high rollers) still don't understand this. Fortunately, their lawyers will put the leash on them if other people complain of harassment.

Most likely, your quant internship will be a pleasant one, even if not as exciting or fulfilling as you had expected. The rewarding part is not the money itself (although New York firms usually pay interns pretty well), but what you learn and what you observe on the job. I hope you'll like your internship enough to pursue a full-time career in quant finance.

Academic Research

If you want to put off job search for now, or if you find interesting research projects in school, it's perfectly okay to gain research experience the academic way. The only advice I have is, get involved in empirical research projects, not theoretical ones. Empirical research means using data to test theory, and that's exactly what quants on Wall Street do. By participating in empirical research – either as a research assistant or carrying out your own research agenda – you learn how to acquire data, how to clean data, how to transform data, how to resolve modeling issues (such as which particular estimation form to employ), how to summarize and interpret results, etc. Even if you are engaged in just parts of the research process, be sure to learn well. Ask a lot of questions. Do your own background research. Gain a thorough understanding of the problems at hand. Explore the pros and cons of potential solutions. Yes, this is a lot of work – probably more than what you have signed up for – but you'll gain valuable empirical research experience.

Chapter Summary

The résumés that come in front of a quant employer all exhibit adequate education. What sets a candidates apart from the rest is usually the practical experience and the skills associated with the experience. Having relevant experience means you've been in the trenches and can get up to speed on the new job faster than someone who's never done anything beyond taking classes.

If possible, find an internship (summer-time or part-time during school year) in quant analysis at some financial firm. Even if the work turns out boring, you'll gain firsthand experience in working in quantitative finance. If you prefer to stay in academic research, be sure to participate in empirical work that gives you ample exposure to data-centric modeling.

Chapter 9: Already a Full-Timer

In this chapter:

You have been working full-time. Maybe you are unhappy with your current job, or maybe you don't like the current career prospect, or maybe you've heard that people on Wall Street make a lot more money. Or perhaps you just got laid off and want to do something different. In any case, you want to become a Wall Street quant. This chapter discusses how you can evaluate your existing experience in the context of quant qualification and how you can acquire quantitative experience if you don't already have enough of it.

Evaluating Your Quantitative Skills

The first thing you need to ask yourself is, "Do I have any quantitative analysis skills?" This is important to know for two reasons. First, it allows you to identify quantitative skills you already possess and can thus offer to your future employer. Second, it also identifies areas where your skills come up short.

In general, you have done quantitative analysis on your current or past job if you have performed *all* of the following tasks:

- Collected data for analysis
- Employed a mathematical or statistical model to analyze the data
- Interpreted the analytical results

Notice that I left out the task of designing a model from this list. Since most junior analysts are not involved in this step, it's common for people to know quantitative techniques (i.e., the implementation) without fully understanding why a particular model is implemented.

In addition, you should have been involved in actually using a quantitative model. This means if all you did was to code someone else's step-by-step formulas, you cannot be considered to have worked in quantitative analysis. After all, analysis requires both understanding the problem and the details of the solution methodology. This is what separates an analyst from a developer, even though a developer also possesses important skills.

If you have never done any quantitative work, you need to start from the beginning. You need to acquire the necessary skills. If this applies to you, simply consult the chapters in the previous section for tips on how to obtain a quant finance education.

If you do have some background in quantitative analysis, the next question is, is your quantitative knowledge relevant to the quant job you'd like to have? For example, someone who has worked in biostatistics and is intimately familiar with survival analysis may find the concepts and techniques in areas like bond pricing and portfolio construction quite alien, as an entirely different quantitative approach is employed. As another example, a good C++ programmer may find it necessary to learn a mathematical programming language like Matlab or a statistical programming package like SAS or SPSS, and the "cultural shock" in using the latter group will likely be enormous.

The good news is, quant finance encompasses an increasingly larger body of quantitative methodologies, and many models previously not in the realm of quantitative finance, such as survival analysis, are being adapted to financial applications. This means people possessing quant skills in all kinds of disciplines can find a "home" on Wall Street. The most important qualification for being a quant is twofold: first, you must be smart – you can think for yourself and find solutions to problems; second, you must be willing to work hard. The truth is, any smart person can learn bond pricing, option pricing, equity analysis, and whatnot. You already have the general quantitative aptitude; all that matters now is the attitude.

That said, if you can show a future employer that you have also acquired quant knowledge specific to finance, you *will* make yourself a stronger candidate (if nothing else, it shows the right kind of attitude!). So, if your existing analytical knowledge is far from what a quant should have, start acquiring quant knowledge now. You may consider enrolling in a specialized quantitative finance program as discussed in Chapter 6, or you may simply read the books I recommended in Chapter 7. Whatever you do, do *not* dwell on your existing knowledge base. Expand it. Make your skills highly relevant to a career in quant finance.

Skills and Starting Position

As you explore a possible new career in quant finance, there's one important item to keep in mind: the level of your starting position – the title, the pay, the status within the corporate hierarchy – depends on how relevant your existing knowledge is. To a Wall Street employer, most candidates for quant positions are pretty smart. Sure, some are smarter than others, but there's no way for an employer to tell ahead of time whether a candidate will make a successful quant, his or her achievements in the past notwithstanding.

Given this information asymmetry between the employer and the candidate, the employer usually takes the easy way out: hire someone who already has the skills and knowledge needed to do the job. (This is a case of *signaling* in economics.) For those readers who already possess quant skills in other fields but not in finance, this has one significant implication for their job-hunting approach: try to find a job that will take maximum advantage of your existing skills. That way, you'll be able to start your new career at a more senior level instead of having to begin your quant career as a junior person possibly at the bottom. Your existing skills will also not go wasted on the new job. Of course, if you are absolutely willing to start from the bottom of the ladder, all options are open to you, but I still recommend first trying to find a job that can leverage your current skills; only when such jobs are unavailable should you broaden the range of quant jobs you would be willing to take.

Leveraging Contacts

In Chapter 3, I emphasized the importance and value of establishing and leveraging your contacts in the finance industry. This is especially true for full-timers, as they usually do not enjoy the advantage of having access to a university career office that can help students reach out to potential employers.

As you search for quant jobs, be sure to inquire among the people you already know – and those you don't know personally but have knowledge of. For example, you might have heard of someone in your field who has made a successful switch into quant finance. It wouldn't hurt to try to contact him or her for advice and help. Or you discover that a coworker's wife's brother's cousin is a hotshot quant; it might be worthwhile to pursue this lead and ask your coworker to set up a social call for you. The possibilities are limitless. All that takes is some courage, maybe even some degree of audacity. If you are the shy type, you can take comfort in the two facts that, first, it never hurts to *ask* someone for help, and second, most people do enjoy lending help to others. Just be polite and explain why you need the help. Never behave in a way that can be interpreted as rude. Remember, patience is a virtue, especially when it comes to seeking someone else's assistance. For example, after you ask your coworker to set up a meeting with a potential contact, give the coworker some time to make the arrangements. Don't pester him or her with the meeting request, or you'll end up alienating the one person who can help you.

Should you ask your current boss for help? I think the answer is obvious: if you are on good terms with him and her and know he or she will encourage you to find the best opportunity for yourself, by all means approach him or her for advice and help. If your boss is a jerk (e.g., he or she is one reason why you want to leave your current position) or if you want to keep your ambitious career plans secret, you should avoid tipping him or her off.

Chapter Summary

If you are currently working full-time but have never used the same quantitative tools Wall Street quants use, you need to acquire the necessary knowledge and skills. Doing so both enhances your chances of finding a quant job and prepares you well for a new career ahead.

BRIGHT FUTURE: GO FAR AND PROSPER

Chapter 10: Evaluating Offers and Starting Job

In this chapter:

Congratulations! After all the hard work, you now have a job offer in your hand. Maybe you have more than one offer. It's time to celebrate… and think about what to do next.

This chapter deals with the euphoria, and confusion, over the offer you just received: how to evaluate its terms, how to negotiate (and whether you *should* negotiate), and how to work two or more offers to your greatest advantage. It also dispenses some practical advice on the first days on the quant job – what to expect, how to deal with new coworkers, and what to do when faced with office politics.

Oral Offer vs. Written Offer

The very first thing to remember about a job offer is, it must be in writing and on official stationery paper – and properly signed by the hiring manager or an authorized HR representative – to be official. Often, the hiring manager (or an employee eager to have you onboard) will call you first to let you know that they are extending a job offer to you. This oral offer serves two purposes: first, as a courtesy correspondence to help alleviate your anxiety; second, probably more important for the hiring firm, to allow you to start thinking about taking the job and to increase *their* chances of having you onboard instead of losing you to a competitor company.

But you should *always* wait until you get the official written offer in the mail before you decide whether to cancel any other impending interviews. Never, ever pause or stop your job search until the official offer has arrived *and* you have reviewed the terms of offer. No matter how much you hate or dread interviews, if you get an oral offer in the morning and have an interview already scheduled for the afternoon (with a different firm), go to that interview! People do make mistakes; for example, the hiring manager might have called the wrong candidate. (This does happen!) Since legally firms aren't liable for such errors, you would only hurt your own interest if you cancel all your interviews without waiting to receive the written offer first.

Occasionally, the employer is so eager to have you joining them that they would pressure you over the phone to say "yes" to the unseen offer. Other times, a small firm like a two-person hedge fund might want to save money on paper and FedEx and insist you say "yes" before they send you the written offer. Whatever the pressure might be, never bulge in your insistence on having a chance to review the official written offer first before making a decision.

When you receive an oral offer, remain calm and the first thing to do is to thank the caller for the courtesy and for the team's confidence in you as a future member. You may want to flatter the caller – and offer him or her some assurance about your plans (which you won't disclose, of course) – by telling him or her how much you liked the team and how excited you are about the opportunity. Again, the key here is to *not* make any commitment over the phone. The only exception is if you already know 110% sure that you won't be taking the offer (e.g., you hated the place when you were interviewing there, or you already have an offer from another place which you really liked much better); in that case, politely decline the offer so some other candidate will get a chance to receive the good news.

Often, but not always, the caller will give you an indication of how much compensation you've been offered. In general, this may not be the best time to leap in joy or sound disappointed, because you need to see the written offer first. Remember, people do make mistakes, and the caller might have quoted you the wrong figure (which cuts both ways). Ditto for things like title and position. It's adequate to simply thank the caller for the information. However, if something stands out to be grossly below what you were told to expect at the interview – for instance, the interviewing manager might have told you the total annual compensation would be in the range of $125,000 to $155,000 but the caller said $98,000 – you can, and should, bring it up and ask for a double-checking. The reason for doing this now rather than after getting the official letter is, if the hiring firm truly made a mistake, it would be easier to correct it now than later when an official letter has been made and the entire recruiting bureaucracy, from the HR to the division head, would have to be awakened to correct even one minor error.

When you talk to the bearer of the good news on the phone, be sure to ask what to expect next. When will I receive the written offer? Will it come by postal service, UPS or FedEx? How much time will I have for deciding on the offer? Whom will I call if I have questions? The first and last of these questions are important, because you'll want to know whom to contact (e.g., the hiring manager, the HR, or the headhunter) if you don't receive the official offer letter in, say, two weeks.

Let's say you now have received the written offer and have just gingerly opened the envelope and taken out the letter. Just to be sure, double-check that it's your name at the top of the first page and the offer is properly signed in ink by the hiring manager or an HR representative (or some high-level executive). Now it's time to read through the letter.

The Money Game

Of course, the one thing that interests you the most is the salary and bonus offered. I bet the dollar sign will be the first thing you look for in the offer letter. You can usually easily pick out the numbers, although I've seen quite a few offer letters that spell out the compensation in English words instead of using the dollar sign and digits! As you look at the compensation number, keep two things in mind.

First, your compensation will likely consist of two parts. One is your annual salary, and the other is your bonus. The salary is also known as the base or the base salary, and that's the paycheck you receive every two weeks, twice a month, or once a month depending on the term specified in the letter. (Also, at many firms, different departments disburse payroll checks at different intervals.) Obviously the more often you get paid, e.g., once every other week, the better, but you have no control over this frequency, and it doesn't really matter that much. How often you get paid your salary should not be a point of contention at all.

As a quant, you'll be known as an "exempt" employee, just like other Wall Street professionals. This basically means you get paid a salary for working x number of hours per week (where x is usually something between 35 and 40), and won't get paid any overtime if you work beyond those hours. That's right: even if you work every day from 7 am to 9 pm without lunch break (that's 14 hours), plus you put in a few more hours every weekend, you won't be paid the customary 1.5 times regular pay that wage earners (as opposed to salaried employees like yourself) are entitled to. When you work beyond the x number of hours per week, you are basically working for the firm for free. The law allows it, and you have absolutely no control over how many hours you work. That's why it's important that as you consider the offer, think back to the interview: hopefully you remembered to ask someone what the hours were like. Even if you didn't, try to recall what the work environment was like. Did people look reasonably jolly and healthy? Or did they look tired, sick and down-trodden? Did you find people chatting with each other or sharing water cooler gossips in the kitchen area? Or was everyone buried in his or her work and the office, though packed with people, felt eerily quiet to you? You may need to rely on your gut feelings to judge whether the job is going to be slavery or offers a reasonable lifestyle beyond work. The two things to keep in mind, though, are 1) as you start a new job you can expect to put in longer hours than the other employees and 2) as you begin your quant career at the junior level you can expect to work really a lot of hours in the first few months. Given that you've made a commitment to entering quantitative finance, you know you'll need to face the tradeoff between career and lifestyle. The number of hours is a more relevant question when you evaluate competing job offers than when you have just one offer.

By the way, offer letters usually do not spell out what the x is, i.e., they don't tell you how many hours you officially put in each week. The implicit assumption is 35 or 40, but like I've just said, it doesn't matter at all. So don't be alarmed if you can't find this x in your offer letter.

Wall Street salary is more or less standardized across firms for the same pay grade – firms, like government agencies, have pay grades for different levels of positions (see later for the difference between position and title). This means that you can expect to be offered the same salary by different firms, unless you will be sent to work overseas. If there are differences, they are usually slight, although at times when the labor market is tight some firms may be aggressive in offering a more attractive salary. The salary offer can vary from year to year, and it doesn't necessarily go up each year. For example, during the dotcom craze Wall Street firms had to pay higher salaries to attract talent who otherwise might choose to go to a dotcom. Then, after the market crashed in 2000 and there was an excessive supply of skilled labor, Wall Street salaries crashed, too, often by 25% or more. But in general, you can expect Wall Street salaries to be relative stable, and once you join a firm, your salary will likely increase each year to keep up with inflation.

Wall Street high rollers don't get rich from their salaries. They do so from the fat bonus checks they receive. The bonus – also called performance award or merit award and almost always paid once per year in the first quarter of the following year – is what sets job offers apart and what sets firms apart. Your bonus will vary greatly depending on a number of factors: the market conditions, the firm, the department, the group, the job, and your expected contribution. The range for the bonus offer is huge. For a junior quant, it can be as little as $10,000 or as much as 100% of your salary. For a senior quant, $20,000 is usually the low end, with the high end reaching $250,000 or more. The thing to keep in mind is that, in most cases, the offer letter gives you an *ex ante* estimate of your bonus. It's a target figure, but the firm usually makes no guarantee you'll be paid that much. On the flip side, you can rake in more than the target *ex post* if the firm, your group *and* you performed well in a given year (and the firm is generous enough to share that extra profit with employees). In some cases, though, a quant offer letter may guarantee you a specific amount of bonus for the first year or first few years. This can happen when you are already established in your current career and the firm feels a good reason to compensate you for switching into finance, or when the labor market is tight and firms feel pressured to offer more attractive terms to potential employees. If your offer includes a guaranteed bonus, be sure to find out whether it's a guaranteed minimum, meaning there's an upside if the firm does really well, or an inflexible amount with zero variance.

Another source for the great variation in bonus offers, and *ex post* payments, is the area you'll be working in, or more specifically, whether you'll be on a trading desk or in a research department. Broadly speaking, if your job offer is for a trading desk, your target bonus will be low – oftentimes, the offer letter won't even mention a target bonus. This is so because trading desk compensation is heavily dependent on the desk's profitability. If the desk fails to make money for the firm or the clients, nobody gets paid (other than the regular salary). That last statement is an exaggeration: at large firms (as opposed to small ones such as small hedge funds), you'll still get some bonus which comes from the firm-wide bonus pool. It'll be peanuts and make you wonder why you bothered working 80 hours a week for the last 52 weeks. On the other hand, if the desk does well *and* the firm as a whole does well, you can expect a big, fat bonus check – and that's the kind of Wall Street fairy tales you hear all the time. Everybody seems to think that traders, such as those working at hedge funds, make a lot of money. What everybody forgets is that, first, not every trader makes money for his firm or clients (many trading activities are zero-sum games); second, even among those that do make money, not every trader makes a killing. The upshot is, as a trading desk quant, your expected bonus will have a huge variance, and the only thing you can do as you evaluate the offer is pray that if you join the desk, they'll be blessed by their lucky star this year and every year hereafter. (As a quant, of course, you know that's statistically improbable.)

If the position is in a research area such as analytical research, strategy research or financial engineering, your target bonus will be likely spelled out, and you can expect the *ex post* payment to be more or less in line with the target, barring a catastrophic collapse of the company's bottom line. The number won't be glamorous; for instance, it's probably 15% or 25% or 50% of your salary. You know it's extremely unlikely your realized bonus will go up to 100% of your salary. In fact, even if the firm quadruples its net profit in the year, all that extra money will go to the top-level managers (i.e., managing directors) and the senior traders and salespeople (including investment bankers, who are essentially salespeople). Research people won't be sharing in the glory of an extraordinary year for the firm. Back in Chapter 1 I made the distinction between the front office and everybody else, and nowhere is this distinction felt more pronounced and real than the size of the bonus. On the other hand, as a back office worker you'll take some comfort in knowing that unless the firm had a disastrous year, you can expect to take home the target bonus (minus taxes, of course).

As you evaluate the monetary offer, you need to keep things in perspective. Yes, there are people on Wall Street who make a lot of money – and when the market is good (as it is as I write this in early 2007), bonuses of over half a million are commonplace. But as someone new to the industry, you need to be realistic. You have yet to prove your worthiness. If you had some prior extraordinary experience that can be valuable to your employer – for example, you developed an innovative, profitable trading system or you published a Nobel-worthy paper on forecasting P/E ratios – then you would, and should, command significant compensation. But in that case you wouldn't have needed to read this book, would you? For us mere mortals, keeping expectations low is probably the best strategy. Disregard all the apocryphal stories you've heard about what *other people* might have made *last year*. It was someone else, not you, and it was history. What matters is your own career, and sometimes it may be worthwhile to take a job with relatively low starting pay but a more promising and lucrative future down the road.

Another important issue to keep in mind is the tradeoff between pay and lifestyle. As I alluded to earlier, higher pay is highly correlated with longer working hours and more stress on the job. There's a reason why salespeople (including investment bankers) and traders get paid fat bonuses – it's to compensate for their shortened expected lifespan as a result of long hours and cardiacally (and possibly psychologically) unhealthy stress. If you want a relatively cushy position where you can have a meaningful life outside of work and get to spend time with your family – things that many quants would value more than money – you can expect the compensation to reflect that flexibility.

This tradeoff becomes even more relevant when you have several offers you are comparing. Don't just look at the total cash compensation (that's salary plus expected bonus). You need to think about what you'll be doing. Which job involves more interesting (however you define interesting) work? Which job will likely lead *you* to a bright future and which one will be more or less a dead-end job? And, of course, which job will allow you to have a life outside of work (assuming you do want a life outside of work) and to pursue your hobbies and personal interests? If you took economics you know the concept of a utility function. Your utility function depends on more than monetary reward. The question is how much weight you assign to each of the factors that enter your utility function: money, sense of fulfillment, future opportunities, stress level, collegiality in the office, working hours, free weekends, free lunch every day, etc. Too many quant newbies make the mistake of going for the money and realizing only a few weeks into the job that they are not happy at all. Learn from other people's mistakes. Like the old MasterCard commercials used to say: there are things money can't buy.

Because the bonus is paid once a year – usually in the first quarter of the following year – there's always a risk that your employment may terminate before the bonus payout day for whatever reason. In that case, you won't get your bonus. That's right: you won't get a penny of that promised bonus money if you leave just a day before the payment day. (If you get laid off as a result of corporate restructuring or cutbacks, you'll probably receive some severance pay if you work for a sizeable firm. The amount of the severance pay depends on your position and tenure at the firm.) The same disaster can strike if you work for, say, a hedge fund that has a huge investment or trading loss right before bonus payment day. So, you may want to perform a risk analysis that balances a package of high salary with low bonus against a package of low salary with high bonus. If you are very risk-averse, you should go with an offer that has a high upfront salary. If you are not risk-averse, the high bonus offer will likely be attractive. If you are in-between or unsure, your decision making will be tougher; how about just tossing a coin?

(Want to know what I personally prefer? I wanted to tell you but I won't because someday I'll be looking for a new quant job and the last thing I want is facing an employer who has read this great book and boxing myself into a specific salary-vs-bonus group!)

In addition to salary and performance bonus, you may be offered a signing bonus. Signing bonuses are not unusual for fresh graduates; it's the employer's way of giving you some "pocket money" in exchange for your signing the offer letter. The typical range is $5,000 to $50,000, depending on the position and the market's health status. If you are already working full-time and switching jobs, you may be offered a signing bonus as an incentive, or as a way to compensate for the year-end bonus you'll lose by switching jobs. Often, you may not be offered a signing bonus. Should that matter? My take is consider the other terms of the offer as well as the attractiveness of the job first. A signing bonus is only a one-time payment. Taxes are deducted, and you are required, almost without exception, to return the entire *before*-tax amount if you leave the firm within certain amount of time, usually a year! (In other words, if you leave the firm that paid you a $20,000 signing bonus after three months, you'll be asked to pay the firm the whole $20,000 back even though, after taxes, you probably only received $12,000 in cash! Now that would be a really bad start for your finance career.)

Large firms, and many small firms, may also offer a relocation (moving) package in addition to, or in lieu of, the signing bonus to offerees who will have to move a long distance to the new job. ("Long distance" usually means 50 miles or more, following IRS guidelines, although some companies define long distance as more than 100 or even 200 miles!) The relocation package can take one of two forms. It can be an upfront payment like a signing bonus and you get to use it however you want – so if you have lived very modestly and have few possessions, your relocation cost may be tiny, in which case you'll get to enjoy the relocation money on other nice things such as splurging it on a beautiful 60-inch high-end Sharp® AQUOS™ LCD HDTV capable of true 1080p definition. (You do deserve it.) Or it can be a reimbursement whereby you are allowed to spend up to a preset amount and submit receipts for reimbursement when you start working. Unless you have a small palace of your own that you need to move to the new locale, the size of the relocation package shouldn't figure prominently in your offer evaluation.

Resting Days

While offer letters usually don't spell out the whole gamut of benefits such as medical insurance and life insurance because these are always provided to full-time employees, they do mention paid vacation days. There are five things to keep in mind regarding vacation days.

First, the number of vacation days varies greatly from firm to firm. European firms, for example, are famously generous in this department, often giving employees (even those in America) four weeks per annum to start with. American firms, on the other hand, usually start with two weeks per annum, although if your position is high enough, you may start with more. At most firms, you accrue 1/12th of your yearly allocated vacation days each month. On paper you are supposed to take off at most the number of days you have accrued up to that point of the year, but most big firms allow managers to decide whether an employee can pre-spend vacation days. Smaller firms such as most hedge funds may not allow this flexibility.

Second, whereas companies used to make a distinction between vacation days and personal days, now most firms have combined the two and give you a pool of paid days off that you can use however you like. For example, instead of having to deal with ten vacation days and two personal days separately, employees now can use the 12 total days with flexibility, subject to the accrual limitation mentioned above as well as specific managerial approval.

Third, what you are entitled to may not be what you can actually get. This may or may not come as a surprise to you: vacation days are both a right and a privilege on Wall Street. It's a right because the law says so. It's a privilege because your boss might not think it's your right. Of course, nobody will physically stop you from taking a vacation or threaten you with dismissal if you take two weeks off – after all, such anti-employee behavior would invite a costly lawsuit. But many Wall Street bosses, themselves workaholics, would insinuate the message that you shouldn't take "too many" days off, even when what you are taking off days within your earned number of vacation days. For example, they may tell you that the project you are working on is very important and you need to take responsibility for its completion on schedule. Or, when you bring up the subject of vacation, they may display an expression of strong disapproval on the face and in the voice, making you feel uncomfortable to actually ask for a vacation. Or, simply, by not taking *any* days off themselves, they make it difficult for the employees to take a vacation without feeling guilty. Such bosses are everywhere on Wall Street, and unless they explicitly forbid you from taking a vacation without a legitimate business reason, you really have no recourse to turn to. My advice here is as long as you know you deserve the vacation, or when you have a true personal or family situation you need to take care of, you should accept no BS and insist on getting the time off you need. You cannot work or live in fear of reprisals from your boss. Besides, as long as you do a good job at work and prove your worthiness as an employee, you have nothing to fear.

Fourth, almost all firms allow you to roll over some unused vacation days from year to year, but there are usually strings attached, such as only a limited number of days can be carried over to the following year and you must use them up in the first quarter of the new year.

Fifth, most big firms allow you to cash out your unused vacation days when your employment terminates. On the flip side, if you have pre-spent vacations days you had not accrued, you may be asked to pay the firm back for those days, usually in the form of a deduction from your final paycheck.

What about sick days? In the old days firms used to spell out the number of sick days employees could take. The prevailing trend, at least among large firms, is to leave that out and allow some flexibility at the manager's discretion. Some employees assume this means "unlimited" sick days, but that's rarely the case. Obviously firms know that with a generously ambiguous sick-day policy (which does not expressly spell out the number of allowed sick days), a few employees will be tempted to play hooky. To prevent this, you may be asked to furnish proof that your sickness or illness is serious enough or contagious enough to warrant your staying at home. If you take too many sick days off during some period, even with your manager's approval, HR will call you to discuss why you may have been malingering on the company's dime.

Besides regular vacation and sick days, the firm might also give its employees days off for marriage (marital leave), childbirth (parental leave), and/or family death (bereavement leave). Large firms will likely pay you for these special leave days, although this is not guaranteed because labor laws don't require it. In any case, these days won't be mentioned in the offer letter; if they interest you, you'll need to call HR to find out. (The good thing is, since you have the offer now, you can ask them pretty much *anything* you always wanted to ask but were afraid to at the interview time!)

Titles and Positions

Your offer letter will tell you what your title and position will be. Now, this is an area that causes much confusion, mainly because there is no standard terminology and each firm treats "title" and "position" differently. For example, you may be told that you'll be an "associate" or "assistant vice president" or even "vice president," but you'll also be told that you are being hired as a "quantitative analyst." What's going on?

You usually get two kinds of titles because one is used internally to identify the level you occupy on the corporate hierarchy and the other is used to identify the kind of work you actually do. So *corporate titles* (or *corporate positions*) like associate, AVP, VP, director, and managing director define your seniority level, whereas *functional titles* (or *functional positions*) like quantitative analyst, quant developer, quantitative trader, and senior financial engineer define the scope of your work and are also used to communicate your function to the outside world.

Let's look at the corporate titles, which signify ranks, first. (You should be aware that more and more quant-oriented firms and departments no longer use corporate titles, which are a vestige of the old banking tradition.)

On Wall Street, the professional ranks start at the analyst level. (It's important to remember that the corporate title of analyst is totally different from the functional title of analyst; for example, many senior equity analysts, people who cover the stock performance of companies, are managing directors on the corporate scale!) If you have just a bachelor's degree and no prior full-time quant experience in the industry, you'll likely start at this level.

The next level up is associate. Most firms give out the associate title to new hires who have an advanced degree or possess prior industry experience. There are exceptions to this, though: a few firms, including Deutsche Bank's U.S. operations, my ex-employer, have got rid of the analyst level and start new graduates off – regardless of their degrees – at the associate level. In fact, more and more Wall Street firms seem to be following this trend so it's conceivable that in the not-so-distant future the analyst level will disappear altogether and associate becomes the entry-level title.

Some firms – especially those on the buy side – have a corporate level called assistant vice president (AVP) that stands above the associate level. Given the trend toward abolishing the analyst rank, it's possible that in the future AVP becomes the new associate level as the latter gets pushed down the corporate food chain. Just keep in mind that the AVP title is not universal on Wall Street.

Next up is vice president (VP). It always makes me laugh to talk about this level. After all, it's quite an impressive title, isn't it? Chances are, if you get this title and tell your non-finance friends about it, they'll be really impressed, thinking you are one of the top executive officers of the firm! Alas, nothing can be further from the truth. While being promoted to the VP position signifies your having gained the confidence of the firm – as a VP you'll be given the power to make some independent decisions – it's more or less a dime a dozen position. It's definitely *not* an executive position, that's for sure. But it's a nice title to have, nonetheless. You may be offered the VP title if you have extensive industry experience, e.g., you have been working as a quant and are now switching to a different employer.

Some firms have a senior vice president (SVP) level, although this does not appear to be commonplace. Instead, most firms promote qualified VPs to the director level. (Firms with the SVP level also have directors, promoted from among the SVPs.) As a director you'll be given significant supervisory responsibility for a functional area. For example, you may be in charge of risk modeling or strategy optimization. It's unlikely readers of this book will be offered this position (except, perhaps, at some very small firms), as a director should already possess not only technical expertise but managerial experience as well. By the way, a few firms call the directory level principal instead, but it's the same thing.

While some firms have a mezzanine level of senior directorship, most go straight to the managing director level. Managing director (MD) is the climax of a successful Wall Street career. A vestige of the old partnership system on Wall Street, MDs are the captains of the various business ships that make up the corporate fleet. Each MD is responsible for the P/L ("P-and-L," or profit and loss) of his or her business unit. He or she is the big boss for that unit. He or she also participates in the executive profit-sharing at year end, and here's where the big bucks are made. (An MD's compensation is heavily dependent on the P/L of his or her unit as well as where the unit fits in the business maze, e.g., front office vs. back office.) Becoming an MD should be the aspiration of every ambitious quant. Of course, it's a tiring job, too, so not every smart quant wants to become one.

What's above MD? There may or may not be a formal senior managing director level. Regardless, the most important MDs become top corporate executives: the CEO, the COO, etc. These important MDs sit on the executive management committee, which is similar to the cabinet in a Western democracy and the politburo in a Soviet-style government. These are the decision makers who steer the entire fleet.

I hope you now understand what the various corporate titles mean. One thing I haven't mentioned is the relationship between corporate title and compensation. Indeed, the corporate title not only signifies your seniority, it also determines your base salary. Anecdotal evidence as well as conversations with various Wall Street people suggest that each corporate title is tied to a salary range. While there is difference in salary among VPs, for example, the difference is unlikely to be huge. But when a VP gets promoted to the director level, there is a jump in salary. However, corporate titles do not play much of a role in determining the yearend bonus. For example, a quant VP who works as a trader (a front office position) may take home more bonus pay than a quant director or even a managing director in charge of basic analytical research (a back office area) at the same firm. Compensation also varies greatly between buy side and sell side as well as among the different functional areas (e.g., prop trading vs. agency trading) of each business unit.

Functional titles (positions) describe what you actually do. These are much easier to understand. For example, if your functional title is "quantitative analyst," well, that pretty much describes what you do, right? I mean, how confusing can that be?

Other examples of functional titles are chief quantitative strategist, senior financial engineer, lead quantitative trader, senior risk manager, head of fixed income derivatives research, and, of course, CEO.

To complicate things a little, there is no standard as to which title goes on your business card. The pattern on Wall Street seems to be, if the corporate title is AVP or below (i.e., analyst, associate, AVP), it's left out and only the functional title goes on the business card; the rationale here is, if you are on the lowest rungs of the corporate ladder, why make a fuss about it? For VP and above, people advertise the corporate title, usually in addition to the functional title. So it's not uncommon to see a business card identifying its owner as "Senior Vice President / Head Quantitative Trader" and such.

Other Things in the Offer Letter

Although an offer letter is not a legal employment contract – indeed, the offer letter will likely make this point clear upfront – it usually contains languages that could only have been written by a lawyer. For example, the letter will describe your responsibilities on the position as well as both your duties and rights as an employee. It will delineate a few conditions that you must satisfy in order for the offer letter to be considered in force. (For example, if the firm finds out you have a drug addiction problem or lied blatantly on your résumé or during the interviews, they may rescind the offer.) It will also tell you which state's labor law will govern your employment, as well as that, by law, you'll be subject to drug testing and/or background checks. (Before or immediately upon your start, you'll be fingerprinted as part of the background check process. All financial firms in the United States are required by Federal law to do the check.) Finally, the letter will tell you when you must give the firm a firm answer (no pun intended) on whether you accept or reject the offer. The response deadline is usually a week from the day the offer was made – not the day you received the letter!

As you peruse the offer terms, you should be aware that while most of the language is standard, you should consult a employment lawyer if you do not fully understand anything or have doubts about anything. Even though the offer letter is not an employment contract – essentially meaning the employment is not guaranteed – once you sign it, you are legally bound by its terms. So, for instance, if the offer letter says you'll be subject to personality testing and later you refuse to be tested, the firm will have a legitimate reason to rescind the offer or fire you, and you'll have a hard time fighting the termination.

If you are a not a citizen or legal resident alien of the country where you seek employment, the offer letter will either detail the steps you and the firm need to take in order to secure legal working status for you or refer you to a separate document. It's important that you stay in close contact regarding the application status of your labor visa, e.g., the OPT or H-1 in the U.S.

Negotiating Offers

While the art of negotiation is way beyond the scope of this book, I can offer some thoughts on this important topic.

First of all, you should know that every offer can be negotiated. You don't even need more than one offer to negotiate, although having more than one obviously places you in a stronger position. Even with only one offer, if any terms – from salary to performance bonus to relocation package to vacation days – don't satisfy you, you can just pick up the phone and call HR. Once the firm has made an offer to you, it can't rescind it just because you want better terms (as long as your demands are reasonable, not exorbitant, of course). In short, you won't hurt yourself by trying to haggle.

Before discussing how to negotiate effectively, let me first give a warning: *never lie about having another offer.* This advice applies to both the existence of this purported other offer (or other offers) as well as its terms. If you have only one offer, never make up another offer in the hope of gaining an upper hand in the negotiation. Firms *will* ask you what the other company is and may just as well follow up with a call to that company – even if the company is not in the same industry. Once I met a candidate who claimed to have another offer, from a software company. I was suspicious of the salary he said he was offered at this other company, so I called their HR to check. They told me they had never even given him an on-site interview. You can imagine what happened next. If you do have at least one other offer, be honest about its compensation terms. If you lie and the hiring manager asks you to produce the other offer letter so he or she can match the terms, you'll be in real big trouble. While Wall Street is not exactly the place where you find a bunch of truly honest people, for your own sake don't cause problems for yourself before you are even hired.

Let's assume you have one offer. You feel that the salary is a bit on the low side, or maybe you had expected more vacation days. Time to call somebody. You can call either the hiring manager directly, or call the firm's HR contact, or call your headhunter if you used one. The important thing is, call them. Do not use e-mail, as e-mail is totally ineffective for negotiating anything – its lack of personal touch actually works against you, plus the other side will know you are too timid to call, so they won't take your request seriously.

When you call, be sure to first thank the other party for getting you the job. Tell them how impressed you were with the group and the people, but *do not* sound you are eager about taking the offer. If you leave the impression that you want the job and want it bad, you have just tipped your weak hand and you can kiss any better terms you were seeking good-bye. So keep cool and let the other person guess how much you liked the offer. In fact, if you can subtly voice a bit of disappointment over the terms that bother you, you can probably tip the negotiation balance in your favor.

I want to emphasize that there is absolutely nothing wrong with negotiating the offer. Hiring managers and HR people expect it. They know how to play the game. The only issue is whether you can play it, too. Don't ever feel embarrassed. If you can't help but feeling guilty about "taking advantage" of the hiring firm, forget about negotiating the offer and just sign the offer letter. But why not fight for your right when everybody else does it?

The key to successful negotiation is knowing how to link the issues to the other party's interests and how to give-and-take. The other party's interests include not only the obvious benefits such as having a highly qualified employee like yourself, but also the less obvious ones such as feeling good about helping out a new employee. In other words, appeal to the other person's conscience. For instance, you can mention how expensive it is to live in the new city and how you still have a lot of student loans to repay. The other person might have gone through a similar experience so he or she might feel sympathetic toward you and your request. As another example, if your parents live far away (e.g., in another country), you may want to ask the other party to consider giving you a few more vacation days each year so you can visit your parents. Do your best to arouse some sympathy, and you'll likely get what you want, in part if not in whole.

How likely you'll get your wishes fulfilled depends ultimately on how important the hiring manager thinks you are and how much leverage you have. This means that how much extra benefit you ask for should depend on your own assessment of your importance. Remember, there's a deadline for accepting or rejecting the offer. You don't want the other person to tell you "I'll get back to you" and then never call you back, which in turn forces you to sign the offer without getting what you wanted. So you want to ask just enough to make the other person feel your request is reasonable and justified. You should also leave some room for back-and-forth negotiating in your request. For example, you might ask for an extra week of vacation time but will gladly settle for two days. Don't be shy about negotiating, but always keep the big picture in mind – the big picture being having a job secured as well as not pissing off the boss before you even start the new job.

For the same reason, never try to insinuate a threat, such as "I don't think I'll be able to accept your offer if you don't give me the better terms I want," during negotiation. No matter how artful or subtle you think your threat might be, it won't be taken well, period. It leaves a really bad taste in the other person's mouth, and may lead to rescission of the offer altogether. After all, nobody likes to be threatened, the least by a candidate who hasn't even proven his or her value to the firm yet. (Someday, when you've become a successful and rich quant, you can use artful threats liberally.) Even if the offer terms are so far below what you wanted or expected that it's impossible to secure better terms that meet your minimum demand, or even if you don't really want the job, you shouldn't burn your bridges – especially if this is the only offer you've got. Besides, keep in mind that when you tell the employer that there are terms in the offer that displease you, you are already implying that you may not accept the offer, so there's absolutely no reason to verbalize that implicit threat in any way. Do your best on the negotiation part. If you feel the final offer is still inadequate, just gracefully walk away and find something else.

When you put forth your demands for new terms, you can expect to receive a counteroffer in return. In other words, don't expect the other person to say yes to whatever you want. It usually doesn't happen that way. (Of course, if it does happen, that's nice.) The original job offer already represents what the firm thinks you deserve – and the offer terms are usually fair and competitive if the firm is of a reasonable size. (Small companies, in particular small hedge fund firms, may try to sneak inferior terms by you.) Negotiating an offer often resembles a game of tennis or ping-pong, with you and the firm volleying terms back and forth. My experience has been that it usually takes two to three rounds for both parties to reach a satisfactory agreement.

When you have two or more offers and none stands out as the must-have, obviously you want to, and should, negotiate among the offers. First, look over the offers and pick out the best offer in each of the important areas: salary, annual bonus, signing bonus (if any), vacation days, and title and/or position. Look out for any unusual perks that one of the offers may contain. Then, call the hiring manager or HR representative at the place you want to go to the most. Be sure to call, not e-mail, which would be ineffective for negotiating an offer. Calmly explain to the other person how you would enjoy working for his or her company, but how one or more of the terms in the offer letter are inferior to your other offers.

Two things to keep in mind as you use other offers as a bargaining chip in your negotiation. First, never lie about the other offers' terms. You just never know if the other person might ask you to fax over a copy of that "other" offer which you claim proffers twice as much pay and three times as many vacation days. Second, make sure the differences between the offer terms are reasonable: the differences should not be so insignificant as to arouse indignation in the other person for wasting his or her time over trifles, nor so large as to make it impossible for the other person to meet even half of your demand. In fact, having other offers can be both a positive leverage and an Achilles' heel: if you have another offer that is so good, the other person might reason, why don't you just take that job? So, always be reasonable, and always have a good reason why you deserve to be given more than the standard offer package.

Regardless of what you negotiate for or how you do it, there's a very important thing that must not be overlooked: after you finish negotiating, be sure to ask for a new written offer with a new decision deadline. Nothing is final unless it's put in writing and properly signed. I haven't heard of any case yet where a firm tries to go back on the negotiated offer terms, but you want to play it safe. Never sign the original offer letter if any term has changed during the course of negotiation.

Occasionally, the other party may promise you that part or all of your demand may be met in the future, but not now. For example, they might cite longstanding company policy or "current budgetary constraints" as the reason for insisting on an oral promise rather than giving you a written agreement. This can be tough to handle. You just never know if the person will be true to his or her words in the future, or how far in the future this "future" is, or if he or she will still be with the same group or the same firm at that future time. You should try to get at least part of your demand met in writing, offering some comprise if needed. At the very least, send the person an e-mail detailing what he or she promised orally after the conversation, so you have a permanent record of these promises. (Federal law requires that all financial firms retain employee e-mails for a number of years. Even if an employee deletes an e-mail from his or her Outlook, a copy of that e-mail remains on the e-mail server as well as gets archived to backup tapes.) Leaving such an electronic paper trail also makes the person more likely to make good on the promise when the time comes.

Starting Your New Job

Long at last, you are now ready to start your new job as a Wall Street quant. You are ready to launch a hopefully successful and rewarding career in quantitative finance. And our journey together is also reaching its end. Before saying good-bye, I'd like to talk a little bit about what to expect on your new job.

Chances are, when you start a new job, you'll be given a "honeymoon" period to get acquainted with the new environment as well as to get up to speed on the work. For example, if you have to master a new programming language or statistical package, you may be given a few weeks to learn it. You'll have a chance to learn by doing, and you'll have access to coworkers who have already gone through that phase and who therefore can be of tremendous help to you in your learning period. Be sure to leverage the experience and knowledge of your coworkers – which, of course, also means you should be friends with your coworkers. Sure, there may be one or two people who just don't click with you, but keep things professional, and at least be courteous with such coworkers. In most likelihood, though, you'll work with relatively pleasant people and benefit tremendously from the mutual learning and mutual support.

Handling the boss is probably going to be the toughest challenge, especially if you've never worked in a corporate environment before. The one key thing to remember is, do not judge your boss on the surface. He or she may seem really nice and understanding, but under the façade he or she may possess a tough and cunning personality. Similarly, a disciplinarian who rarely smiles or chitchats may turn out to be a completely fair and supportive manager. Recall the section on dealing with interviewers in Chapter 4; the same principles apply here. But there's a big difference now: as an employee, you'll have to face and deal with the boss every day, versus meeting someone only briefly (and never again). So it's vitally important you understand how your boss thinks. You don't have to agree with him or her or even like your boss. But if you can see things from his or her perspective, you'll be able to handle him or her better.

Of course, all this is easier said than done – and the task is made all the more difficult when the boss turns out to be a, uh-hum, jerk, or if you two just don't get along. (Don't you wish you had a secret portable scanner to scan each interviewer for their personality at interview time?) As long as the boss is not harassing you or otherwise abusing the boss-employee relationship, there's little you can do other than focusing on your own performance. Get into the habit of frequently e-mailing your progress and milestones to your boss and coworkers; keeping a paper trail, even an electronic one, is the secret to surviving office politics. (Of course, if it's you who did something wrong, the paper trail can really come back and bite you, too. Hint: before you click that submit button...) When things do get to a boiling point – we all hope that won't happen but in real life, it occasionally does occur – you can always pack up or leave.

If you perceive a boss – or a coworker – being less than professional in his or her conduct, you have two choices: face up to the person directly and have an honest face-to-face conversation about the problem, or go to HR directly and ask them to talk to the person. In this day and age, no one should be stressed out by an abusive boss or a hostile work environment. Remember, the law is on your side (at least here in the United States), and if your grievances are legitimate, HR and management will pay attention and help you get the problem resolved – after all, the last thing they want is a lawsuit from an employee who feels he or she has been unlawfully treated and abused. Even when you aren't sure if the treatment you are receiving is fair or right, talk to HR. In my experience, HR folks are usually interested in keeping employees happy and productive, often more so than the business-line managers. If a faceless Wall Street firm has a personal side at all, it can be found among the HR people. So don't let that resource go wasted when you need the help.

After the honeymoon period, you'll be working at full steam, and things will quickly settle into a routine. You'll also become part of the office gossip circle. The key thing to remember about water cooler gossip is, what goes around will also come back. If you enjoy talking about others behind their backs, you can be sure that other people also take delight in talking about *you* when you are not around. So try to stay out of office gossip, both as a messenger and as a subject.

It's likely that, at some point during your quant career, you'll be drawn into some type of office politics. This is not surprising, because quants are people, too, and smart people are ambitious and self-confident. When ideas collide, conflicts arise. While oftentimes both sides to the conflict can emerge as winners so nobody loses, a lot of times only one of the parties is "right" or gets to have the ear of upper management and thus comes out ahead of the other party. When you think about it, interpersonal conflicts take place all the time. They happened with our siblings when we were growing up, they happened with our classmates in the first grade as well as in the tenth grade, and they happen with our social friends all the time. I don't know why people shake their heads every time the term "office politics" comes up. Well, when you have people with brains who've got their own ideas of what works and what doesn't work, why wouldn't there be conflicts? And when you have conflicts, there will be politics.

Philosophical musings don't help you actually handle a tough situation, though, so a little bit of advice may be in order. If you are caught in the middle of office politics, the best course of action is to not take sides. I've seen ambitious quants who thought they could take sides and get ahead when their side won. Well, it didn't always turn out that way. Besides, why waste your time and energy on these things? Your goal is to gain experience and become a successful quant in your own right, not to become someone else's ammunition in office politics. If your boss wants you to do something, obviously you do it (as long as it's a legitimate request). But if the task you are given may harm another person or another group, you should bring this up with your boss and make it clear to him or her that you will not allow yourself to be caught in the crossfire. If a manager who's not involved in your line of reporting (i.e., not your boss or your boss's boss, etc.), politely decline to take on any work without talking to your own boss first. Remember, even if you take sides and your side wins, you might become a scapegoat when upper management comes to town and investigates the complaints of the losing camp.

For many people, playing office politics can be fun – may I recommend Sun Tsu's *The Art of War* (Amazon link to special paperback edition with bilingual text and what's widely regarded as the best translation: www.amazon.com/exec/obidos/ASIN/0976072696/pd_bk-20, ~$12) if you are interested in how to cunningly handle office warfare – but ultimately it's tiring and distracting, and all too often someone ends up being the total loser. And often, even the winner walks away with a bad reputation and may end up being a loser in the long run. As you gain more experience in the corporate world, you'll become better at judging how to handle office politics – or maybe even become a politicking master yourself. But at the beginning of your career, it's probably best to stay away from such distractions as much as possible. Besides, quants are seen as intellectuals. Upper management likes quants who bury themselves in real work, not in extracurricular activities like office politics.

So, here we are, time to say good-bye. I hope you've learned a few things of value from this book. Be well and best of luck! I do hope to hear from my readers, so do drop me a line and let me know how you are doing!

INDEX

Colophon

This book was written, formatted and laid out in Microsoft® Office Word 2003 on a Sharp® Actius™ PC-MM20 laptop running Windows XP Home Edition SP2 and a Sony® VAIO® VGN-FE880E laptop running Windows Vista™ Home Premium. The body text is in 12-point Times New Roman, with chapter titles in Arial and Internet addresses in Courier New. The manuscript was converted to the Adobe® PDF format on the Sony VAIO laptop before being sent to the printer.

About the Author

Brett Jiu, Ph.D., currently works as a senior financial engineer at a major technology-driven equity agency-broker firm that serves institutional investors. Prior to his current position, he worked as a quant in private wealth management (buy side) and economic strategies (sell side) at Deutsche Bank. He started his finance career as an analyst and trader at RGNCM, a Manhattan-based hedge fund. In addition to his finance career, Brett also spent some time working as a management consultant at McKinsey & Co.

Brett has published articles on algorithmic trading, investment decisions under uncertainty, and mergers and acquisitions. An electronic gadget fanatic (current favorite: Playstation 3), he was featured in the *New York Times* in 2005. Brett received his bachelor's degree, *magna cum laude,* in applied mathematics from Harvard College and his master's and Ph.D., both in economics, from New York University. While at Harvard, he was a staff reporter, columnist, news editor, and photographer for the daily *Harvard Crimson.*

Printed in the United States
87040LV00005B/130-132/A